The Friend

Who Got

Away

Edited by

JENNY OFFILL

AND

ELISSA SCHAPPELL

Introduction by

FRANCINE PROSE

DOUBLEDAY

NEW YORK LONDON TORONTO SYDNEY AUCKLAND

THE FRIEND

WHO GOT

AWAY

_____

Twenty Women's True-Life

Tales of Friendships

That Blew Up, Burned Out,

or Faded Away

PUBLISHED BY DOUBLEDAY

a division of Random House, Inc.

DOUBLEDAY and the portrayal of an anchor with a dolphin are registered
trademarks of Random House, Inc.

Book design by Chris Welch

Library of Congress Cataloging-in-Publication Data
The friend who got away : twenty women's true-life tales of friendships that
blew up, burned out, or faded away / edited by Jenny Offill and
Elissa Schappell.— 1st ed.

p.   cm.

1. Friendship. 2. Loss (Psychology) 3. Separation (Psychology)
I. Offill, Jenny, 1968– II. Schappell, Elissa.

BF575.F66F694 2005

158.2'5—dc22

2004058259

ISBN 0-385-51186-8

PRINTED IN THE UNITED STATES OF AMERICA

June 2005

First Edition

1   3   5   7   9   10   8   6   4   2

FOR AMANDA DAVIS,

who is dearly missed

I have lost friends, some by death . . . others through sheer inability to cross the street.

—VIRGINIA WOOLF

ACKNOWLEDGMENTS

Many thanks to our agents, Sally Wofford-Girand and Joy Harris, and to our editor, Deb Futter, for their invaluable help with this book. And to David Hirmes and Rob Spillman, whose unending support and patience made it all possible.

CONTENTS

FOREWORD

Jenny Offill and Elissa Schappell

YOU HEAR THE name, and your heart starts to pound, your palms sweat. You catch a glimpse of a familiar face on the street and suddenly you find yourself sideswiped by memories better left forgotten. It may have been years since you last spoke, and yet it all comes back in a moment, the first giddy rush of talk, the shared confidences and sudden adventures, the certainty that your friendship could survive anything, and the startling heartbreak when it didn't.

We all have one. A story about the friend who got away. A tale we replay on sleepless nights, turning it over in our minds, chastising ourselves for our cruelty or betrayal, our longing or jealousy. Sometimes we mourn the loss of a friend; other times we celebrate the break, but no matter what, we don't forget it.

The loss of a friendship can be nearly as painful as a bitter divorce or a death. And yet it is a strange sort of heartbreak, one that is rarely discussed, even in our tell-all society. Tales of disastrous loves abound, but there is something about a failed friendship that makes those involved guard it like a shameful secret. Whatever happened to your friend? someone asks, and more often than not the answer comes back carefully crafted to give away nothing. *We had a falling out. It's complicated.*

Why does the thought of seeing an ex-friend sometimes stop our hearts in a way that seeing an old lover doesn't? Why is it so difficult to trace the arc of a failed friendship, to shape it into a recognizable narrative? Even country music, with its laundry list of heartache and longing, won't touch it.

Perhaps this is because stories of lost love feel somehow universal. Behind each bad breakup or broken marriage there is a litany of complaints, such as infidelity, alcoholism, or bankruptcy, but no matter what the sordid details, the fact that a romance has failed is never all that surprising. That love can end suddenly, inexplicably, is the refrain of a thousand pop songs. No one expects anything less.

But friendship is supposed to be made of sturdier stuff, a less complicated, more enduring relationship. Because of this, the story of a breakup with a friend often feels far more revealing than that of a failed romance, as if it exposes our worst failings and weaknesses. After all, an ex-friend is someone who knew our deepest secrets and then vanished, someone we drove away or who chose to leave us. Often this person knows a self we have kept hidden from the rest of the world, a self we may have hoped to retire or to pretend never existed. The passing of time or an expensive therapist may make us believe that we can erase an unpleasant past, but ex-friends are nagging reminders that this is a false hope. They know our history, and they remember it. And for this reason they haunt us.

Among the threads that tie the stories in this anthology together are the surprisingly fierce emotions that are released when a relationship based neither on blood nor on romantic love is forged and then broken. Every close friendship offers the same fundamental thrill; someone has singled you out and chosen you, someone who had no obligation to do so. No wonder that when a friendship ends it feels like being cast out into the cold again.

There are countless reasons that friendships fail or end, but each broken bond feels deeply personal, as the pieces in this anthology will attest. In order to protect the privacy of others, some of the writers have changed names or small autobiographical details so as to allow themselves greater freedom to tell their stories. The result is that these essays represent the truth as each writer sees it. No doubt some of the people depicted in these pieces will dispute their former friends' version of events. How dull it would be if they didn't. The dizzying subjectivity of such emotionally charged experiences makes questions of guilt and innocence impossible to pin down with any assurance.

How much to trust their own account of events is something many of the writers in this anthology have grappled with in their pieces. Some have worried about the ambiguity of their final conversations or the haziness of their memories; one writer even conjured up the voice of her ex-friend, disputing and debating the facts as she tried to get them on the page. And two writers, once best friends, took the extraordinary step of telling both sides of their painful breakup, allowing readers to observe up close how a shared experience can be refracted very differently through the prism of emotion.

It is a measure of the complexity and difficulty of this topic that so many writers who were initially eager to be a part of this anthology retreated when it came time to sit down and revisit their lost friendships. Some fled out of guilt or fear of retribution, some because they were afraid to open the door to all that confusion and pain again. A few writers even began essays, only to find, somewhat eerily, that the friends they'd thought they'd severed ties with had suddenly reappeared in their lives, hoping for reconciliation.

In the end, because these stories of betrayal and loss and longing involve such revelation, the decision to tell them requires an act of faith in the reader, one we are very thankful the twenty brave and eloquent writers in this book have chosen to make.

AMONG MY ACQUAINTANCES is a woman infamous for the stormy high drama of her female friendships. This woman and her dearest friends are almost perpetually embroiled in dramatic arguments, raging feuds, and tearful, bitter breakups. They part ways and spend months or years refusing so much as to hear the others' names mentioned. Then, at last, something gives and inspires them to initiate remorseful reconciliations, to swear their undying loyalty, enjoy brief periods of grace, inevitably followed by more real or imagined slights, more betrayals, more accusations—and so the cycle begins again.

I've never quite understood why she would act that way with her friends, since it's always seemed to me that theatrics of this sort are meant to be the exclusive province of love affairs. That's why we have boyfriends, husbands, families—so we can behave like that. Our friendships are—or are supposed to be—our most uncomplicated, sustaining, and reassuringly reasonable relationships. Unlike our families, into which we're born without being consulted, we can choose our friends for their many admirable and endearing qualities. Unlike our love affairs, into which we are drawn by all sorts of inchoate, mysterious, and often purely chemical forces, our friendships have to do with shared interests, lively conversation, and the certainty that our friends will care for us, wish us well, and be there for us when we need them most. And though the start of a new friendship can feel like the early stirrings of love—there's a similar excitement, that same drive to find out who this new person is and to spend as much time as possible in her company—it often feels superior to a romance, or in any case far healthier, less disturbing, and more sustaining, free from tests of passion and fidelity, and the hurt feelings that result when those tests are failed. For unless we've reached that period of our lives at which we are ready to settle down, the first stages of a love affair are a bit like standing on the top of a mountain from which we can already see how things will end—most often, badly.

But when we begin a friendship, there's no reason to believe that it can't last forever. If our family ties are bonds that we cannot shake loose, if our romances are flames that suddenly flare up and just as suddenly die down, our friendships are steadily burning fires that we can remain beside, taking consolation in their comforting warmth and light.

But, as so often happens, experience has proved otherwise. The twenty searching and insightful essays in this collection have shown me how complicated these relationships can be—as if I didn't already suspect it, as if I didn't have my own legions of former friends from whom I've drifted away, from whom I have been separated by geography, life, and death, whom I no longer see but who continue to haunt me. Like former lovers, they are the ones whom, from time to time, I seek out on the Internet, in the phone directories of distant cities, in the faces I pass on the street. For it's almost as if they still hold some Proustian key to the mystery of lost time, the answer to the question of who we were when we were friends, and of what has become of us since.

By focusing on the ways in which friendships end, on the sudden fractures or gradual diminutions that turn out to be as singular and various as the individuals involved, these essays explore the meaning and nature of friendship, the arc of these simultaneously unique and emblematic alliances, and all the complex and compelling reasons why we choose certain friends at certain critical moments in our lives. A number of these pieces deal with the ways we form youthful friendships at a time when we ourselves are only partly formed, and still see our friends as mirrors in which we desperately hope to glimpse a sharper and clearer, or simply more interesting, image of ourselves. Some address the ways young women's friendships can at once express and mold their identities, and in the process help them to define who they are, and who they hope to become. And these narratives manage to convey all the pain and frustration of watching a friend move into a different world, or reveal a hidden self wholly unlike the dear, familiar person we thought we knew.

Lydia Millet's essay "Flawless" concerns the sort of friendship we sometimes have with someone who seems to represent an ideal we long to resemble, an alternate and more pleasing alter ego until, at last, we realize that the other person is not only not like us but also not like anyone we would ever wish to be. The "flawless" freshness and fluency that the younger American abroad admires in the beautiful, worldly-wise Columbia graduate student turns out to be a kind of moral Teflon that permits the older woman to ignore an ugly truth for reasons of passivity, laziness, or simple convenience. Elissa Schappell's "You'll Be All Right" captures the particular thrill of finding that friendship can cross barriers of background and social class, of discovering that we can be friends with someone who seems very different from us or from anyone we've ever known. And it evokes the way in which a friend can appear at a critical juncture, like some heavenly messenger dispatched to tell us what we most need to hear—and then vanish from our lives. Katie Roiphe's "Torch Song" not only allows us to recall a time in our lives when "people didn't belong as absolutely to other people," when the "barriers that in adult life seem so solid and fixed . . . did not exist," but also a time when the urge to self-destruct melded seamlessly with the compulsion to test one's powers, and when friends still seemed somehow replaceable, the least important factor in any equation that involved sex, and men.

Ann Hood's "How I Lost Her" and Kate Bernheimer's "Other Women" examine the dissolution of friendships even after age and sad experience have taught us that our friends are not in the least interchangeable or expendable. Helen Schulman's "First in Her Class" looks at the tragic way in which death can at once strengthen, intensify, and ultimately even sever the bonds of friendship. Jennifer Gilmore's "The Kindness of Strangers" is partly an inquiry into the ways that competition and personal ambition can sabotage a friendship and turn it into something not merely unfeeling but parasitic. Finally, Vivian Gornick's "It Felt Like Love" and Beverly Gologorsky's "In a Whirlwind" disclose the extremely important and seldom emphasized truth that women's friendships are not restricted to girlish giggles and gossip, to shared beauty and fashion tips, but can have their bases in the intellect, in politics, and in a reasoned and adult view of the world.

What all these different voices and wonderfully various essays share in common is the ability to conjure up these lost friends with remarkable tenderness and veracity. And they frankly acknowledge something that is far too rarely talked about: that losing a friend is painful, even wrenching. A loss of this sort leaves a void that is impossible to fill, since it is impossible to re-create the quirks and qualities, the gifts and strengths, and even flaws, that draw us to a particular person, that move us to chose one person, rather than another, as our friend.

The loss of a friend upon whom the heart was fixed, to whom every wish and endeavour tended, is a state of dreary desolation in which the mind looks abroad impatient of itself, and finds nothing but emptiness and horror.

Thus Samuel Johnson wrote about the death of friends, but as these essays show, he could just as well have been writing about a loss that occurred through more ordinary and less tragic circumstances. The nature of friendship is, after all, as mysterious as the nature of love, and the stories of our friends—how we found and lost them, what they taught us, how they sustained and comforted us, or betrayed and hurt us—are among the building blocks from which we construct that wondrous, beautiful, and highly unlikely edifice which, for want of a more capacious term, we have learned to call the self.

The Friend

Who Got

Away

TORCH SONG

———

Katie Roiphe

MY MEMORY OF Stella, at nineteen, is neither as crisp nor as detailed as it should be. It's only with a tremendous effort of will that I can bring her into focus at all. She is wearing a complicated black outfit that looks like rags pinned together with safety pins, and black stockings, with deliberate runs laddering her legs. Her skin is translucent, the color of skim milk, and her matted, dyed blond hair looks about as plausibly human as the hair of a much loved doll. Under her eyes are extravagant circles, plum colored and deep. She always looks haggard. No one that age looked haggard the way she looked haggard. And yet, as one came to know her, that was part of her romance.

Stella was from the South. I remember her being from a trailer park, but it may have been a small, sleepy town. She had some sort of unspeakable tragedy in her background, which added to the quality of southern gothic she cultivated. In my picture of her, she is curled up on a mahogany windowsill, with a

Faulkner novel, but in reality, she was one of those brilliant college students whose minds are clamoring too loudly with their own noise to read much.

On good days, Stella looked as if she were late to the most important meeting of her life; on bad days, she looked if she were being hunted down by organized and insidious forces. She was also one of the most powerful people in our Harvard class. She was monumentally, conspicuously damaged in a way that was, to us then, ineffably chic. She had an entourage of followers and hangers-on, mostly men of ambiguous sexual preference whose mothers had given them exotic, weighty names like Byron and Ulysses. She had an authentically doomed streak that was to the rest of us, future bankers, editors, lawyers, future parents of one point five children, and mortgage holders, uniquely appealing. And the whole time I knew her she was writing something—a detective story? a play? a thriller?—something with a murder in it, I think, but whatever it was, it added to the impression that she was engaged in more important endeavors than the rest of us. She talked in the cartoon bubbles of comic book characters: "Oh ho." Or "Jumping Juniper." Or "Iced cold beverage," or "Eek." This was part of an elaborate, stylized defense, against the softness associated with sincerity.

And yet, the perfection of her cool was pleasantly undermined by an ambience of frazzled vulnerability. She was overweight, and had a flinching relationship with her own body. If you caught a glimpse of her coming down Plympton Street at dusk, you might mistake her self-deprecating shuffle for that of a homeless person. In retrospect, I can see that she was kind of wonderful looking, with her fabulous, disheveled gestalt, but at the time being overweight was an enormous, almost insurmountable, taboo. She had a great, pure throaty laugh, which went along with a child's pleasure in the smallest things. I can see her clapping her hands in delight over a chocolate sundae or a gardenia-scented candle.

She was one of the few girls at school that I could talk to. We would sit on her bed and chatter for hours. She would smoke insane amounts of cigarettes. I would drink insane amounts of coffee. In the background a scratchy Lou Reed song called "Waltzing Mathilda" might be playing; a song which for some reason we couldn't get enough of. It was about a party interrupted by the inconvenient discovery of a female corpse.

Over the years the sting of what happened between us has died down to an anecdote repeated at cocktail parties, where I had found it could be interesting sometimes to reveal something odious about yourself. "Will you listen to how you sound?" I can hear Stella saying. "It's still all about what a colorful character *you* are, isn't it?" In my mind her voice is perpetually and sharply sarcastic, which it wasn't always. There was plenty to Stella besides her considerable satiric gifts. But that is, after all of these years, what remains.

Stella's one conventionality was that she was in love. The boy in question was very tall and very green-eyed. He wore ripped jeans and fake gas station attendant's shirts, and was a Buddhist. He had a funny, fluid way of moving his long arms and legs that was attractively effeminate and moderately vain. And he had elegant, sharply arched eyebrows that gave him the aspect of one of the wickeder Greek gods. I won't bother to say what his name was because he could have been anyone, and his specific personality, which was fairly annoying in a number of specific ways, would only be a sideshow and a distraction. I knew the night I met him and Stella that they both were and weren't together; both facts were equally apparent after being around either of them for five minutes. They orbited each other, but anxiously. They spoke the same weird patois, a mixture of baby talk and archness. ("Who was that female person you were talking to?" "I don't know to whom you are referring, doll.") They seemed, if anything, like a brother and sister engaged in some kind of incestuous love under the magnolia trees of an old plantation.

The secret was that Stella and the boy sometimes slept together. In retrospect, I can't think why it was such a secret, unless it was the boy's vanity that demanded they remain officially unattached. Their spotty, intermittent affair depended on him not seeing a more conventionally pretty girl, and was extremely damaging for Stella, who remained in a state of dramatically heightened jealousy at all times. There was a whiff of scandal to the whole thing, which came, in a world where surfaces were everything, from their being so mismatched in looks.

In other words, it was hardly an ambiguous situation. There was, Stella would later point out, no shortage of boys: there were boys with prettier eyes or a more refined knowledge of Proust; boys with more original neuroses, and less saccharine forms of spirituality. But the fact is that attractions are contagious. I spent hours sitting at "Tommy's Lunch," drinking lime slushies and listening to Stella take apart the peculiarities of his character; hours listening to her fits of jealousy over the irresistible odalisques sprawled across his dorm bed. This is what happens when an overly intelligent woman brings all of her talents to bear on an infatuation: Without either of us realizing what was happening, she somehow persuaded me of his attractiveness.

My flirtation with the boy, if you could even call it that, was beyond furtive. The three of us were often together, and he and I behaved toward each other with an irreproachable mixture of mannerliness and hostility. He came to visit me alone once when I was sick and brought me magazines and orange juice. Our conversation was innocent bordering on banal. I think we talked about the declining quality of the cereal selection at breakfast. Neither one of us told Stella about the visit.

And yet somehow we both knew. It was as abstract and agreed upon as an arranged marriage. I felt it when I stepped into the cool morning air, and gulped down a milky cup of coffee before class. I felt it when I walked next to the slate-colored river, watching the shallow crew boats skim the surface. It was with me, in other words, all the time: a low-grade excitement about this boy I barely knew. From this distance in time, this may be the most foreign and inscrutable part of the story: the attractions that could at any moment flare up and end your life as you knew it.

At this point I may as well offer a slight, very slight, argument in my defense: people didn't belong as absolutely to other people then. There was a kind of fluidity to our world. The barriers that in adult life seem so solid and fixed, literal walls defining your apartment, your bedroom, did not exist at that age. You listened, for instance, to your roommate having sex; you slept easily and deeply on someone else's couch; you ate breakfast, lunch, and dinner with everyone you knew. And somehow nothing was quite real unless it was shared, talked about, rehashed with friends, fretted about and analyzed, every single thing that happened, every minute gradation of emotion, more a story in the process of being told than events in and of themselves.

Over the summer the boy came to visit me in New York. I remember him standing in the doorway to my room, grinning, with an army green duffel. Had we pretended it was a platonic visit? It seems far-fetched that he would have come all the way from New Hampshire to New York to see a casual acquaintance, but I have a feeling that was what we told ourselves. We climbed up to the roof of my parents' building and watched the boats go by on the Hudson, the sun silhouetting the squat water towers a dark silvery green.

I am aware, even now, of some small part of me that would like to say that it was worth it, some adolescent, swaggering side that would like to claim that the sexual moment itself seared the imagination, and was worth, in its tawdry, obliterating way, the whole friendship. It was not.

Of the act itself, I remember almost nothing at all. It seems that when one is doing something truly illicit, not just moderately illicit but plainly wrong, the sex itself is forgettable. The great fact of the immorality overshadows anything two mere bodies can achieve. All I remember is that he was gentle, in the way that sensitive boys were supposed to be gentle. He brought me a warm washcloth afterward, which sickened me slightly, and embarrassed me.

Stella, red pencil tucked behind her ear, would notice that I haven't described the actual seduction. That I've looked politely away from the events, because they are incriminating and, more important, banal. I wouldn't want to debase my great betrayal, my important, self-flagellating narrative with anything so mundane as what actually happened. That's how she would see it, anyway. Two people taking off their clothes, however gloriously wrong, are, in the end, just two people taking off their clothes.

But really, the problem is that my mind has thrown up an elegant Japanese folding screen, with a vista of birds and mountains and delicate, curling trees, to modestly block out the goings-on. And it does seem after all of these years, that a blow-by-blow would be anticlimactic. I can say, in a larger sense, what happened, which is this: I didn't care about him, nor did I delude myself into thinking that I did. I had enough sense to know that what I was experiencing so forcefully was a fundamentally trivial physical impulse. And that's what makes the whole situation so bewildering and impenetrable. Why would one night with a boy I didn't even particularly like seem worth ruining a serious and irreplaceable friendship?

I suppose, in accordance with the general and damaging abstraction of those years, I was fulfilling some misplaced idea of myself. I was finally someone who took things lightly. I thought a lot about "lightness" then. Even though I wasn't someone who took things lightly at all, I liked, that year, to think of myself as someone who did—all of which raises another question in my mind. Was at least part of the whole miserable escapade the fault of that wretched Milan Kundera book everyone was reading, *The Unbearable Lightness of Being*? That silly, adolescent ode to emotional carelessness, that ubiquitous paperback expounding an obscure eastern European profundity in moral lapses? The more I think about it the more I think it's fair to apportion a tiny bit of the blame to Mr. Kundera. (Here Stella would raise her eyebrows. "A book forced you to do it? How *literary* of you, how *well read* you must be. . . .")

I suppose, also, in some corner of my fevered and cowardly brain I must have thought we would get away with it. I must have thought we would sleep together once and get it out of our systems. It turned out, however, that the boy believed in "honesty," an approach I would not have chosen on my own. He called Stella at the soonest possible second and told her. It was not hard to imagine the frantic look in Stella's eyes when he told her. Stella looked frantic when she had to pour cornflakes in a bowl. I hated him for telling her. I couldn't bear the idea of her knowing. Strangely enough, I felt protective of her, as if I wanted to protect her from the threat of myself.

I don't think I grasped right away the magnitude of what I had done. It felt—thanks to Professor Kerrick's Representations of Anomie in Twentieth-Century Art—like waking up in the middle of a René Magritte painting and finding tiny men with bowler hats suddenly falling from the sky. It didn't make sense, even to me, and I was startled, in a way, to find that it was real. To have the boy in my house the next morning, wanting coffee, and to have his soft blue-and-green flannel shirt spread out on my floor, was for some reason extremely startling. Cause and effect were sufficiently severed in my mind that I had not apprehended the enormity of the betrayal. In the light of day, it seemed a little unfair that I couldn't take it back.

I don't remember if the boy called Stella from my house, or if he waited a few hours and called her from a phone booth in the train station. I do remember him reveling in his abject abasement. I couldn't believe how much he reveled. He was, among other things, a religious nut. But back to Stella. It's funny how even now my mind wanders back to him. This man I did not even delude myself into thinking that I cared about. This man I did not even *like*.

Stella, needless to say, was furious, mostly at me. I've noticed, in these cases, one is always furious at the person of the same sex, and one always finds the person of the other sex contemptible yet oddly blameless. To further complicate things, Stella and I were supposed to be roommates in the fall. This made everything infinitely worse: undoing our roommate arrangements proved to be more arduous than one would think. We had to disentangle ourselves officially in the eyes of the bureaucracy, and on paper: it was like getting a divorce.

Before I go any further maybe I should say something about self-destructiveness in those years. That warm July night, there was the pleasure of destruction, of Zippo lighters torching straw huts, of razing something truly good and valuable to the ground; there was the sense, however subliminal, of disemboweling a friendship. I remember filleting fish that I caught with my father on the docks, and seeing liver, kidney, roe splayed open on the slick wooden docks, for all to see. There was something thrilling and disgusting about it. Tearing open my friendship with Stella had the same effect. I felt sickened. I felt the freeing thrill of ruining everything.

And then again, it may be deceptive to talk about this whole phase of life in terms of feeling. Maybe the problem was the absence of feeling. Maybe the problem was a kind of annihilating rage that swept through me. Maybe I did what I did because, at that age, I couldn't yet feel the way I wanted to feel, the way Stella felt, about a man. A few lines of Wallace Stevens were starred and highlighted in my Norton anthology: "Knows desire

without an object of desire, / All mind and violence and nothing felt . . . / Like the wind that lashes everything at once."

From this vantage, the story is quite chilling. I would like to
say something in my defense, but what could I say? This is, by its
very nature, an act that cannot be defended. I will say that my
sense of morality shifted, that the last remnant of childhood,
that last puritanical streak of self-righteousness, vanished, that I
learned to be less rigid, because you never know. Fundamentally
nice people have done deplorable things in their pasts. Fundamentally deplorable people change.

One could say that the seeds of the end of my friendship with
Stella were embedded in the beginning. I met both her and the
boy at once after all; and I may have been attracted, in a way, to
both of them at once, to the impossible triangle as it was being
assembled. Stella may even have known, on the long nights
the three of us spent together sitting around her fireplace, him
slumped down on a chair, long legs gracefully crossed, listening
to the whine of the Velvet Underground, that she was creating a
problem; the temptation was that rooted, that inherent in the situation.

But back to the girl standing next to a tall boy by the water
towers. The seconds before she leans into him, or he leans into
her. The sky a glowing navy blue. How would the girl herself
have explained? I am afraid that she would have come out with
something like "It felt like the right thing." (I can hear Stella
launch into this one: *It felt like the right thing. Of course, it felt
like the right thing. But did you stop to think for one second in
the midst of all of this exalted feeling?*) I am aware of how feeble
this sounds, how predictable, how mundane, but I am trying to
be as accurate as I can. In the moment it felt like one of those
exceptional situations that rises above conventional morality, "in
the moment" being another of those phrases one heard all the
time back then. In the moment one is not thinking; in the

moment the physical takes precedence; this is, of course, the businessman's excuse with his secretary; the politician's excuse with his intern; the tired cliché, in fact, of every single adulterer with the gall and the paltriness of spirit to try to explain themselves, and yet it is true: in the moment, it did not feel as if there was a choice.

Afterward I tried to wheedle my way back into Stella's affections. I had great faith in my wheedling back then. I wrote her a series of elaborately contrite letters. I remember quoting Auden in one of them: "In the deserts of the heart / Let the healing fountain start." But the heart remained a desert, as it tends to. Ornate apologies, overly flowery expressions of the self-contempt I did, in fact, feel would not do. This, of course, is because nothing would do.

As it turned out, my efforts to explain myself bothered Stella to no end. I think, in retrospect, that all she wanted me to do was accept responsibility. I think the whole conversation about what happened exhausted her. Who cared why or how from her point of view? Who cared what particular frailties of character led me to be vulnerable to this sort of thing? What matters in the end is the irrevocable act. Even if I was able, through sheer force of will, to create a little ambiguity in a wholly unambiguous situation, there was something insulting, finally, about doing it. My impulse, it seemed, was to take the whole thing apart like a car motor, to take out the pieces and look at them together; of course, if I could engage her in this process, if I could get her to look at each one of these oily mechanisms *with* me, then I would be part of the way to regaining our friendship. It is the two of us doing something together, however awful. Stella, in her own way, sensed this and refused.

As for Stella, she hated me with aplomb. It was not a partial or forgiving hate. It was a deep, ardent hate. It was so seductive, this hate, that it pulled in other people who hated me too. Stella's emotions were charismatic that way. There were whole tables in the dining hall I had to avoid.

One could ask if I really wanted to save the friendship. I admit that I might not have. I admit that there may have been something in the friendship that was crowding me. Why else would I have done it? Why else did I have so few close women friends in the first place? I have four sisters, and it may be that I already had such an abundance of intense female love and ambivalence that my friendships with women seemed just the tiniest bit disposable. But this sort of psychoanalytic thinking has its limitations, especially when it comes to a nineteen-year-old. Because there may have been something entirely accidental in the crash-up of the friendship; it may have been a random act of violence, like someone taking out a gun in a school one day and shooting a secretary to the principal. It might have been that same sort of stupid, senseless act.

I remember once when I was five my class was going on a trip to Staten Island on a ferry. I had been looking forward to this trip for weeks, had in fact, drawn several pictures of the boat and stuck them to the refrigerator. The morning we were leaving, I had the signed permission slip from my parents. I had my cheese sandwich packed in a paper bag, and my cardigan buttoned over my school uniform. And yet, when we got out onto the boardwalk, the wind blowing from the East River, holding hands in twos, like the little girls in the Madeline books, something happened. I started crying. The teacher stooped down, and I told her I had a stomachache. I told her, in fact, that I was about to throw up. I was sent home, and I missed the boat ride. Why had I done it? My mother asked, somehow knowing that I was faking. But I didn't know why. I sat at home miserable by myself, thinking of all my friends floating away on the deck of that lovely boat: it was my first purely anarchic moment of self-sabotage.

But then again, there *are* reasons that I could go into. There are myriad possibilities as to why I would do something so patently absurd: I could go all the way back to Teddy Fairchild, the first boy I liked, with shoulder-length corn-colored hair, who left a bag of Russell Stover hard candies in my locker at camp, to my enormous shock, and then, at the end of the summer, never answered my letters. Or Henry Powers, who had caffe latte colored skin and dark curls, and decided, after our idyllic romps through the dunes in Nantucket, that he would rather play with boys. If I wanted to I could delve further into the great gaping insecurity that is always responsible for this sort of bad behavior: when I was thirteen I was dangerously ill, and in and out of the hospital for a year. By the time it was clear I was going to be alright, I weighed sixty-two pounds, my skin had a distinctly greenish cast, and clumps of my hair had fallen out in the front. While my friends were cultivating the usual romantic dramas, I was oddly removed. The boys I knew would confide in me their feelings about other girls, because the question of their liking me, or of my feeling like a possible prospect of their affections, was so remote as to not even occur to them. I read books, and resigned myself to not being part of the game; and this resignation, this astonishment that a boy would like me, lingered dangerously. It turned me, to be honest, into something of a monster for a little while. Somehow this feeling that I was outside the romantic comings and goings of my peers got mingled with the idea that I wasn't going to live, that I was somehow outside of life. You can see where I am going with this. You can feel, in this explanation, the silent doctor nodding in the corner. So many years on the couch. So many exquisite explanations of appalling pieces of selfishness. And yet they are all true and not true; it may just have been a warm night and a beautiful boy.

If she were here now Stella would say that all of this analyzing, all of this cyclical, wordy remorse, all of this endless trying to understand, or saying I'll never understand, all of this throwing up my hands in the face of human nature, or extolling the self-destructiveness of the age, is just another way of making this about me, rather than her. She would be right, of course.

Shelter

_____

Emily White

RAYMOND WAS TALL and towered above me, his black hair shining, his loud laugh drowning out the world. He wore sharkskin suit coats and narrow ties; he was never at rest but always alert and impatient, as if he was on the verge of a getaway. In the hall at school, girls surrounded him. We called ourselves fag hags, scrambling for a place next to him on the courtyard bench. He provided shelter from the world of boys while also allowing us entry into it. Holding hands with him at lunch, you could almost convince yourself you were part of a love story.

This was in Portland, Oregon, at an elite private prep school. Both Raymond and I had been sent there by relatives—Raymond by his aunt, I by my grandfather. Our classmates were some of the most privileged kids in Portland, and their parents regularly appeared in the society pages. My mother would read the page aloud and say, "Now, don't you know that Schnitzer girl?"

With its manicured gardens and attentive teachers, the school made us feel like the future would be kind to us. There were no grades, no punishments. Faculty members were called by their first names; they wore ponchos and fought for admirable causes. The cafeteria was not a cafeteria but a converted barn in which the cinematic light flattered even the plainest faces. Sometimes when I think about Raymond, when I try to unravel the question of why I idealized him so insistently, I blame the light itself. The light made it hard to see him clearly.

Before Raymond I was a grim, save-the-animals girl, hiding in my coats, which became increasingly large and boxy as my body developed. I was the kind of girl to whom people said, "Smile, it can't be that bad!" and "Aren't you hot in that?" Raymond saw me as his project. "You are really something," he would say. "Come out of your shell." I craved his attention and tried to do as he instructed. Under his influence I started wearing flimsy thrift store dresses with Eiffel Towers or insects patterned on them, and waxy white lipstick. I became an "eccentric" girl. I developed an anomalous, high-pitched laugh.

Most mornings I'd rendezvous with Raymond on the city bus. My younger sister and I waited for the 70 every school day, huddled in the doorway of a diner. Inside an old couple sat at the counter coughing into their handkerchiefs and talking about when their checks might come. My sister always had a few Star Wars action figures nestled in her back pocket, although at thirteen she technically should've outgrown them ("They're friends," she explained). Hunched beneath our backpacks, we searched the horizon for the bus. When I saw it approaching, I wondered anxiously if Raymond would be inside waiting for me. I wondered if he would like my outfit. When the door closed, the 70 was as hot as a terrarium.

On a bad day he'd missed the bus or skipped school. On a good day he was perched in the last row, saving a seat for me with his backpack. Because he lived in rural Oregon, he'd already been riding buses for an hour and a half by the time he arrived at my stop. If he'd fallen asleep on his corduroy coat, he greeted me with ridges on his face. He said, "Let me look at you." Back then he was never cold or shut down; he made me feel safe, necessary, central to him.

Out the bus window, as we rode the last few miles to school, there were graveyards where kids met for beer parties, forested hills with mansions set back in them. Other kids from school rode the 70: a girl with slicked-down hair and cat-eye glasses who was determined to write her final paper on Edie Sedgwick; a pothead with a disintegrated laugh; a girl who claimed to have made a perfect score on her SATs.

Our closest friend was Gillian, a half-Jewish, half-Korean girl with an impenetrable gaze that drove boys wild. "Where are you from?" the boys asked, and she wouldn't tell them. Gillian's parents were swingers, and her mother's boyfriend lived in the attic. The boyfriend was a bus driver with a red beard, and sometimes he drove the 70. As I boarded the bus, he said, "Hello, young lady," and although there was nothing sexual in his voice, I couldn't help but think of him naked with Gillian's mother, her father listening outside the door.

Raymond and I could talk incessantly about Gillian's mother fucking Redbeard; it was an opportunity to talk about forbidden sex. Neither one of us had actually had sex yet, but we had a tremendous amount of desire coming off of us; we wanted to shake off our feeling of constriction and monotony, and sex seemed one way to do it. Also drinking, which we wanted to do as often as possible, and traveling, which we were determined would happen soon. "New York," we'd say to each other, "we're definitely moving there." But how would we get out? The only vessel we had was the 70.

We disembarked at the foot of the school property, trudged up the hill, and said good-bye to each other, promising to meet at lunch. It was only a few hours until I would see him again but already I missed him—I was not content to be away from his side for very long. I depended on him, and the need made it hard to be alone in my skin. After school, we'd rummage around in thrift stores, walk down the street drinking gin out of Pepsi cans, see movies we'd seen before. Raymond was a cinephile and read every film and gossip magazine. He knew the lives of movie stars as some people know the lives of saints.

At a café we frequented after school, one of the waiters looked like a movie star, with a long neck, a thin waist and a white belt, bangs that almost covered his eyes. On his break, he smoked clove cigarettes and put them out on the floor: "The whole world's an ashtray," he said.

"God, he is something," Raymond whispered. We were hungry for this waiter, and we drank his rotten coffee until our stomachs ached. We bought his brand of cigarettes, hoping he'd ask for one. "Put the cigs on the table so he sees them," Raymond said. But the waiter never took the bait, and our desire for him just kept unfolding, the way all desire does when it can't quite meet its object.

LYONS, OREGON, POP. 10,008, was where Raymond lived with his mother, Carol, her husband, Andy, and their three young sons, all under the age of seven. Carol and Andy were wild-eyed, broke, back-to-the-land hippies. I can't remember if they smoked pot, but they seemed like the kind of people who wouldn't hear the oven timer no matter how long it had been buzzing. For ten years they'd been building a boat in their garage; the outside was finished, but it was hollow on the inside. The plan was to make enough money to finish the boat and sail out of there, to travel all over the world, dinners straight out of the ocean, no permanent address, no taxes. Raymond thought the boat was a piece of junk. He thought Carol and Andy were too loopy to ever get out of there. He predicted they would always be stranded in Lyons under the exact same boring tree branches.

One night I took the long bus ride home with him to meet the family. The half brothers sat at the table overturning their dinner plates and blowing bubbles in their milk. They were little princes, little darlings. Although I'd always thought of Raymond as beautiful and graceful, here he was like a lumbering adolescent babysitter who should've gone home an hour ago. Raymond was Carol's son from a one-night stand—she'd met the father on the beach on a trip to Hawaii. She was there on some kind of spiritual quest, and indeed she returned transformed, but not in the way she'd hoped. The father lived in New York and knew nothing of his son, or this is what Carol told Raymond, and it infuriated him that through some kind of rude hippie magic she'd turned his father into a shadow. Raymond knew the man's name but he'd never seen his face, not even in a photograph. He thought of himself as a bastard and made jokes about it. "I'm a mistake!" he said. "That's why I'm so fucked up!"

That night the brothers circled around Raymond making duck noises as he tried to write his art history paper—"Kandinsky: His Life and Work." Later that night, as we lay in bed, he talked about the brothers in sentimental terms with love thickening his throat, but he was an alien among them. In the morning, his mother barely noticed as we left the house, so preoccupied was she with the wailing, legitimate children who had not been on the earth as long as Raymond and who were not suspicious of her as he was.

Three things I remember him saying:

"I hope my brothers don't turn out gay."

"Gin is good."

"You are a goody-goody with a bad streak a mile wide."

I've realized since then that people who feel like mistakes often recognize each other, and like Raymond I was not quite sure what I was doing in my parents' house, if I should really be there or if I was one of the uninvited. This alienation was the bond between Raymond and me, the overriding code. My house was a world of perpetual drinks, where if the glass was not full, someone had to be sick or asleep. For lunch my dad often had three serious martinis. These he consumed at the Captain's Corner, a place of nautical decor and no windows. He tippled throughout the afternoon and continued to drink at home after work, a gallon of wine carried off into the living room. Gonna watch TV, he'd say as he breezed past my sisters and me bickering at the table. Gonna get drunk, my older sister whispered. An entirely different man emerged as the booze took effect. Here I am, the man said. Don't try to deny my existence. He had a different accent and walk, his feet hit the ground differently; he might as well have had a different name.

Perhaps because of these frequent unsettling transformations there was a depression in the air of home; depression was the weather of the place, it was the smell soaked into my bedroom rug. My sisters and I had a sinking suspicion that maybe we had overstayed our welcome. The more depressing it became the more I'd wish for the sound of Raymond's voice; even after too much gin he seemed glamorous, talking about art films and escape, not like my dad, who did not talk about anything coherent and seemed on the verge of turning to stone.

My older sister lived in the bedroom on the other side of mine, and she watched television constantly. She memorized all the shows, collecting *TV Guide*s and arranging them alphabetically, becoming an expert on the sitcoms offered in the new fall season. Sometimes while she watched TV she read books about animals, or sorted through her bead and rock collections. But she never wanted to go outside, and she didn't want to be disturbed. KEEP OUT, the sign on her door said. Through the wall I could hear the laugh track at regular intervals.

For my sister, television was a destination, a crossing-over, a necessary light source. New York was like that for Raymond and me. We were hypnotized by a fantasy of moving there—"Remember NEW YORK," we would say to each other as once again the weekend elapsed without anything happening to us. We turned it into a kind of Jerusalem. Portland was merely a layover in our journey to the great city. We pooled our money for the mythic apartment we'd share in the East Village. We studied maps of subways. We started using the word *borough*. Now I see we were not so different from Carol and Andy with their boat. Like them we believed that if only we could launch ourselves out from under the rain and the terminal sky we'd be cured.

One Friday after school, I was hanging out downtown with Raymond. We'd gone to the café to look for the waiter but couldn't find him. The approaching weekend was like a chemical in our brains making us restless. Would anything happen? Would it have anything remotely to do with sex? At this point, I'd lost my virginity with a soccer-playing boy who played soft rock on his car radio, music that reminded me of going under at the dentist's office. He did not fall in love with me nor I with him; perhaps I was too in love with Raymond to fall for anyone else. Raymond had managed a few trysts, but he did not tell me many details, only that the men did not talk much, they just signaled to him in parks and stores.

At the bus stop, we ran into a couple of girls from school: the perfect-score girl and her friend Jessica. Jessica said if we came to her house we could probably drink a bottle of her parents' wine. I knew Jessica wanted to be part of Raymond's circle. She looked up at him smitten, her cheeks reddening whenever he returned her glance. Suddenly, he put his hands under her armpits and lifted her off the pavement. She thrashed around, said, "Stop! Stop!" Her rhinestone earring rolled onto the sidewalk, but he kept carrying her. He said, "Relax, let me transport you." She said, "But you're hurting me!" Then she started to cry. "Raymond put her *down*," the brainiac ordered in her slow voice. I wondered if she sounded sedated because she knew the answer to every question. Raymond freed Jessica, and she scurried to the phone booth to call her mom.

For weeks we made fun of her, called her chicken, poor baby. She was sad and left out in her blue peacoat, eating weird rice mixtures packed in Tupperware for lunch, meals that looked already digested. "Call your mommy!" we said as she walked past. "All I wanted to do was lift you up!" Raymond said.

BIT BY BIT we saved money to pay for our passage out. During the summer I worked in the food court at a fish and chips restaurant where the clam strips tasted like rubber bands. Each day a crazy man visited me at the counter and made a speech about the origins of chowder. "Did you know, young lady, that clam chowder comes from Boston?" he would begin, his hair slicked to the sides of his face. Raymond worked around the corner at a pizza place where he was forced to wear a pilled red sweater vest and a matching visor. When our shifts coincided we'd visit each other on break, sometimes drinking screwdrivers out of paper cups and returning to our positions suddenly pleasant to the customers, our breath powerful with corrective mints.

Raymond was brilliant, but he was animated by a feeling of failure. The year we were to graduate he dropped out of high school. Before he dropped out teachers convened special meetings with him; obviously, he'd been designated the troubled homosexual, a kind of mascot. They told him, "We know you can do more. We know you just need to push past your obstacles. If there is anything you want to talk about..." With burning cheeks, he'd recount the meetings to us. "They treat me like a doomed gay bastard," he said.

Soon after he dropped out of school, Carol and Andy finished the boat. The day they took off on their journey the story was picked up by the local news: a feel-good, end-of-the-hour feature about one family's gumption and pluck. A hair-sprayed anchorwoman interviewed his mother, and she said the boat was a new beginning for her family. She introduced her three sons but never mentioned the fourth. The boys looked into the camera: they had the look of people who are adored. It was a redemption story in which Raymond was not and could not be mentioned—he complicated it. They were sailing off in the ark to save themselves, and he was left here on land. Later, they'd drift into shallow water and rip a hole in the bottom of their boat and Raymond would feel vindicated.

After they disappeared, he rented an apartment and decided to change his name. I accompanied him on a series of errands filing the necessary papers—he'd decided to take the name of his aunt, the aunt who paid for school. He hated his mother and wanted their relationship annulled. We marched around town to various government offices and waited for our number beneath the fluorescent light. Soon he was given a new social security card and a new identity. He bought a new wallet to celebrate. I celebrated with him, but now I wonder if I should've taken the name change as a warning: if he could erase his name, what else or who else might he want to erase?

In a photograph from that period, we're in the public square again, and I'm wearing so much white lipstick my mouth is undetectable beneath it. Raymond is lifting me up like he lifted Jessica, but I'm smiling. I'm not telling him to stop as she did. We both seem strangely overjoyed, like religious fanatics. For a while, this photograph lay beneath the glass on my mother's dressing table, but after our final falling-out I took it back, put it in an envelope labeled LIES, and sent it to him along with every letter, postcard, and photograph I could unearth. I was trying to purge myself of all that evidence. But I didn't find all of it. Sometimes a card or letter turns up among my raft of possessions. I immediately recognize his handwriting, but now I see it as a cruel script where I used to see it as a promise of love. YOU ARE WITH ME FOR GOOD, he once wrote at the end of a letter, the bastard.

WHEN THE TIME came to leave Portland, we emerged from the mall with our final paychecks and walked out into the daylight blinking, as if emerging from a cave. My hands smelled of grease. Yuppies flocked toward the riverfront park for a concert by a white blues singer, a man who never sounded like he truly had the blues but instead like he was having a conniption fit. "That guy is a perfect representation of why I hate Portland to death," said Raymond. We rode the bus to his apartment. He'd given everything away except for some clothes and books. Dust devils swarmed in the empty corners; I felt giddy and hollowed out, like everything I'd done up until that moment had been a form of waiting: for buses, for a resolution to desire, for a city that was not this city, for the drink to take effect. A forlorn palm tree rotted in the corner of the apartment and Raymond decided he should throw it off the roof and put it out of its misery. We heard the pot shatter on the sidewalk below but were too afraid to look over the edge and survey the damage.

The next night was our long-awaited flight, a red-eye for which tickets were so cheap they couldn't guarantee our bags would arrive with us. "You might have to come back to the airport and get them if there is too much other cargo," the attendant said. We accepted this, and my father took our picture at the gate. You can have a million send-offs, the picture says to me now, but you can never really get out of here.

At 2:00 A.M. in Detroit, falling asleep against each other as we waited for a connection, Raymond and I were pilgrims who'd almost arrived. On the last leg of the journey, a little boy squirmed in the seat in front of us as his parents slept. He turned around and made a series of faces at us: the tongue out, the nose turned into a pig's nose, et cetera. Raymond filled the boy's ears with quiet monster noises until the boy was feverish, beside himself. Suddenly he pulled a blanket off his father and threw it over Raymond's head. Now we were hysterical; the stewardess cleared her throat. Raymond left the blanket on his head for a long time, until the boy shrieked, "Take it off! Take it off!" He was afraid Raymond had disappeared under the shroud. The next morning, we said good-bye to the boy as we filed out of the plane. He was crabby by then, as tired of us as we were of him.

We didn't find an apartment in the East Village as our fantasy dictated; instead, we ended up in a railroad flat in Chelsea with a skinny girl roommate who took speed after work and talked about how she felt like her mind was expanding to contain the universe. The whole time we lived there cockroaches and water bugs occupied the kitchen. They'd been there before us and they would outlast us. One day, as I pressed my job interview clothes, baby cockroaches crawled out of the iron.

New York was the city of his father, and Raymond believed that he was out there somewhere, taking elevators up into the high-rises, or riding in the cabs we couldn't afford. He wanted to track him down and tell him he existed, to say, Hello, hello, I am here. A few times he tried to find him in the phone book, looking up different permutations of his name and trying the numbers. No real voice ever answered, just machines. This was before the Internet, before you could really waste time searching for people.

Raymond found a job working for a film company, answering phones and running errands. He became increasingly obsessed with celebrities—not with movies but with the people in them. He found his way into greenrooms so he could see them in the flesh. At cocktail parties he stood next to men who'd won Oscars, although he never spoke to them. He loitered in bars frequented by actors, and he knew which hotel doors they were likely to emerge from. We always walked slowly by these doors, waiting for the rush of air and the famous face.

I suppose he felt legitimized by celebrities after such a long story of illegitimacy, as if being in their presence meant he had arrived and he too was someone with an important name. For a while, the celebrity he worshiped most was Sigourney Weaver because she seemed half man, half woman. He imagined himself talking to her and her listening to him. He hunted down her home address on his boss's Rolodex. When she lost at some awards show he sent her a dozen white roses, writing his phone number on the card. He waited for her to call. After three weeks, he declared her a fucking bitch. He took all her pictures down from his bedroom wall. I never heard him refer to her again.

I preferred the celebrities on the screen. In real life, they often seemed small and made of wax, their eyebrows plucked too clean. I was beginning to realize New York was too much for me. I couldn't handle the crowded air or the cockroaches; I was accustomed to harmless bugs that curled up when touched, not giant creatures that could live until the end of time. Each morning, I took the rush-hour subway to my job at a publishing house, and like a creature born without the last layer of skin, everything seemed to get to me: the gamy tunnel smell, the legless man sitting on the ground selling carnations, the crush inside the car, everyone so smashed up and exhausted they seemed to be going extinct. At work, a kind old receptionist looked at my pale face and said, "Honey, you look like you need to go to Mexico."

Raymond started taking ecstasy, hanging out at gay clubs all night. He didn't invite me along. "You wouldn't like it," he said. "Too much noise." While he'd had a few furtive affairs in high school, he'd never had boyfriends—just older men with wives who hurried him into their motel rooms, or boys whose clothes he hated. Now he'd discovered a world of beautiful proud boys who shaved their chests and listened to underground dance records and wore designer T-shirts. They were like his Sirens, and he vanished into the city searching for them. He came back spellbound, like my dad he had a different accent, and he kept secrets from me. He took so much ecstasy it stopped affecting him. He needed three hits to feel what he used to feel with one.

Some mornings he was so exhausted he'd start running a bath

and forget about it. He'd fall asleep, only to be awakened by a pounding at the door. "You're flooding my apartment again, you idiot!" the woman from downstairs shouted. "I am going to get you back for this!" She was four feet tall, her face white with rage. I worried she had the power to put a curse on us.

One night my high school poetry teacher came to town and took me out with his old college friend. They were forty-three-year-old men who were obsessed with eighteen-year-old girls; they said women their age looked too sad and worried. "They have these lines around their mouths, I can't stand it," the friend said. They talked about their college days, when they led protests and became campus heroes. I saw their eyes light up over my young flesh, and I felt a surge of power; soon I started dating the teacher's friend. In retrospect, I wish I could've taken myself out of that bar, but you see this was what I'd always been looking for, ever since the days with Raymond on the bus: for someone's eyes to brighten over me. I'd take that brightening any way I could get it.

The forty-three-year-old had a car, so I no longer needed the subway. He promised soon he'd take me on a trip out of town. He said he'd written books, although later I'd find out he'd only started them. He collected records and played songs for me from the Golden Age of rock and roll. He said, "Put your ear right up to the speaker and let the music deafen you." I learned the names of the rock gods and tried to impress Raymond with them, but he wasn't impressed by any of it. "He is a macho, homophobic creep. I bet he beats up fags in his spare time," Raymond said. "You should get away from him." "I will," I said, but it took me years. I became addicted to the dinners he bought for me on his maxed-out credit card. After a night together, he'd drop me off and I'd drift into the apartment as Raymond was drifting out. "Out with the geezer?" he'd say. "Probably the last date," I'd reply. "Sure," he'd say. "Famous last words."

We knew something was happening to us, that we were cracking up. The forty-three-year-old brought this to the surface; he became the embodiment of it. In an attempt to repair our disintegrating bond, we took a trip to Philadelphia to see Raymond's aunt, the woman who'd sent him to school and after whom he'd named himself. She drank a pint of scotch a day and collected lipstick. She said lipstick cured sadness, and she could gauge how sad she'd been by the color of lipstick she bought. Fuchsia meant she'd been down pretty far. Raymond loved his aunt and believed she should've been a celebrity. Together, we visited the Liberty Bell and the stairs Rocky climbed; we helped his aunt recycle all her whiskey bottles. We made a dinner of Cornish game hens whose necks we forgot to remove. We sat in her courtyard garden beneath rustling birch trees and said, I love you. On the train ride back it seemed we were the same people from the red-eye flight, people who have built a fortress of loyalty and there is no getting in or out of it.

For a while after Philadelphia, it was fine. Raymond discovered the films of John Cassavetes, radiant stories of people who can't contain their free-floating grief. Raymond became obsessed with these movies, playing them over and over again and reciting the dialogue aloud. He was determined to become the next Cassavetes, or maybe an actor in one of his movies. He tried to write scripts in the style of Cassavetes, but he was too tired after work and clubs to sit at his computer. Under the influence of Cassavetes, frustration built up in him, an impatience that made it impossible to stand in line at grocery stores.

I think it was this frustration that electrified his hand one night when he hit me in the face. We were arguing about my boyfriend ("a sixties casualty," he said), about whether *Shadows* or *Faces* was Cassavetes' first movie. I can't remember exactly how it came about, or whether I saw it coming, but suddenly there it was. Blood on my shirt, ears ringing, the whole sordid picture. Raymond didn't apologize or flinch, he just stood there as I held the side of my face. Maybe he wanted me to rise up and fight him, but I didn't have the constitution, and I was wearing a skirt that was hard to move in. So I left, and for a few weeks I didn't speak to him. I spent most of the time at my boyfriend's apartment, where he showed me pictures of himself in the sixties, when he was the hippie to end all hippies.

Eventually, I went back to Raymond. I buried the memory of the fist in my face—the way it so clearly said: Get away from here. Don't come back. We were friends again when I enrolled at Sarah Lawrence that fall; he came to my dorm room and helped me hang a curtain to block out my roommate. But he was skeptical of the girls in their cashmere sweaters and their highlighted hair, and he didn't visit very often. While I dreamt in the library, AIDS arrived in New York; it arrived with its claws out. He was always coming home from hospital rooms when I managed to get him on the phone. But he didn't want to tell me about it.

One evening, I took the train into the city to meet him, and we went to a gay bar where he met a group of his ecstasy friends. On a giant screen, porn films were playing, men with penises so large they seemed like jokes. Raymond and his friends only occasionally glanced at the film, and I tried to train my eyes away from it, but after a while the boys around the table started laughing at me. They said my face was turning red. "You should check it out," one said. "Breeders don't get to watch this kind of stuff." I tried to seem relaxed, but I felt hot and angry with Raymond, angry for the way he made me feel like an awkward appendage from the past, a possession he couldn't figure out how to shed.

The next morning we woke up hungover in his apartment. One of the boys from the night before dropped by and we smoked pot. For a moment, I felt like I knew where I was and why I was there. Raymond had never looked more like a celebrity. He said, "Let me massage your leg, you need to loosen up." He pulled on my ankle very hard. "Stretch!" he said, like a P.E. teacher. Maybe the pot made it hard to feel what was happening, but I thought I felt a muscle in my knee tear. "Oh, my God, Raymond, something happened," I said. "It'll be okay. Just stop being such a hypochondriac," he told me.

Raymond and his friend left for a wedding, and he promised to call and take me to dinner later. I sat in the apartment watching *Rosemary's Baby*. My knee swelled up, hot and damaged. Raymond never called, and I waited for him in his apartment all night. I counted to one hundred and back again, trying to hold myself together. His roommate saw the light on and came in. He was a nice ex-Mormon whose scalp was always stained from hair dye. He gave me something to wrap around my pulsing knee. "If it makes you feel any better," he said, "he abandoned his brother here without calling one night just like he's left you. And he's only ten."

Of course I know now that Raymond needed to abandon people just as he had been abandoned; I know that easy story of reenactment. He wanted to be the person who wasn't coming home, who wasn't there no matter how many times you tried his phone number.

I saw him one more time after that long, swollen night in his apartment. He agreed to meet with me after I begged him for an explanation. "Let's take a walk. Maybe it will feel better," he said. I was still limping. We were walking on a sidewalk in the East Village. Garbage was heaped in the gutters, maybe there was a strike. The air smelled of spoiled food and incense. "I'm sorry," he said. "Sorry for not coming back to the apartment and getting you." "It's okay," I said. "I'm just glad you called." He was quiet for a moment and then he said, "You know this is bigger than the both of us and what it really is is that you never listen, you really never listen. Never!" Then he ran away down the sidewalk. That was more than ten years ago, and it was the last time I ever saw him.

I try to go back to that moment on the sidewalk and retrace the steps that led me there. I wonder what he meant when he said I didn't listen, if there was something I should've heard, something he tried to whisper in my ear, something that was carried off by the wind. Maybe there was a moment when I should've taken a different course, a plane I should not have boarded, a moment when I should've spared myself the grief. I blame it on ecstasy, on his mother in the boat. It depends. I feel like a fool for all the drama and wish I'd acted differently, with self-respect. But there are voices in the wall I listen to, there is a strong undercurrent of self-destruction in me. So even after our love became a mean, dangerous thing, I embraced it, I followed it, I pushed my way into its ruined interior.

Later, I hear rumors; someone claims he saw Raymond's picture in a porn magazine. From this, I imagine a good-and-evil story about the sweet boy who goes down into the underworld and abandons his friends. Out of the light and into the darkness! But I can't quite convince myself of this cliché. I try to think of what we could've become to one another: lifelong roommates, collaborators, dinner party companions who complete each other's sentences and say, "Remember? Remember?" until people say, "Enough of high school already." I wonder what it means when a history ends the way ours did, so abruptly, if you can ever repossess that history and put it on display or if it remains locked up and sealed shut in some cold part of yourself. I return to Portland and walk past his old apartment, past the place where the plant we threw off the roof must have hit the pavement. That night I have a dream in which Raymond calls and tells me, "It was all a big misunderstanding. I'll be right over!" But even in the dream I know he'll take forever.

END DAYS

Jenny Offill

—————

WAS AFRAID TO sleep over at her house. I thought that in the night the Rapture might come, sweeping up Mary and her family. Mary had shown me a passage in the Bible that spoke of such things. *One will be taken and one will be left. Two will be sleeping in a bed and one will disappear.* Only the believers would be taken up, she told me, and this was bad news because I didn't believe.

Not in Jesus at least. I was twelve that year. I believed in ESP and positive thinking. I believed in my horoscope (Scorpio) and my lucky number (3). I believed that animals were more trustworthy than people and that trees had feelings. I believed that prayer was useless because I'd prayed, *Make my mother happy*, and nothing had changed.

But Mary wanted me to believe that the end of the world was coming. One night she kept me up for hours talking about heaven and hell and everything in between. She said that the end would come like a thief in the night, that no one knew the hour or the day.

I had never read Revelation before, but somehow the words seemed familiar to me. I was used to worrying that I was living in the end days. For months now, my mother had talked of disappearing. Already I knew it could happen in a hundred ways. And so I waited and worried, thinking: *Some hour, some day.*

"What if you died today?" Mary asked me. "Don't you worry where you'll go?"

"No," I lied.

"A thief in the night," she said, "just think about how quick that is."

In the dim light, her face shone with certainty. I thought of how calm she always seemed. How she didn't chew her pencils or bite her nails like I did. How she didn't make her statements sound like questions. Adults would have called her poised, but it was something simpler than that. Mary was sure of her place in the world, and this made her content. She reminded me of my dog in a way. Sweet, loyal, trusting—a completely different species.

I told Mary I didn't want to think about the end of the world, but that wasn't the truth exactly. As unnerving as I found her doomsday talk, there was a part of me that thrilled to it. It was strangely exhilarating to lie in her pink canopy bed and consider the same questions philosophers had for centuries. Would the world end? Did hell exist? Could suicides go to heaven?

Yes.

Yes.

No, Mary said.

She turned away and pulled the covers to her chin. "Sleep well," she said sweetly, as if she hadn't ruined any chance of it.

IN THE BEGINNING, of course, it was Mary who seemed doomed. She showed up the first day of school wearing an ankle-length skirt and a sweater appliquéd with tiny hearts. Even worse, she'd brought her own lunch in a big paper bag. "Good luck, Mary!" someone had written on the front of it. She was the only new girl that year, a seventh-grade transfer from Holy Trinity. All anyone knew about Trinity was that cheerleaders had to wear culottes instead of skirts and no one was allowed to dance, not even at homecoming.

The funny thing about Mary was that she didn't even try to fit in. She wore dowdy clothes, never spoke in class, and spent her free periods reading the dictionary. When the cool boys made jokes, she didn't laugh, and she sometimes went to Bible study instead of basketball games. She was strange looking too, not ugly, but not conventionally pretty either. She had blond hair and blond eyelashes and skin so pale it looked as if she'd never spent a day in the sun.

It didn't take long for the rumors to start. One of the girls said Mary was an albino, another that she was a hillbilly from Kentucky. But it soon became clear that Mary was impossible to tease. She had a disarming way of answering taunts directly as if they were intended as innocent questions. Albinos have pink eyes, she'd explain patiently. They're not just blond like me.

She wasn't a hillbilly either. She was from Illinois like the rest of us, she said. Her father was a businessman, and her mother was a housewife and a member of the Junior League. She had one brother, Johnny, who was ten, and a cat named Popeye. In the beginning, she had no friends, but eventually even the mean girls were won over by her. Mary baked cookies when people got sick and gave Popeye's kittens away for free. And she never told if you cheated off her during a test.

You have to admit she's kind of nice, the girls started to say.

We became friends by accident because of the school spelling bee. The year before, Mary had won the school, city, and state competitions, and made it all the way to the nationals in D.C. The first-place prize was a college scholarship and a chance to meet the president. Mary placed twentieth. As soon as she got home, she started studying again. She was determined to win the following year, the last year she'd be eligible to compete. That was why she was always in the library reading the dictionary.

Word got around about Mary's spelling talent, and when it was time for our school's annual bee, the auditorium was full. A local news show even came to film the competition.

I was a good speller too, but I didn't think I had a chance to win against Mary. But one by one the contestants fell away until we were the last two left. I spelled *miasma* and *perpendicular* and *galoot*. Mary whizzed through *luminary*, *baklava*, and *carbuncle*. Then Mary misspelled *firkin*, and a hush fell over the crowd. I stepped up to the microphone and painstakingly spelled *firkin*, then sailed to victory on *ephemeral*. "E-P-H-E-M-E-R-A-L, ephemeral," I said.

After Mary lost she cried, but the next day she came back to school and said she and her mother would like to tutor me. They already had an arsenal of dictionaries and spelling lists, she said, and if I hoped to make it to nationals I needed to train aggressively. The whole thing seemed weird and probably Christian, but I wanted to win and go to Washington, so I agreed.

The next day, I went home with Mary. Her house was quiet and perfectly neat. Mary told me to take off my shoes and leave them by the front door so I wouldn't dirty the carpet. I liked the soft swish my socks made as I tiptoed into the den behind her. Mary showed me our study area, a large wooden table covered with file cards, markers, and dictionaries. Her mother came in with a plate of cookies. She was young and pretty and wore a gold cross on a delicate chain around her neck.

"Are you girls ready to spell?" she asked brightly.

I nodded. I worried that she could tell my hair was dirty. My mother said if you brushed baby powder through it, it worked like shampoo. You could never tell with my mother. Most of the time her Richmond, Virginia, background kicked in and she wouldn't let me leave the house unless I looked perfect: clean hair, ironed clothes, shoes that had been shined until they gleamed. But every once in a while she'd say the baby powder trick was good enough.

Mary's mother put down the cookies and suggested we begin our studies with a short prayer. They bowed their heads, so I did too, but I kept my eyes open.

Dear God,
You made this world and all the words in it.
Help us to learn the splendors of your dictionary.
Let us spell with humble hearts for the glory of your son,
Our Lord Jesus Christ.
Amen.

"God made the dictionary?" I asked Mary after her mother left. "Was that what she was saying?"

"God made everything," she said.

"Pencils? Socks? Toasters?"

"Everything," she said.

That night, I had trouble falling asleep. It had never occurred to me that God had such a hand in things.

It took a few weeks to get used to, but after a while I started to like it when Mary and her mother prayed. They bowed their heads and screwed up their foreheads as if they were really concentrating. It was the only time I ever saw Mrs. Larkin with an unpleasant look on her face. To me, she looked like a mother in a magazine, pretty, efficient, a little blank. Mostly, she seemed like an ingenious machine whirring from one task to the next, vacuuming, dusting, cooking, gardening. Tulips on the kitchen table, fresh laundry folded in the drawers. Once I asked Mary if she thought her mother was happy, and she was so startled she didn't answer at first. "Why wouldn't she be?" she said finally.

That was the winter my mother wished she was dead, the

winter everything was unraveling. The new headmaster at her school had started firing faculty, and my mother got cut in the first wave even though she was one of the school's most popular teachers. She was given notice in January but was supposed to finish out the year, and her strange lame-duck status took a terrible toll on her. She could hold it together until the end of the school day, but as soon as she got home, she'd collapse in tears.

On bad days, she would lock herself in the bathroom and cry, saying we'd be better off without her. My father would knock tentatively on the door, then leave a cup of tea outside. Sometimes he wrote notes to her and slipped them underneath. One night when my mother had been in there for hours, I wrote a jagged line like a seismograph in my diary and under that in capital letters "WORDS ARE STUPID." Immediately, I felt guilty, wondering what Mary would think. The day before she had quizzed me on *lucent*, *polyphony*, *sanguine*, and *numinous*. Don't you just love words? she'd asked me when I got them right, and I had nodded happily.

I tore the piece of paper out of my diary and ripped it into little pieces. The way my mother cried was a secret I was keeping from Mary.

In some ways, it was easy not to tell her. The dark fact of my mother's despair seemed impossible in the pretty, sunlit rooms of Mary's house. Everything about the place seemed charmed to me. In Mary's bedroom there was a pink canopy bed with flowered sheets, a white desk with special cubbyholes, and a dictionary as big as the one in the library. Inside her bureau, all her clothes were organized perfectly. Mrs. Larkin had even made a special divider to separate Mary's socks from her underwear. In the bathroom, she had color-coded the towels for each member of the family. The same was true with their toothbrushes. When I marveled at the system, Mary shrugged. My mother's just like that, she said.

Sometimes when no one was looking, I would peek in the

Larkins' closets and drawers, hoping to find a pocket of messiness, some sort of disorder that would prove they weren't what they seemed. But I could never find it. Every drawer and cupboard was perfectly arranged.

My mother had always been the one who kept the house organized and clean, but when she fell apart so did our family's housekeeping. Once a week, we would all make an effort to clean the front rooms, the part of the house that a visitor might see. But there was always a junk room, secret and shameful, filled with laundry, old magazines, and broken games. It was meant to be the guest room, but it had been a long time since it had been used for that purpose. Every time my mother looked in the junk room she'd start to cry again.

All winter, I never invited Mary to sleep over at my house. I always said it was better to stay at hers so we could use the good dictionaries. If Mary was suspicious of my excuses, she never let on. She had only been inside my house a few times, and never in the junk room, but the day before the spelling bee she did a spooky thing that made me think she knew about it anyway.

"Here," she said, handing me a little book as I got out of the car. The book was called *Open Your Heart to Me*. On the cover was a picture of Jesus knocking on the door of a vine-covered heart like a vacuum cleaner salesman. The story was about Jesus coming into a woman's heart, going from room to room, clearing it of sin, until finally he reached the one room that she still kept locked, the room with the hidden key.

"No, it's too messy," the woman said. "I can't let you in." Then the picture showed that behind the door was a room filled with envy and hate and jealousy piled up on top of lust and greed. The woman tried to keep him from going in, but Jesus told her that this was the one room he wanted to see. "Open the door," he said. "Give me the key."

After I finished the book, I tried to fall asleep, but I couldn't even though Mary had warned me that I had to get at least eight hours before the bee. I tried to count prefixes and suffixes like sheep, but after an hour of this I was still awake. When I closed my eyes, I kept seeing the vine-covered heart and Jesus knocking and knocking until someone let him in.

Finally, after tossing and turning for hours, I got up and went into the junk room. There was a pile of papers on the bed with some panty hose and a box of safety pins jumbled in. There was a half-opened Advent calendar and some tattered fairy wings from my Halloween costume in third grade. There was an expensive dog bed that the dog never wanted to sleep in. There was an exercise cycle and a pair of roller skates. I went into the kitchen and got some garbage bags, a few boxes, and some Magic Markers. I started in the back and sorted through every pile, boxing and labeling and finally stacking each box inside the walk-in closet one on top of another. I felt giddy with excitement, thinking of how much order I was creating. On and on I went, clearing out each nook and cranny with feverish intensity. By the time I finished, my nightgown was filthy and I had Magic Marker stains all over my fingers. I sat on the blissfully uncluttered bed and watched the sun coming up over the hills. Everywhere I looked there was a clear surface. I thought that this must be what it felt like to get religion.

When my mother saw the room, she was happy. "I can't believe this," she said. "What a wonderful gift you've given me." But then her face clouded over and I saw that she was worrying that everything would just fall apart again.

I promised her that I would keep it clean, that I'd take care of the room every day and keep the junk from rolling in.

My mother smiled. "You make it sound so easy," she said. She lay down on the smooth bedspread and motioned for me to lie beside her. We looked out the window, which had been hidden by boxes before.

"Look," my mother said. "Sky."

A FEW HOURS later I woke to the sound of Mrs. Larkin honking in the driveway. I was so tired I felt like I was in a trance, but I forced myself to get up and get dressed. I combed my hair with baby powder and put Visine in my eyes to make them look less red. I spelled silently as I brushed my teeth, but already I knew it was hopeless.

Mrs. Larkin looked upset when she saw me. "You look as if you haven't slept a wink," she scolded. "Didn't you to go to bed early?"

"I had bad dreams," I said.

Mary reached up and touched my head. "You must have seen a ghost in your sleep. Look, your hair turned white."

"It's baby powder," I explained. "It works in a pinch when you don't have time to wash." I looked at my hands and saw that they were still spotted with Magic Marker stains.

Mrs. Larkin pursed her lips tightly, but she didn't say anything. When we got out of the car, she took a brush out of her pocketbook and brushed my hair briskly until all the white was gone. "There," she said. "That's better."

My parents arrived just before the bee and sat in the front row with the Larkins. They both seemed excited, and my mother had put on a pretty dress for the occasion. She had even covered the dark circles under her eyes with concealer so that she looked as if she was well-rested.

Mary took my hand in hers. "Don't be nervous," she said. "Just pray that God gives you the right words."

My mother gave me a hug. "You're such a good speller," she told me. "I'm sure you'll do well."

I shook my head. "I'm not going to win," I said. "I can tell I'm not."

Mrs. Larkin frowned at me. "That's no way to think now, is it?" she said.

But I was right. I only made it to the sixth round. The word I struck out on was *nebbish*, defined as a pitifully ineffectual, timid, and luckless person. Backstage I cried, stung by the thought that the winning word at my school spelling bee had proved horribly prescient. *Ephemeral*, meaning short-lived, lasting only a day. Mary said God must have other plans for me.

That night I couldn't bear to go home, so I asked if I could sleep over at Mary's house for one more night. "Of course," Mrs. Larkin said. "You girls deserve to have some fun after all this work." We made popcorn and watched movies, but as soon as Mary fell asleep, I started crying again. I tried to be quiet, but she woke up anyway.

"What's the matter?" she said.

"I don't know," I told her. "I just started crying."

"If there's something wrong you can tell me, you know."

"I think I'm just tired," I said dully.

Mary was quiet for a while. "If you don't want to tell me, you can tell God," she said. "He's always there to listen if you believe in him."

I thought about a book I'd read once that told about the fantastic creatures that lived in the dark depths of the sea. There were giant squid with eyes as big as saucers and jellyfish the size of Christmas trees. There were transparent minnows that glowed like lights and eels shot through with electricity. Why in the world would the maker of such terrible and marvelous creatures care if I believed in him?

"I'm sick of God," I told Mary. "That's all you ever talk about. God. God. God. Who cares about all that anyway?"

To my surprise, she looked like she might start crying too. She hugged a pillow to her chest as if to guard herself against my words. "I just don't want you to get left behind," she said finally. "I want to know you'll spend eternity with me."

I couldn't think of anything to say. I was sick of eternity and Jesus and talk of being swept away. I was sick of hearing that this world was merely a way station on the road to heaven.

"Just leave me alone," I said. "I'll be okay."

Mary didn't answer. For a long time, I could hear her sniffling, then she turned her back to me and went to sleep.

It was cold in the room. I looked out the window and wondered what time it was. It was still dark, but the stars were beginning to fade. A few more hours until morning probably. I decided I should stay awake until dawn just in case the thief came. I imagined him like a shadow that moved across the wall, changing from one thing to the next, impossible to fix in place.

Mary had a night-light shaped like a shell, and after she fell asleep, I stared at it for a long time, trying not to think about eternity. I remembered a game I used to play with my mother when I was little. *Don't think about a beach ball. Don't think about an airplane. Don't think about a red elephant,* she'd say. And, like magic, the forbidden thing would appear in my mind as if my thoughts alone had called it into being.

I tried to think about the shell and only the shell, but somehow the game kept creeping in again. *Don't think about the Rapture. Don't think about the end-time. Don't think about what happens when you're dead.*

THE SUMMER AFTER the spelling bee, my family moved to North Carolina. On moving day, Mary and I cried and swore we'd keep in touch, and for a little while we did. I don't remember what we said in our letters, only that Mary always ended hers the same way: *Know that you are in my thoughts and prayers.* Her words irritated me. Knock, knock, knock, they said. Knock, knock, knock.

When school started, I stopped writing Mary back. Her letters piled up on my desk, pink and blue envelopes with my name written on the front in girlie curlicue script. At first, I opened and read them, but after a while I didn't even bother to do that.

Finally, the letters stopped. I stuck all the old ones in a box under my bed and forgot about them.

I had made friends at my new school quickly. A bunch of punk rock kids who dyed their hair jet-black and wore accusatory buttons on their jackets. Most had home lives that made mine seem completely idyllic. Ingrid's dad was a drunk who couldn't hold down a job. Maggie had a sister in a mental institution, and Lisa's mom had a boyfriend who preyed on her until she learned to double-lock her door at night.

It was thrilling to be the normal one again. Despite my fears, my mother had not disappeared. She had climbed out of her despair and become a sturdy presence in my life again. She had started a successful tutoring business and was deeply involved in an Episcopalian church that had just been founded. All signs pointed toward a happy ending, but still I watched my mother nervously, careful to make sure she was tethered to the world securely. It took a while, but slowly, I began to believe that the worst was over, that nothing terrible would happen.

I brought my friends over to the house now. They liked my mother because she was smart and kind and knew how to talk to teenagers without condescending to them. "You're so lucky to have a mother like that," Lisa told me once, and I didn't even explain how things used to be.

Sometimes we skipped school and went to the park to drink cheap wine and smoke clove cigarettes. We listened to the Sex Pistols and swore we'd try heroin if we ever came across it. My new friends thought it was funny that I'd come from a state even lamer than their own, and it didn't take long for me to turn my old life there into a joke. *My best friend was a Christian who believed that the end of the world was near,* I told them. *Once she cried when I said I didn't believe in Jesus. We spent hours and hours just reading the dictionary.*

One time I even read some of Mary's letters aloud to Lisa and Maggie. After that, they took to whispering *Know that you are in my thoughts and prayers* every time they said goodbye. Every-one agreed I was lucky to have escaped from Illinois before the big bad Rapture came. "At least here, you won't be the only one left behind," Lisa said. "We'll all meet in the park and have an end-of-the-world party."

IT'S BEEN MORE than twenty years since I last saw Mary, but I think of her sometimes now that doomsday talk is in the air again. No one I know now believes that God will end the world, but some days the news makes it seem like we will bring about our own ruin. How much simpler the Rapture seems than this. To think that this life is not the end if only we believe it isn't.

On bad days, I watch the news and listen to the radio compul-sively. Sometimes in the blare of warnings Mary's gentle voice comes back to me: *You must be prepared. You must be vigilant. You must ask yourself, Will I be ready?*

I am no more ready now than I was then, but I have taken cer-tain modest precautions. I wear my glasses now on the subway so as not to leave this world in a blur. I have memorized the chem-ical smells to fear: bitter almonds, Juicy Fruit gum, geraniums. I look up when planes fly low overhead and keep three hundred dollars in a coffee can. I cross my fingers if the subway stops mysteriously between stations.

It embarrasses me to admit that I think this way. To see myself once again drawn to these apocalyptic visions. But the truth is at times I feel oddly exhilarated by all of this, the way I used to when I listened to Mary outline the stark choices before me: heaven or hell, stay or go. There are only two kinds of time that matter, she used to say. This very moment and eternity.

I still wonder which would be better: to disappear or to be left behind. Both seem impossibly lonely. Mary, of course, would say it was better to disappear. Otherwise, you'd have to live through the end days, when everything man touched turned to ruin and there was nothing beautiful left to see. I try to picture a ruined world, but for once my apocalyptic imagination fails me. Instead, I see Mary and the other believers floating away from earth like astronauts, spun out into the dark beauty of the stars, released at last from gravity.

FLAWLESS

Lydia Millet

I SPENT THE SUMMER between high school and my freshman year in college in a small town in the Italian Alps, where I had a fellowship to improve my Italian. Every day I went to classes at a small language institute for foreigners. The town was full of fat black slugs I couldn't help stepping on as I walked the hilly path to school in the foggy mornings; the school was full of tall blond Norwegians, terrifyingly beautiful and clean.

In high school I had considered myself to be one of the pretty girls, but I looked at the Norwegians and saw for the first time that I was a mud creature. I was born from dirt and in the dirt I would remain. I was fit only to sniff around at their feet.

I instantly fell in love with at least two of them.

Also at summer school were several other Americans, but only one of them was as beautiful as the Norwegians. Her name was Wendy and she was from New York City. *Manhattan*, she said. *The Village.* She was taking time off from her MBA program at Columbia. When I first met her she affected me the same way the Norwegians did: she was flawless, fresh and perfect of tooth and skin, a soap commercial. She spoke Italian like a native, her accent warm and fluid and without a hint of the comic Yankee twang most Americans have when they try to speak other languages.

I admired her, but I was also afraid, as I was afraid of all of them. There was something inhuman in their lack of blemish, something alien. Their hair always shone, their breath was always pristine, and even after serious physical exertion they smelled only of laundry detergent and Lagerfeld cologne. Still, they were benevolent aliens. They came in peace. And when they approached me in their genial and democratic way, I was receptive to them. I trooped around in their company gladly, a grubby, ungainly girl by comparison, plump around the edges, who started conversations abruptly and suffered the occasional glaring pimple.

In the six weeks of the language course, Wendy and I became friends. She was an opera buff, her father a concert pianist, and I had taken classical singing lessons in high school, so we talked about how we liked Verdi. She lent me Deutsche Grammophon opera cassettes to listen to on my Walkman and educated me about famous European tenors like Fritz Wunderlich and Jussi Björling, whose early deaths she found romantic. With the tapes in my trusty Walkman—which had previously held only the likes of A Flock of Seagulls, Men at Work, and Falco—I wandered the cobblestone streets of that misty Italian village feeling lofty and transported. I was grateful to Wendy for that.

Possibly the common touchstones were what interested her, the fact that we both had a taste for music most of our peers didn't like and both read good books. But in fact even years later, knowing what I didn't know in high school—namely, that even in this Extreme Makeover culture appearances aren't quite everything—I'm still mystified by what drew her to my company. She was sophisticated and cosmopolitan in her early twenties, and wore tasteful designer clothes without wrinkles that exuded wealth. I was a seventeen-year-old rube from Toronto who had just recently given up her tennis shoes with the light blue swishes on the sides and the double-tied laces stamped with multicolored hearts.

Probably the answer was simple: I was the only other woman in the group who was roughly her age, spoke English as a first language, and came from an educated middle-class family. Probably she was lonely.

She was also clever, good-natured, and warm. There was nothing to dislike.

By the time we left to go back to the United States, she and I had promised to keep in touch, and we did. She came to stay with me in my dorm room in North Carolina that fall—it was 1986—and I spent a short spring vacation with her in Florida, where her mother lived. She made us crepes and breaded eggplant in the tasteful kitchen, which shone of copper and stainless steel, while I confessed that only Kraft dinner was within my culinary repertoire. In fact I ate it many times weekly, whenever I was not dining on similar fare in the school cafeteria.

But Wendy was a strict vegetarian and did not eat processed foods. She warned me of the dangers. I was discovering that Wendy lived what I considered to be an ascetic life. She did not eat candy or drink cheap beer; did not listen to *rock music* or watch television, except for PBS; did not wear synthetic fabrics next to her skin. She barely wore makeup—why would she?— but the small bottles of skin-care products on her mother's bathroom counter had French names, and when I turned one upside down and saw a price tag I had to stifle a startled laugh.

The following summer she flew to Toronto while I was staying alone at my parents' house, and we lay on the beaches of Lake Ontario and baked in the UV rays. I continued to worship her impeccable face and body and admired her composure, but I strove to keep my pathetic adulation a secret. To that end, I adopted a purposefully casual attitude toward the friendship.

It was the summer of my junior year when I first went to see her in New York. She lived in an elegant brownstone in Brooklyn Heights whose foyer featured oil paintings warmly lit from above so that they had the patina of copper. The place belonged to her wealthy boyfriend, David, who was away at work when she ushered me in. Orchestral music played on the high-end stereo, and as soon as Wendy's back was turned I shot a stealthy glance at the album cover and saw it was something called *The Rite of Spring*. I filed this away to use in conversation should she bring it up.

My footsteps were silent on the thick carpet. I felt an urge to take off my shoes, as though entering a temple.

It was not a large apartment, but like Wendy it was perfectly groomed. Nary a greasy fingerprint graced a doorjamb. On the walls hung Japanese watercolors of weeping trees and arched wooden footbridges, and a black-and-white bamboo screen divided the bedroom in half, hiding the double futon. In the peach-colored bathroom there was also no sign of dirt, only the faint chemical smell of oranges. There was a static quality to the place, as though the walls were so thick nothing unwanted could ever penetrate.

Later we met David for cocktails and then went to dinner. He was a quiet, well-mannered blond man in his thirties, wearing a gray suit. He spoke softly and smiled gently, and everything he said was careful and bland. He treated us both to several courses in an upscale restaurant—*Would you care for an appetizer, Lydia? I recommend the tapenade*—and then strolled with us at a leisurely pace through the West Village. We stopped to look at break-dancers spinning on the ground, and David watched them patiently with a look of faint indulgence, like an anthropologist studying primitives. Wendy leaned her head on his shoulder and smiled. Further along we listened to street musicians from South America playing on pipes made of wood. I looked at David as he listened to them play and saw he approved of them more than the break-dancers. Then we bought Italian ice creams in sugar cones and ate them as we strolled through the light crowds, basking in the warm July dusk.

It occurred to me that David seemed more like a benevolent uncle to Wendy than a boyfriend, but I had nothing against him.

Then he left on business for a few days and we had his apartment to ourselves. We drank wine, about which she knew everything and I knew nothing, and then sat up late talking, getting deeper and deeper into disclosure, tongues happily loosened. We talked about men, of course, and our relationships with them and the sex that we had. At the time I was seeing a flamboyant drama student whose interest in me was waning after a year and half, though I did not yet know it. I lamented our business-as-usual sex life like a woman twice my age. Wendy said her sex life with David was good, except for some minor peculiarities.

—Like what? I asked, budding with prurient interest.

—Well, for instance, he won't go down on me unless I scrub it first with disinfectant. And he watches me to make sure I do it right.

—What?

—You know. Down there.

—Huh, I said, nodding slowly, trying to keep my face impassive though I was fairly sure she could not see it too well in the dimness of the candlelit room. I thought of how immaculate she always was, every hair in place, not a fleck of dirt under her French-manicured nails or a single pore visible on her smooth caramel skin. It occurred to me that if I was the one David was dating he would probably make me wash myself with an industrial sander. —That seems kind of, I don't know. Disturbing?

—Oh, I don't know, she said, and shrugged. —It's not that big a deal.

Later, as we lay side by side on David's king-size bed with the lights out, she asked me if I could keep a secret.

—Yes, I said, not sure if I was lying.

—You can't tell him I told you. And you can't tell anyone else.

—Okay. Sure.

—When he was a little younger? David and these other guys raped this girl. They were in high school I think but she was only twelve. It was in this church, on the altar.

I was silent for a long time.

—Huh, I said finally.

—They were never caught or anything. I mean no one knows it was them and they never told. But they raped her. No one believed she was raped and she got thrown out of school for being pregnant.

—Really.

—So anyway. He's got some issues around it and he's trying to work through them.

I did not know what to say. Wendy talked a little more about the aftermath of the rape, how the twelve-year-old girl had been ostracized and David and his friends had seen it happening but never come forward. For years they had lived in the same tightly knit Polish community with the young girl and had never done anything to relieve her burden.

Wendy did not put it this way. She related the story with a casual neutrality, as though the facts of the case were almost incidental. What was important was that David was sorry now, she said. There was nothing he could do, of course—the girl had grown up and become a woman, and he had a career and a lot of money—but he was now sorry.

Finally we fell asleep, tired of talking, listening to the faint rush of traffic in the distance. When I woke up in the morning I was instantly anxious, until I recalled that David wasn't due back from his business trip until after I left the city.

I spent two more days with Wendy in New York. She did not

bring up the subject of the rape, but I found myself returning to it in idle or lonesome moments and keeping my thoughts from her. I would see David in a ring of boys around an altar covered in white linen, with a dark-haired, skinny girl spread-eagled among them, her skirt hitched up around her waist, screaming shrilly as they held her down. Or I would instead see Wendy naked, standing in front of the sink in the peach-colored bathroom with one foot lifted onto the toilet, scrubbing herself as David looked on to make sure she was doing an adequate job.

Between these ugly flights of fancy I found myself impressed by small things, like Wendy's intricate knowledge of the subway system or her confidence in her summer job. She was working at the offices of a multinational corporation in midtown, speaking her fluent Italian on the phone to customers. She wore an elegant dark skirt suit that made her look like a flight attendant, and kept her long, soft hair expertly twisted into a bun on the top of her head. I met her for lunch, and we sat in the park and ate sandwiches. I worried about the crumbs and mustard around my mouth as I watched her even white teeth bite precisely into a thin carrot stick.

Then my thoughts would stray to the altar, the kicking girl, and the boys' hands fumbling at their flies.

Shortly after I got back to North Carolina I realized that something about Wendy's seamlessness had silenced me when I was in New York, made it difficult for me to bring up the subject once it had been broached and then shelved. I could not talk to her except in a way that went along with her. And I had been afraid that if I asked her about the rape it would distort something in the façade of her that I clung to, something I relied on. I was frightened of the disruption of anger.

So I decided to sit down and write her a letter. Even the phone was too intimidating. *Dear Wendy, it was so great to see you again* . . . and then I moved on to the heart of the matter. *But are you sure David is good for you? I don't know if I'll be able to act normal around him knowing what you told me. It just makes me uncomfortable that he hurt that girl and never did anything to help her afterward.* I'm sure the tone of my letter was more high-handed than this, but that was the gist of it. I did not know if David was healthy for her and in fact I did not know if he was healthy even for me, who barely had to see him. No doubt the letter was arrogant, but it was also honest: and now when I remember it I regret mostly the style, and less the intent.

I was nervous after I mailed it, and it was weeks before an answer came, prolonging my discomfort. I worked on forgetting the letter as leaves turned yellow and red in Chapel Hill, flutter-ing down to dapple the rolling greens of the campus. I knew that Wendy would feel I had overstepped, though I believed my let-ter to have been reasonable; I knew the friendship might well be over. But I told myself repeatedly that it did not matter, and when I was walking quickly across campus with a zealous sense of momentum—this happened to me often when I was eighteen and nineteen, a sweeping euphoria at the prospect of my own future that seems to me now a sweet artifact of adolescence—that none of my old, fading friendships mattered, that they were all ephemeral and real life was only just starting up.

Finally Wendy sent a short, neatly written note on a stiff card saying she did not wish to have further contact with me. She could not continue to be friends with someone who did not "respect" her "choices."

With that we went our separate ways. I had no doubt I had acted correctly. In fact, the way I saw it, my behavior had a tinge of nobility. I had struck a blow for upstanding citizens every-where, raising my voice in defense of an innocent twelve-year-old victim and refusing to bend.

And instead of upsetting me, the friendship breakup came as a relief. I noticed the relief only in passing and reasoned that if Wendy was so ready to throw in the towel over a single argu-ment—the only one we'd ever had—most likely the friendship hadn't been worth much in the first place. After all I had not asked her to choose between her boyfriend and her friend; I had only said I did not know how to be comfortable around him in the wake of her startling confidences. I had only been asking for elaboration from her—an acknowledgment of the vileness of the act, an outcry, a reassurance that she too was horrified by David's crime. I had been looking for something—admittedly, something I had not named. But she had refused to give me anything at all.

Besides, what was she doing with a gang rapist of prepubescent girls who demanded she sanitize her genitals for his protection?

My relief was not caused by the matter of David's offense or my own rationalizations about the weakness of the friendship. Rather I felt released from my subservience to Wendy's brand of hermetically sealed beauty. I admire beautiful people to the point of fatuousness, giving their beauty far more credit than it is due—and though I'm hardly alone in my exaggerated reverence for good looks, my superficiality has sometimes led me to ignominious places. Even recently, steadily heading for middle age and supposedly more mature than I was at nineteen, I have let myself be humiliated for the sake of attractive company.

I wondered what David thought of Wendy, whether some pathology compelled him toward her precisely because of her seamless and clean aspect. Did he feel, as I did, that she was the true light of the sun and people like me were mere shadows cast on the wall of a cave? Did he make her wash herself with peroxide because of some furtive shame of his own or because he held himself apart from the baseness of flesh? I wondered whether the rape had spawned a repulsion toward women's bodies or whether his repulsion had spawned the rape. I wondered if for him desire itself felt unclean, and whether therefore he blamed the object, whether he wanted the object cleaned in order to erase his desire or to provoke it.

I want to erase old versions of myself, and it strikes me that David must have felt this way far more strongly than I do. He must have—unless he was a sociopath, and possibly even then— wanted passionately to take back his actions in the church, or at least the memory of them. (And why had he told Wendy about the rape in the first place? A high-risk gambit or a provocation? Why had he told her, and why had she told me?) Past versions of ourselves are both set in stone and irretrievably distant. Partly, for an instant, it can seem tragic that we are held responsible for them.

David and I had only one thing in common, namely our attraction to Wendy. Mine was platonic and his was not, but probably both of us were drawn to her more for the visible shell than for the subtleties within. There between us was an object of desire, and we moved along parallel tracks of selfishness toward the object and then away from it. Wendy must have wanted to include me in her confusion when she told me about the rape; she must have needed to create a companion who could share the burden and mirror her own position of complicity, knowing an ugly secret and struggling to reconcile it with the allegiance she felt. In her eyes my refusal to take on the task must have consti- tuted a betrayal, because what are friends good for if not to stand in each other's shoes?

A few years later Wendy sent me another letter, saying we had both probably written things we regretted. She told me she had broken up with David long ago and was living in a different city, and she asked if we could rebuild our bridges and be friends once again.

Yet instead of taking the opportunity she offered me in this second letter, I stubbornly maintained a position of rectitude. I wrote her that, although I would like nothing better than to renew our friendship, I could not apologize for my previous con- duct because I did not think I had said or done anything wrong.

Rather than be friends again I wanted to show her how right

I had been. Implicitly I was demanding an apology from her, an admission that I had been right to distrust David and she had been wrong—not as part of a friendly conversation but as a precondition to a new friendship. I wanted to show her that while she may have embodied external perfection, it was I who held the higher ground when it came to the spirit. This time, I wanted her to be sure, I would not be subservient. I wanted her to know my moral purity had trumped her perfect skin.

There was satisfaction in this for me, the smugness of believing myself to be a superior being. At last. Wendy might look good to the passing gaze, but I, at least, despite my compromised flesh, could boast an inner light.

DANGEROUS

Dorothy Allison

THE FIRST TIME I kissed my friend Carla, I suspected I was doing something dangerous. Maybe she would laugh. Maybe she would not respond. Maybe she would stop me and that would be that. That was the risky part. But it's just a kiss, I told myself, no big thing.

I turned my head so as to stroke my cheek against hers, but Carla moved quickly to more fully put her lips on mine. She stopped only to whisper, "I've been wanting you to do that."

I pulled back a little and saw that she was trembling. I felt another momentary uncertainty. Maybe Carla was a lot more serious about what we were doing than I was. That was not something I had considered. I'd been sexual with friends before. Sometimes it worked; sometimes it did not. Usually it was obvious fairly quickly. The times it did not work, it had mostly seemed to be that we laughed too much. Giggling proved anathema to sexual focus. But then there were the moments when kissing a friend had moved smoothly and easily to terrific spurof-the-moment sex—heated enough for satisfaction, relaxed enough for no dangerous repercussions. Of course the latter generally took place at parties or gatherings where sex was more or less expected. This did not feel like that. This was immediately heated and dangerous and momentarily daunting.

"I love you," Carla said.

"You don't know me like that," I told her.

Carla smiled and put her fingers flat against my belly. "Don't be so scared. Nothing bad is gonna happen. And I know you better than you know yourself."

I stopped myself from pulling further away. I looked into her face and tried to figure out what made me so anxious. I trusted Carla. Of course I did. Kissing didn't mean we were going to act out some romantic entanglement and wind up months down the way screaming in fury or stomping away in despair. This was my good friend. I knew who she was. And maybe she did know me better than I knew myself. Maybe I was being anxious for no reason.

I wanted to believe that. I wanted to believe it so much that I kissed her again. She's a grown-up, I repeated to myself. We know what we are doing. I ignored the anxiety that continued to bubble somewhere in my nervous system—the part of me that suspected I was making a mistake.

I tried to adjust my attitude. Obviously, what we were doing was not casual. We were going to have to talk about it a whole lot more. We would be careful and clear, make sure that we were thinking about everything the same way. That was the danger. Certainly we could move back and forth along the median of friendship and sexual desire. We just had to keep the trust and the communication open and easy. We just had to figure out how that was done.

I did not want to believe that sex was so powerful it invariably undermined friendship, though I was perfectly aware that desire is one of the most powerful and subversive emotional mechanisms. But why was it so easy sometimes and so difficult others? I knew where my own trigger points were located, what I had to fear and control and make plain. Didn't everyone have such a list? I had told Carla some of the most painful of mine, she had told me some of hers. She had never been loved as she wanted, never treasured as she deserved. I knew that as her friend, but it felt different after I started sleeping with her.

Still there was something that kept going wrong, moments of confusion and uncertainty when I was not at all sure that I understood what we were doing. We were not "in love." That was something we had agreed on. We loved each other but we both had lovers, others to whom we had made commitments and whom we did not want to disappoint.

Slowly, painfully, I found myself not wanting to be around my friend, not wanting her to make love to me. I could make love to her. I did not stop loving her. But no matter how close and naked we got, it seemed there were more and more moments when I wanted to get away from her. How had I gotten myself to a place where I would be happy to see her until I actually did, and then want nothing so much as to get away? I did not understand what had happened. I kept trying to puzzle it out.

SHE READ MY journal.

I had kept notebooks for years, carefully when I was young, and more freely once I left my stepfather's house. But even when I lived on my own, it had taken me a while to learn to write in my notebooks freely. It was a piece of becoming a grown-up— being able to write anything down and look back at it later. It was the beginning of making ideas over into story, and the core of figuring things out. My journal was where I kept track of what happened, tried out different versions of stories, and most of all puzzled out what I did and did not understand. It was full of bad poetry and long, tedious rants, as well as notes on things I wanted to do or feared to do. It was also where I kept track of my own uncertainties and passions, and this thing with Carla that I was not sure I should be doing at all. I had written about her a lot in that journal, her and me and what we were doing and how unsure I was of whether I wanted to go on being sexual with her.

I wish I had not done this, I wrote. *I wish she would start sleeping with someone else so that we could be friends again the way we were. I wish it was a year from now and she had a new girlfriend so I could be helpful and supportive when she complains about her.*

When Carla told me she had read my journal, I was stunned. I had left it in my bag, and she simply pulled it out when I was out of the room. It was an act I had never imagined, but I felt stupid even saying that. I had showed her a lot of my writing. I had read her stories, poems, and even some of my journal entries, but it had never occurred to me that someone I trusted would read what I had not intended that anyone read.

Carla cried, but I could not even think. How had I *not* imagined that she would read my journal? How?

"It is so easy for you," she told me. "You don't know how hard it is for me."

Maybe I didn't. The more Carla stared at me with that desperate expression, the more I wanted to be anywhere else but near her. The more she told me I had hurt her, the more I wanted to get away from her. I would have done anything to keep her as my friend. Anything—except bury myself in the role she wanted me to occupy. How had she not known that about me, she who knew me so well? But why had I believed her when she said that anyway?

By the time Carla stopped speaking to me, I was simply grateful not to be hearing one more time how much I had hurt her.

THE FIRST WOMAN I loved was Kathy. An Arab Israeli runaway, completely incongruent in Central Florida. Fedayeen, she called herself and laughed every time as if it were an intimate joke. But when I said it jokingly, she didn't like that. She was serious. She was serious when she climbed into my bed. She was serious when she showed me what I was for. I was for her. I was hers. She showed me that. No question. I wanted to be her friend, but she wasn't interested in being friends.

Love her? I do not think I loved her. I think I was taken up by her. I think I was lifted up out of myself by her. When I met her I was a girl, I had no notion what life meant. But from the first, any time she shot me a look or even moved her hand I would shift to her side and give over anything she asked. I had not known myself to be that kind of person, and from the first I realized that forever after I would have to be careful with that part of my nature.

I gave myself to Kathy, lost myself in her, her crazy daddy, her dangerous boyfriends, the crying jags that were like those of no one I have ever seen since. She did not cry as if in grief, only in anger. No. Rage. Her fists would pump and pound, she would curse and kick, and finally howl. "God damn! God damn!"

I could never let go like that, turn the air to steam and the heat of it to outrage. I would never tear my own skin the way Kathy would. Long, glittering nails on her like red-black shark's teeth. She would drag them up the insides of her arms, where the skin was tender, or back around her shoulders, where it was harder to tear but possible if you were as crazy mad as she was. The skin peeled off in parallel lines. In the naked Florida heat, the white lines scarred her arms up and down and curled around her shoulders like the marks of torn-off baby angel wings.

Of course, she was angry. She was mad with anger, and I worshiped her. We became the halves of one sundered person— angry female hurting herself more than anyone else. She eased her rage with heroin. I offset mine with the touch of her sweat and the taste of her tears.

When she died—from an overdose I should have anticipated—too far away for me to intervene, or even to slap her face for the waste of her life, I swore to give up that part of me that I had given over to her. Afterward, when women would reach for me or pull me too close, there was always a wingless, stubborn part of me at a distance, holding back just in case.

I MADE RULES for myself, never letting myself have sex with a woman with whom I felt a risk of falling too much in love, or if I did, I never did so without another woman there to cushion my desire—another lover in the room, or present in both our imaginations. As a barrier to injury, grief, or loss, I kept myself at a distance from "falling in love" while loving and making love freely. Friends were fuck-buddies—a familial connection. We got naked with each other on the most basic level in the moment of orgasm—completely exposed—but then pulled up our jeans and stepped apart as if nothing of great importance had taken place. It took a deliberate kind of armor to manage that. Odd how easy it was to put that armor on and how difficult it was to peel it off once it was in place. But for many years I did not even try. I needed that armor. It made me stronger and frankly made it possible for me to do what I most wanted—figure out how the world worked one woman at a time.

SEXUAL DENIAL, I used to think, was one of the greatest injuries we women experience. I believed that salvation lay in confronting that denial and in demanding genuine erotic autonomy. Coming out of a childhood of violent abuse, I had found it very hard to get to a place where I could let myself be naked or vulnerable with another human being. Doing so had been revelatory to me. That I could experience sex and be made not only happy but transported with joy—that had been life-changing. I became an evangelical advocate for erotic mastery. I wrote on the subject, volunteered as a peer counselor, and helped found an organization for women whose erotic imaginations, like my own, had been labeled sick, unreasonable, or anti- or non-feminist.

You want someone to spank you until you orgasm, but you are scared about what will happen if you actually do anything about that desire? "No problem, come sit over here," I'd say. "I'll see if I can't find you a suitable partner. You want a him or a her? You want her to be kindly or stern? Come on, girlfriend, tell me what you are looking for, and let's see if, together, we can't manage to make it happen." Pragmatic, dogmatic, evangelical. My approach seemed innocent to me, innocent and logical and completely reasonable. It was innocent in the sense that I was blissfully convinced that I was doing something right and good, and that sex itself was as simple as scratching that peculiar itch we all had but were hesitant to discuss in mixed company.

I swore I'd never marry, take no life partner, no sanctioned pair bond. I would make no compromise with society's misplaced moral obsessions. I was a feminist. You didn't have to buy me dinner or seduce me with promises to plot your way into my bed. You simply had to be sure enough of yourself to ask me for exactly what you wanted, and I would feel duty bound to try to provide that desire. Sisterhood, to me, meant not just feminist advocacy, it meant fervent solidarity, a literal and full commitment of the body as well as the mind.

My romantic self-image was that of an independent, self-contained comrade who'd stay an hour or a day but never take up residence—the ardent friend who would always be there, but not too much there. What I also wanted was a life shared with committed friends, women whom I could trust to love me as I loved them, to care for me as I cared for them, allies and partners in the best sense. We would keep each other's secrets, come in crisis, and answer miserable 3:00 A.M. phone calls or alerts spread by phone tree. We would find funds when none were to hand, give the warning that no one else would risk, or arrange that vital erotic adventure that would recharge even the most numbed and enervated soul. It was the romance of a family of friends, and the idea can still inspire me—even as my notions of how it might actually work have become a great deal more prudent and down-to-earth.

WHEN WE FIRST became friends, and before we ever tried sleeping with each other, Rickie and I used to talk about the kinds of women we were attracted to. Rickie wanted mysterious, dangerous, high-femme seducers—particularly the kind that would let her play out her fantasy of being a female version of Sal Mineo or Steve McQueen. I wanted only grown-up, fully acknowledged, blatantly perverse women. Not just lesbians, not just dykes; I wanted perverts. I wanted girls who smoked stinky cigarettes and cut their hair in ragged styles, women with facial scars or persistent bruises. Rough trade was what the faggots called it, but I knew that was only a part of what I was after. I wanted wounded girls who had made strength out of damage, stubborn, angry, and absolutely determined not to be victims in any way at all. Oh, you could spank them, but only if they let you. And you could bet your butt that, afterward, they would flip you right over on your belly and hit you twice as hard as you had dared to hit them. Those were my weakness—those sharp-eyed, desperate girls who were just as eager to get up and go back to their own beds as I was to get them out of mine.

God, they were mythic! I knew it and so did they.

"James Deans" my friend Rickie labeled them. "Female James Deans." They knew what they looked like when they hooked their wrists over a pool stick laid suggestively across their shoulders, or swiped grimy fingers up a faded stretch of blue-jean thigh. "Look, there's another one," Rickie would whisper in my ear at Peaches 'n' Cream on a Friday night. And together we would look at her, dark-eyed and absolutely focused, until she would look back, and then we would set about getting her to ignore Rickie's nicotine-stained teeth and that giggle I had still not learned to completely suppress.

"Come here, little girl, got something you don't know you gonna like, but oh, you are going to like it." We were shameless. We would have been predatory, if we had not been exactly what those women were hoping to find.

THE ADVENTURES I shared with those women in my twenties and thirties became our own little urban legends. Tough dykes and adamant feminists, we wanted no part in the victim ideology we held in such complete contempt. We were ruthless with each other, daring each other to be yet tougher and more outrageous. The ideology that we preached may have been a product more of our own desires than of any carefully thought-out critique of patriarchal culture, but we were honest in the most stringent sense. We were true to the criterion we had fashioned. No lies, we swore. We permitted no falsehoods in our ruthless exposure of our most secret lusts. When we called ourselves survivors, we meant we were surviving ourselves, our own reconstructed broken selves, and if we had not shared such a highly developed sense of irony, there would have been no power in what we did.

I make it sound more exciting than it was, but it was at any rate unpredictable and totally absorbing. Two decades of my life are gauzy and lust-scented. I lived in a collective household or in a single apartment. I worked ungodly long hours at my day jobs, and wrote innumerable bad poems and short stories when I was not climbing out of some woman's bed in the middle of the night, or leaning back half asleep on my way to some other woman's apartment. My revenge against the stepfather who had blighted my childhood was to be a sexually active, happy adult woman, very sexually active if somewhat unexamined in the realm of what exactly constituted happiness. Could any of us expect to be genuinely happy in patriarchal America? I used to say that jokingly, but with great seriousness. It took me a while to develop ironic distance. Given a paradoxical appreciation of struggle and an abiding hope for how the world and I were changing, I thought I was as happy as I could expect.

HER NAME WAS BEA. She was an orphan, an orphan with property who never touched her own money and understood things I had no way to conceptualize. The rich are different—to me they were practically inconceivable. Bea lived on the kindness of girlfriends, and she made me one of those. I had thought I had nothing for anyone to take, nothing to spare, until she showed me how much I could provide for her. Not having much made no difference. She did not ask for much, only what I had. In the end, I have to say, she did not rob me, she just showed me how much I had that I had never measured until she came along.

The extraordinary thing about her was her face. She had cultivated an almost ritual emptiness—blank, passive, almost always watching, but that mind was alive. She knew so much, had been so many places and done so many extraordinary things. She had gone to school in Europe and been the last woman fucked by a famous dying poet. She had written a poem stolen by a woman who rewrote it as a song and won an award. "Things I have done," she would begin, and then laugh gently. How extraordinary, I thought, to have that kind of rueful perspective on your own life.

Bea swore that sex had pretty much lost interest for her, just wasn't that big a deal anymore. Still, if I really wanted, she would manage to get herself interested. But really, she seemed always to have other things in mind. She spoke of books she had read that I had not, and I prided myself on reading more than anyone. She could talk philosophy, or music, or inheritance law, and make you think you understood those subjects in completely new ways. It was a marvel just sitting with her at dinner, getting her to talk, putting my hand in hers and watching as she laced her fingers between mine.

Her face could go so still, her eyes become so distant. Even in the most violent romantic moments, she could become dispassionate and far away. I wanted to know how she did that. It was as if she had studied her own features and concluded that it was at rest that she was best presented. Ruthlessly, she seemed to have taught her muscles that artless discipline the great beauties know. I was in awe. When she was pulling my hair with a clenched fist, that face above me was so bland, so impartial, that I would begin to struggle to get free, fighting not to weep, not to be ugly while she watched me. Eventually, I learned that was what she liked—making me scream, making me become ugly in passion while she kept herself aloof and undisturbed. I kept trying to understand, to appreciate what she wanted from me, even to give her what she wanted, but it was impossible.

We were misunderstanding each other from the first. When she left to live with a cousin who had enough money to keep her engaged for the rest of her life, I got completely drunk and made love in the basement room of a bar down on Tenth Street. The woman I was with growled and screwed up her face when she came. Looking into her eyes, I felt like a woman dying of thirst being given a full, deep drink of water.

EVERYONE HAS A TYPE, girlfriends used to tell me. I always denied it, but perhaps it is true. Not black hair and a swimmer's shoulders but a particular kind of mind was what I found over and over. Bossy oldest girls or only children, someone who had boxed off her emotions in the way I had done—letting herself love but not too much, never letting herself need the beloved too much. One can do that—put up barriers against desire of that nature. One can starve need. I had done it, and I was attracted to women who, I believed, had also learned the trick. Keep busy. Satisfy all the easier desires—the immediate lusts and the tenuous emotional connections.

It is possible to starve both the imagination and the libido by focusing them in other directions. Anyway, the women to whom I was drawn—first as friends and then as lovers—always seemed smarter than I. That was part of what I loved about them. They were tough—couldn't hurt them—tough enough to be trusted, and tough enough to be safe for me to love in my careful, measured way.

Don't want too much from me was the message I gave the women in my life. Don't expect too much. Don't cling and I won't do that to you. No, really. I won't.

"You're a lot like a man, you know." It was remarkable how angry that statement could make me.

"I'm a dyke."

"Yeah, well. You think like a man."

That was not true. I thought like a survivor, a hard-edged, stubborn, grown-up girl who simply did not want to risk being deeply wounded. But maybe the prejudice that frames the dynamic in those terms is also a clue to the way men sometimes become so armored and angry.

HER NAME WAS JUDITH. She told me there was only one sin that you could commit in bed, and that was the sin of making love to someone you genuinely did not want.

"No pity fucks," she said. "That's a crime I do not commit. I take you to bed, you better believe I want you there. No one else in that moment but you."

In the moment. All right, I could understand that. Passion for its own sake, not for property or safety or reassurance or hope. No confusion. No bullshit. Just head-tossing, screaming, leg-spreading, do-me-now-and-do-me-right action.

I believed her. I took up the goddess she worshiped with only a quick wink to the violent Baptist god of my childhood. No pity. No compassion. Judith was like an old testament heathen prophet. And damn! She was astonishing in bed. She was, without exception, the best damn fuck of my life. What talent was that? Mad, crazy, immediate, she gave me what I had been wanting all along—someone even more armored than I was, someone who could keep desire at such a distance it was all the more enticing. I did not know I was falling in love with her—until it was plain she was losing interest in me. That was when I realized I had not learned to see around the corners of my own desires, to see how desire could trump friendship. To be friends with her, I had to root out my own desire and not resent her for that. Of all the things I have done in my life, that struggle might have been the hardest.

Only years later could I stand next to Judith and draw a breath without pain, look at her and see her as a person separate from all that we had shared. I had thought what I wanted was an armored heart—safety from loss or grief. But there is no safety behind those kinds of walls. I had thought it was a straightforward trade-off, losing some intimacy in the creation of a kind of strength. And there is strength in holding yourself back from intimacy. It had served me well when I was at my most wounded and vulnerable. It was just not the way I wanted to live my life.

I don't believe that there is any true friendship without a bond of honor, and the honor in friendship is the respect you give the other that she also gives you. Respect is a kind of love, second cousin to love or perhaps even first daughter. There is no friendship without love.

All these years later, I dream of them, each of those I women I write about now. I dream their eyes and speech patterns, their happy exclamations and angry shouts—but not the sex. With all the focus I put on sex for so long, I find it remarkable that sex is not the essential thing I remember.

What I fell in love with were eyes that looked right back into mine, and the slow talk that followed. She would bend forward so that her hair would fall into her eyes. The trick was that I had to lean in and look close. Then she would start talking, and a world would spiral out of her like smoke off a candle flame— shaping up in the air between us. Every time it was the same. There was a world I did not know, and she would take me there—her daddy, her mama, her neighborhood, the first book she loved, and the first time she got naked with another human being. That was what drew me in and caught me. That was when I fell in love. And yes, very often, that was when I retreated. It took me longer than I can explain to learn not to retreat, not to run away.

THE FRIENDS THAT I fell into bed with always had different but complementary families from mine. We would talk books, and women, and history, and politics, but come back over and over to our misguided, blundering, painful families. I remember the first woman who told me about loving women who did not love her—how she had made herself not care. I told her how much I admired her for that—that I had done the same thing. I told her how much I loved how she stood up to the contempt of people who knew nothing at all of how extraordinary she was—even as I told myself that I was nowhere near as strong or admirable as she. With every word I leaned further into her, absorbing every word and gesture. In every case, learning to love her was learning to love myself. After all, she was always, like me, an oldest girl on whom expectations had descended. We had exceeded all expectations, but in areas our families neither expected nor understood, so it didn't work out as the vindication it should have been. Over and over again, I fell into fascination with women who had acted out in one way or another the very dynamic I had struggled against and overcome as an adolescent girl.

I DO NOT regret climbing into bed with friends. I regret the times we misunderstood each other or ran away before we had sorted out what we were doing. Sex with friends seems to be possible only if you are both clear about what it is that you are doing. You are messing around, sport fucking, or getting off—not making love, and not making promises unspoken but implicit in the naked acts each of you imagines the other understands.

If one of you thinks that it is only a matter of time before the lightning bolt of true love strikes and you can move in and acquire a cat, then you are definitely going to lose something—if not the friendship, then the ability to be together and pretend that you are not in pain. Desire engages so much of the contrary, messed-up, and labyrinthine human psyche that it invariably subverts simple aboveboard intentions—if there were such things as simple aboveboard intentions. I am neither so simple nor so easy with my own labyrinthine emotions as to assume there is not a whole lot going on underneath that I might not know at the time. I have just learned to trust that little anxious muscle that runs up the back of my neck. If it pulls tight, I slow down. If what I am doing seems mysteriously dangerous, I trust that it is just that. I take my time. I think about what I am doing. Then I make a decision, deliberate, grown-up, and ready to be wrong if it comes to that.

YOU CAN FALL in love with an idea—the idea of who you think a person to be, or who you want yourself to be. You can fall in love with a dream or a fantasy. You can fall in love with an extraordinary human creature crossing the room and looking back at you, the mind housed in that body, the soul shining out of those haunted eyes, the profound regard held back in those stubborn features. Falling in love is an act I examine with a novelist's wary distrust and a feminist's weathered suspicion. For all the reasons it is dangerous, it is still the most powerful act of hope I can imagine.

I don't think I would risk a friendship for even the most powerful erotic attraction these days, but of course I never did see the risk the times I did exactly that. Have I changed or have the expectations of those I know? Perhaps it is that I am past fifty and finally feeling a sense of resolution with my own erotic matrix, or perhaps it is the impact of a genuinely loving long-term relationship, or the fact that my girlfriend keeps me so thoroughly satiated that I don't tend to brood on the subject anymore. I'm an old dyke now, and have been being entirely too forthright on subjects most people avoid for a long, long time. I don't know how to be a different kind of person.

In my life, I have loved and been loved, at times profoundly, and at others momentarily or just briefly, or with only the most limited kind of understanding. It is love itself that seems to me the act that genuinely changes who we are. That girl I used to be, that adventuress, that legend, she would not understand who I have become. She would shake her head and wonder what happened. I doubt anything I could tell her would sort it out. Perhaps if I showed her pictures of the women we loved who are gone now—some dead, some lost, and some so different as to be unrecognizable to themselves.

It is not the intimacy of sex that explains it all, I would tell her. It is intimacy itself—all those shared understandings, risks, and revelations, and long, stubborn years of not walking away when things become complicated.

That is the most astonishing thing. Not those I have lost, but those I have kept.

TOADS AND SNAKES

Elizabeth Strout

OFTEN, DURING THE autumn months of my freshman year in college, in the late afternoon before the
dining hall opened for dinner, I would sit in the lounge of the
dormitory with a group of other girls. *Women* might be the word
used today, but we thought of ourselves as girls, and we were. We
would slouch down in the navy blue couches, notebooks on our
stomachs, our feet on the sturdy wooden coffee table, some of us
smoking—because smoking was still allowed most everywhere
then—and sometimes Janie Zabrinsky would walk by. Janie was
a junior, and whenever she passed through the lounge, she would
give us a small, distant smile, and then glance down. I assumed
she had no interest in our company, that she had better things to
do than sit and talk with us. But I would watch her carefully.
Janie was small and full figured, with long, dark, ropy hair that
was often pulled back loosely, tied in a knot. Her eyebrows were
dark, her skin clear, her eyes were large and brown. "What's her
story?" I kept asking people.

Her mother, I found out, was Mexican, her father a steel-worker from Pittsburgh, and she had several brothers. Her mother named her Jane, because it sounded so American. Janie had taken two years off from college before returning now as a junior, and during that time she had traveled, gone all over the place: to Mexico, Morocco, France, even Iceland. She had done all this alone. This was amazing to me, who had moved an hour away from home to attend college and often returned home on weekends. No one I knew had traveled the world alone. I thought her aloofness must come from the fact that she was older than we were, had seen the world, and that her decision to return to college was one made with reluctance.

But as the weeks passed, Janie began to join us in the lounge, and in her quiet way, she was very friendly. I found it curious, though, to see her take a liking to Pam, another girl in our dorm. Pam was always angry and complaining. "I *hate* the guy who checks our IDs for the dining hall," she'd say. Or "I *hate* that stupid dance class, everyone in it is an *ass!*" I had grown up with a grandmother who was prone to outbursts of anger, who had no qualms about taking part in sudden altercations with store clerks or neighbors, and I had decided at a young age that when my turn came to be a "grown-up" I would not raise my voice. I would be agreeable and easygoing—that was my plan.

Back then, I did not seem complicated to myself. My goal had been to get myself out of high school a year early and straight into college, and I had managed to do that. So when I sat in English class at three in the afternoon, and saw through the window the final, yellow leaves falling from the maples, and heard the chimes from the chapel playing, I was sometimes in a state close to ecstasy. By the time I made it back to the dorm to lounge around the lounge, I was ready to listen to everything.

Mostly, I wanted to talk to Janie. She asked me about my classes, my family, what my parents did, and said she thought it was lovely they were both teachers. Her father, she said, was very intelligent. He read T. S. Eliot in the evenings. It was a shame he'd never had a real education. Her mother had worked in the school cafeteria. "Wearing one of those hairnets," Janie said with her soft laugh. "Jeez." Her brothers, she said, had a multitude of problems, but she was not specific about these problems, and I did not ask. There was something in Janie's quiet demeanor that let you know when she had said all she cared to say. There was a mature discretion to her, it seemed to me, at a time in life when many people would stay up the whole night talking about themselves. But Janie was a private person. Instead of her problems, she spoke of her travels, of the different friends she had around the world. Some of these friends were divorced, raising children alone. One friend who lived in France had been engaged to a man who was manic-depressive, and broken it off with him. All of this intrigued me. The problems the rest of us had seemed like nothing in comparison.

But when Pam sat in the lounge sobbing one night, because her hometown boyfriend had written her a letter saying he was now in love with somebody else, it was Janie who seemed to care the most. While the rest of us spoke flippantly about boyfriends who dumped their girlfriends, Janie said a number of times, "Pam, I'm so sorry," and asked her questions that were penetrating and kind. "When was the last time you spoke to him on the phone?" "When did the tone of his letters start to change?" Janie shook her head with each answer. "What a dreadful person," she said to Pam. "I'm so sorry you have to go through such a terrible time."

Later that night she said to me, as we wandered back toward my room, "I loved a fellow"—that was her word, *fellow*—"in high school, and it was just terrible when we broke up." She said this with a quiet seriousness that touched me. It occurred to me then that Janie Zabrinsky had a soul exceptionally sensitive and tender.

There was something very gentle about her. She spoke quietly, and listened well, her head leaning toward you. For a long time, I was the one who knocked on her door, though eventually she knocked on mine, and we would go eat in the dining hall together, or go for a walk, or just lie around and talk. She told stories of the different people she knew, and she told them well. The woman in France who had to break her engagement was still reeling from it. Another friend in Iceland had a ten-year-old girl to support, but the divorced father paid her nothing. We shook our heads over this.

"That would make me so *mad*," Janie said.

"Well, sure," I agreed. But privately I knew that I would never get divorced. I was not going to end up one of these women who were mad.

And Janie wasn't either. I could tell that from her quiet nature, and the way she spoke of her family. Her mother, she said, did not like living in Pittsburgh, her brothers were scattered all over the place, one went to live in Mexico, another became a real estate broker, another apparently had some trouble with alcohol. Janie was never clear on that. When she talked of her family she had a way of saying only a few things at a time, and I didn't know if this was out of family loyalty or if there were things there that embarrassed her. She admitted that her father was hard on one of her brothers. "My father is not an easy man," she said. "Every Christmas he hates his presents." And she laughed. "Every year I think and think what to get him, and every year he says, Why in the world did you get me this?"

"That's kind of sad, Janie," I said.

"No, it's fine," she answered. "He doesn't mean to be difficult."

In the spring, she told me she had a crush on a fellow in her religion class. I knew who he was, a tall, dark-eyed man who seemed sensitive and shy. "Perfect," I told her. And it did make sense. "But, Janie," I said, "you have to look him in the *eye*."

"I know," she agreed.

But she didn't. I saw that she didn't. I was with her a number of times on campus when this "fellow" walked by, and I saw that he looked at her with interest, that he was ready to greet her, and I saw Janie, every time, drop her eyes and remain silent, while I was the one to say, much too loudly, "Hi!"

"He hates me," she decided.

"He doesn't at all," I argued. "You have to give him a chance." But I was frustrated. And I was confused. If Janie had traveled all over the world making friends with all different kinds of people, why couldn't she say hello to an ordinary boy on campus?

She stopped mentioning him, and so did I. Janie didn't seem to date anyone that year, or the next. I had gathered from her devastating high school breakup that Janie would take a relationship very seriously. Perhaps it was this that made her cautious, but it was not something I could really understand, as I was not cautious myself in matters of the heart. But Janie was lovely, and I was sure she would eventually find someone to love. Besides, our college was small—once out in the world, Janie would find her man. I felt certain of this, and had the sense she believed it herself.

There is always the question of college friends—who will you stay in touch with? I would not have guessed Janie, as much as I liked her, because she had gone off to graduate school in the South, and my life continued on in the North. Still, we stayed in touch intermittently, mostly through letters, and the occasional phone call. There was no e-mail then, nor were there cell phones, and so the immediacy of keeping in touch was not there. Her letters were funny and vague; her phone calls the same. There was something in her attitude that remained light-hearted, or so it felt to me; even when she admitted to not being happy with the journalism program she was in. The men were pigs, she wrote. They got drunk and talked of guns. After a year she dropped out. "More student loans to pay," she said to me, laughing. I didn't worry about her—she still seemed older and wiser than I was; she would get her life figured out. At that time, I still lived with the idea—and perhaps she did as well—that life was something that would get "figured out."

It was after I finished college and moved to Boston that our friendship resumed again in full force. I was cocktail waitressing, and Janie was now in nursing school there. On weekends we took long walks. She was not happy with nursing school, either, and she told stories of the different women in her class, complained that her teachers were stupid. "Why are you doing it?" I asked.

"Because journalists are sharks and I'm not swimming with them," she said. "Besides, I like the idea of wearing a white uniform without the hairnet like my mother." A couple of times she said, "And maybe I'll meet a nice doctor, and settle down and have kids." We both wanted to get married and have kids. It was not something we spoke of frequently, because it was a time when women were expected to do more than that, and in fact, we both did want to do more than that, but my desire to be a mother was deep and fierce. How deep this was for Janie, I don't know, because there was something that stopped me from asking her, specifically, what she wanted to be doing in ten years. The shock of leaving college and being dumped out into the working world had frightened me, and I barely dared to wonder what *I* would be doing in ten years. But Janie already had friends who were married, some with children. And Janie often, in her gentle way, was critical of them. "Jeez," she said. "Naomi makes her husband breakfast every morning before he goes to work. I'd tell him to scramble his own egg." Privately, I thought I would scramble an egg for a man I loved, but I didn't say this. Janie was much more of a feminist than I was. She was more worldly than I was. But I was beginning to think she needed to be more flexible, though I never would have said such a thing.

A year into nursing school, Janie dropped out. She got a job as a city social worker. "Social workers are idiots," she would say. "And the money's so bad I can barely live, let alone pay back my student loans. Boy, is my father mad."

"About your school loans?" I asked.

"About everything." She shrugged.

I was young and self-absorbed and, as the result of a kind of panic, had decided to go to law school, and was piling up student loans myself. I still had that sense that Janie would get her life together, but I think the first doubts began to whisper in my mind around this time, that there was something in Janie that was preventing the things she wanted from occurring. She complained increasingly of her co-workers. "I don't understand my supervisor," she said. "He was so nice to me at first, and now he barely speaks to me."

I suggested maybe he'd liked her and felt rebuffed. "You can appear intimidating," I said. "Men don't know you're kind of shy."

She didn't like that. "Thanks a lot," she said. She laughed, but her face got red.

"I only mean the guy is single, and you're a really attractive woman to have in his midst. I'm just saying he might have felt uneasy." On some level, I was beginning to understand that I had to be careful when I talked to Janie.

"At first I thought he liked me," she admitted. "But now he hates me."

"Did you like him?" I asked.

Janie just shrugged. "He's pompous," she said.

It was puzzling to me that someone as warm and attractive as Janie was not involved with a man if she wanted to be, and if I was beginning to notice an edge to her nature, a hint of defensiveness, I let it go. I had other things to think about—like myself. I was not happy in law school, and dropped out after my first year. But six months of working in a department store and a mill and a medical office had sent me back to law school.

Janie was still restlessly switching from job to job. She had stopped being a social worker and was managing the office staff in a nursing home. "You have no idea how hard it is to manage people," she said. "Someone always hates you."

Meanwhile, I moved in with the boyfriend who was to become my husband, and Janie was happy for me, and gracious to him. She teased him like an old friend. "Going to make your own breakfast?" she asked him. When I told her my future husband didn't eat breakfast, Janie laughed. "Perfect," she said. The three of us spent New Year's Eve together. Janie drank too much wine and fell asleep in the chair in the living room. She had lost some of the fullness that gave her face its youthful look but was still beautiful, and that softness in her personality showed in her face. I remember looking at her fast asleep in the chair and thinking, I love Janie.

And I did. In fact, often in her presence I would think the words *I love you*, and while I loved other friends, it was different with Janie. She was sweet and funny, and attentive. And she was certainly loyal. She had even stayed in touch with Complaining Pam, who was married to an investment banker in Boston. "He's a nice fellow," Janie said. "Pam seems to be doing fine."

"She's stopped complaining about everything?" I asked.

Janie looked puzzled.

"I just remember her as someone who was always getting mad," I said.

"I don't remember that," Janie said, then changed the subject to tell me about what went on in the nursing home where she worked, how poorly run it was. She spoke of grown children who never came to visit their parents. And others who did; a grown man wept at the sight of his mother, though he came every week to visit. The man was married, and his wife never came with him. "He deserves better," Janie said. "Whoever she is."

"You just wait," I said. "Somebody single and wonderful is going to snap you right up."

"Gee, I hope so," she said, and I think she believed it was true. I know I did.

I got married, and almost fainted during the ceremony. Janie was the only one who mentioned it to me. "I thought we were going to lose you there," she told me at the reception.

"I was so scared," I said.

"I know," she said. "I was scared, too."

After I got married, Janie visited us often, and I liked it— because I liked her—and also because I felt she was having a good time. She'd frequently raise a fist to her mouth to cover a laugh, a gesture of shyness that was endearing. It was more and more surprising to me that she didn't seem to date, but I didn't outright ask about it because there was that aspect to Janie that seemed private. In a way, I admired it. I felt that I did not remain private enough myself—though I had my secrets.

But my husband would ask her about her love life. "So, Jane Louise, you have a boyfriend these days?" She'd smile and say, "I'm holding out for someone better than you."

I became pregnant. One night Janie and I were in a Laundromat when the man who ran it told us it was time to close, that I should hurry up with the dryer. I started folding things as fast as I could. But Janie got mad. "Isn't there any respect for pregnant woman anymore?" she asked him sharply. She said this so directly, her pretty face furious, the man mumbled we could take our time. I'd never seen her act like that before, and I was impressed. We laughed about it, repeating it to my husband.

That night she told me of an altercation she'd had with a woman who worked with her at the nursing home. The woman had slept with the boyfriend of her best friend when the friend was out of town. "When I heard that, I stood there right in the hall and said, Well, fuck you. I yelled it," Janie confessed, her fist covering her mouth. "I just yelled, Fuck you. People turned and looked."

"You did?" I asked. "Janie, what's happening to you?"

She just laughed, but I had noticed other odd changes. Janie was losing weight, and it had begun to affect her looks. Her face began to seem pinched, drawn. She cut her hair to right above her chin, and while I preferred her hair long, I still thought she had the same lovely, shining eyes. But she didn't laugh as much. She quit the nursing home, took a job with a small newspaper. She hated it. "Everyone there is an idiot," she'd say, when she came to visit.

When my daughter was born, Janie stopped visiting as often. After a while, she barely visited at all. One time when she sat in the living room, and I tried to breast-feed my new baby, I had the distinct feeling that Janie was irritated because she couldn't have my full attention. And it's true—she didn't. I was overwhelmed and exhausted. I'd had no idea how much care a baby required, and my husband was still in law school, so I spent many hours of the day and evening alone. Often, I was so nervous I did not produce enough milk and breast feeding was a struggle. Janie sat quietly and watched. And then she stopped coming by for quite some time.

Now we get to the part where I see—sadly, and clearly—how much became my fault. I know that when she called I would be tired and often feeling harassed, and the office gossip Janie wanted to chat about was not interesting to me. I pretended it was, but of course she would have known. She would have noticed how less and less I called her, that she was now, almost always, the one to call me.

One evening a week I took a French class at the New School. I sat next to a young woman who, after finding out I stayed at home taking care of a baby, asked, "But what do you do all day?" I could have asked the same question a year earlier, with the same innocence. In fact, caring for the baby required far more than I ever dreamed it would, bathing her, feeding her, dressing her, no sooner was one task done than another was needed, and while this was overwhelming for me, and separated me in many ways from the rest of the world, it also connected me to my daughter in a private and wonderful way. I adored my child.

One day Janie came to town and brought along Pam, who though still married to her investment banker, did not yet have children. And as usual she was complaining about her life. "My mother-in-law gave me this silver bracelet for my birthday," she said. "And it was so *cheap*." We were sitting in a diner, with my baby daughter in a booster seat, and I was jiggling keys for her, keeping the glasses of water out of reach, leaning and kissing her tiny nose.

Janie laughed. "Oh, Jeez," she said to Pam.

I thought, How can Janie not see what an angry person Pam is? My daughter drooled and smiled and slapped at the table happily. I said to Janie and Pam, "Did you ever see such a beautiful baby?"

Neither of them answered.

It took me years to understand how obnoxious that was to say. It took me years to understand that people talk too much about their kids. But I was embarrassed that day—at my own gushing, and at what I perceived to be their rudeness in not being interested in my child. I seemed on one side of the world, they on another.

Still, Janie would show up from time to time at our house, always bringing a small gift, a tin of cookies, or special coffee. While she never particularly related to my daughter, she was an easy houseguest. She joked with my husband. "Putting on a little weight there? Marriage does that, you know."

When my husband went off to work, I said, "Janie, you're getting skinny. Are you sick?"

"Thanks a lot," she said. "You sure know how to make someone feel good."

I told my husband she was starting to depress me. "Why?" he said. I didn't know what to answer. What I never told anyone was that I was starting to depress myself. It's true that I wanted to stay home and raise my daughter. Yet the monotony of preparing meals and doing laundry and arranging play dates made me feel I was living a life that belonged to someone else, and it was a terrible feeling, private, furtive. My husband did not want to hear complaining, and I didn't blame him. So I didn't complain. Or at least, I didn't think I did. In my mind, whatever I spoke of revealed only a fraction of my sense of unease. I went about my life, determined to do things right. I folded laundry while my husband watched TV. I did not ask him to fold it; he, after all, had worked all day in an office. I had no idea that every T-shirt I folded and stacked up was kindling getting ready eventually to ignite. I had no idea of this at all. If I was depressed sometimes, it was my fault. Even when I read a study that claimed the most depressed section of the population was women at home with small children—I still felt that it was my fault. I planned meals that had different colors, bought bubble baths so I would smell good, arranged fresh flowers on the table at least once a week. There was some gratification in doing this.

When Janie visited, I certainly never told her that I had moments of feeling a sense of huge disappointment. At least, I thought, I wasn't Janie, who was out there on her own, drinking more and eating less. One day Janie showed up with her hair dyed blond. "Whoa, look at you," said my husband.

"It's very cute," I said quickly, because it wasn't. It was startling and seemed, given her natural coloring, all wrong. It is one thing to lie to a friend about her new hairstyle, but I was beginning to realize that lately I was lying to Janie a lot. The lying came not only in my not speaking to her honestly about my own life—that barely seemed a lie, since I wasn't speaking to myself about my own life—but in my never confronting Janie's view of reality. More and more she spoke of altercations with her brothers, her father, people at work. Even Complaining Pam seemed no longer to want her visits. She said this was because Pam's husband hated her. Whatever she said, I supported her view, not because I thought it was what a friend should do but because it seemed easiest.

She was still working at the newspaper, writing a weekly column on the local arts, but she had started to complain that people were talking about her behind her back. "The fellow who does the obituaries told stories about me, so when I go to the cafeteria now, people sit at a different table."

"What stories, Janie?"

"I have no idea, but I see people look at me now like I'm crazy, and I know it has something to do with him."

"But *how* with him?"

"I don't know. He just has something against me."

I gave up trying to find out more, assured her that the offending party was indeed offensive. This sort of conversation with her had become a pattern. She continued to lose weight. She cut her hair very short, dyed it red, and spiked it with gel. "I see men looking at me a lot more," she said, with an expression of pleasure.

"Well, great," I answered, but it was hard to imagine the Janie I had first known. Her expression began to match her hair—there was no longer the softness in her face, or even in her voice. What exactly there was in Janie's background, or in her inner life, that caused her to bounce around from job to job, unable to find a satisfying relationship when she clearly desired one, I simply did not know. But I knew that her life was not working out as she had planned, and that the sweet-natured Janie I had met years ago was increasingly bitter. Bitter I could not abide. So I focused on the idea that Janie was depressed. And I think she was. I talked about therapy, knowing that with her natural reticence she would be wary. I spoke of my own therapy in tones of gratitude. She agreed to see a therapist that mine had recommended.

"The woman was *dreadful*," she reported later on the phone. "I will *never* go back."

"Try another one," I said. "You have to find the right one."

"She *hated* me," Janie said. "I could see it from the moment I walked in."

Then Janie called one day to say her mother had died. It was the only time I remember ever hearing her cry. I said I was sorry, and asked for details. Janie's mother had had a heart attack, and Janie had not made it to the hospital in time. The call has always stayed in my mind because I could tell as I was talking with her that I was not saying what she needed to hear—I didn't know what she needed to hear, but I heard the anger in her voice increase through her tears. "It's not your fault you didn't get there in time," I said.

"The doctors could have kept her alive on life support until I got there," she answered.

"But would she have known you were there?" I asked.

"Forget it," she said, angrily, and hung up without saying good-bye. Horribly, I felt almost angry myself, as though I had been put on the spot.

It was months before she called again. I am ashamed to say I did not call her. My own life was in crisis—my husband had surprised me by saying he was not sure he wanted to stay married and, in fact, had been feeling this way for some time. He said we never had fun anymore. He liked to scuba dive and was upset I never bothered to learn. He liked to hear live music and was upset I didn't hire babysitters often enough so we could go hear live bands. These statements, and more, terrified me. There was truth in much of what he said. If I felt angry—and I did—about some of the problems arising, I squelched that anger. I didn't want to be angry. I wanted to be a good wife. But I was over-whelmed.

And when Janie started to call again, I felt a dread rise in me, because it was work now to talk with her. I did not speak to her of the problems in my marriage. I had invested years in making my home life seem "right," and to acknowledge its failure was too painful and humiliating, so I let Janie do most of the talking. More and more her conversations were about friends who let her down, co-workers who no longer liked her. I had neither the desire nor the energy to discuss her own role in any of this. But when I hung up, I was exhausted. Lying is exhausting. Still, these phone conversations continued for some time. I was busy trying to keep my family in one piece, and there was always something needing to be done—laundry, food, the plumber. I pretended everything was fine, and agreed with Janie that who-ever it was she complained about was, of course, in the wrong. This went on and on.

The last time I saw Janie was in Boston. We met for dinner. Her hair was still red and spiky, and she wore a great deal of brown-toned lipstick that made her face look ghostly. She had on more eye makeup than I had seen before. I did not tell her what a friend had told me regarding cosmetics and age—the older a woman got the less makeup she should wear. Instead, I lied and told her she looked good. It seemed an easy, simple lie.

Janie spoke sharply to the waiters a number of times, and each time I winced, but I did not say, Janie, they're doing the best they can. I said nothing about them at all. But she was angry that night. Everyone had let her down—her brothers, her father, her friends. I could not wait for the evening to end. "It's always good to see you," I said, standing on the curb. We hugged, and I got into a cab.

In the cab that night, a slow, enormous anger of my own rose within me. I said to my husband, "I'm not going to see her again."

"You can't do that," he said.

"Yes, I can," I said. And I did.

She called and left messages, and I did not call back. That last night spent with her is one I think about often. Not long after, I made the decision to leave my twenty-year marriage, having no idea how difficult such a thing would be. The sense of trauma felt so great, that often I could barely manage to talk with friends at all. And I knew that I did not want to talk to Janie.

I think I stopped seeing Janie because I could not face the anger I had built up in my own life. In a way, her anger—just like Pam's years earlier— represented my own worst fear. And by the time I last saw Janie it had begun to feel as though everything I said was false. I felt like that character in the fairy tale who opens her mouth and has toads and snakes come out. Because there seemed no way to be with Janie and not be false, I chose to stop seeing her.

Do I regret it? I could pick up the phone, and perhaps she would be forgiving, even after all this time. I think, though I don't know, that her essential goodness never left, even as it became hidden by her own bitter disappointments. But I don't pick up the phone.

When I think back to that image of young Janie walking through the dorm lounge all those years ago, I am baffled to think her life turned out as it did. But what I should really be wondering is not what was in Janie that I didn't see those days but rather, what was in myself? Not the innocence I like to think—the innocence would be only in my not knowing myself, not knowing that I held the seeds of anger so deep down inside of me that the idea of angry women put me off for years. And yet Janie's response to the world and to her life—twisted as it often seemed—was, at least, honest.

I do not pick up the phone because I know that after I said, Janie, how have you been, she would ask me the same, and even now—after all this time—I have neither the courage to lie to her nor the courage to tell her the truth.

OTHER WOMEN

————————

Kate Bernheimer

ONCE UPON A time, there were three. Three of us. Whenever we were together, people would think we were sisters. How could this be? Anne is tall like a statue. She purses her lips, bends toward you to listen. Laura has a small and furtive body like a night mammal. When she talks to you, she glances sideways. I'm not that small and I'm not that tall. Neither imposing nor evasive, I'm in between. Or was. Now they are the same. I alone am different. Yet still, strangers approach us in stores. "Are you sisters?" they ask. "Are you triplets?" We don't look alike but there is an impression of similarity, an abstraction of it: we part our hair on the side, we tend toward brunette, we nod our heads in a particular manner. And we share a sort of made-up language like children. But one set of green eyes, one of blue, one of brown!

Laura, Kate, and Anne.

When we first met we were young and didn't know it. We had all moved to the same desert town to attend a graduate program we each immediately despised. None of us can remember precisely how it was we became friends.

When we met I lived alone on a gritty street in a tiny house with one piece of furniture in each tiny room: a single bed, a card table, a couch. I'd bought everything at a motel-hotel used furniture store. Vagrants knocked on my door day and night. Laura rented a room across town and used cardboard boxes as her bureau, night table, and desk; she'd painted them green. Her mattress she'd found on the sidewalk. A man who rented the room beside hers slipped notes under her door every morning that said he liked hearing her breathing at night. Anne slept in a plywood shed that had been advertised as a guesthouse. In the driveway of the main house, men on motorcycles often handed her warm cans of beer. Generally, we convened at my house and drank wine from miniature cardboard cups decorated with fairy-tale characters which my mother had sent me—to remind me of home, her card had mysteriously stated.

We all rapidly quit the graduate program and got whatever jobs we could find. I had two part-time positions, one on the breakfast shift at a chain diner under the highway, where Anne and Laura would visit to drink endless cups of hot chocolate; in the afternoon I answered phones at a plastics company near the airport, and they often called to hear me say "Triple S Plastics, this is Kate, may I help you?" Laura worked downtown in a freezing air-conditioned building, coding documents for a law firm. During her two daily breaks she would sit on the hot concrete outside, trying to put life back into her body. Anne hit the jackpot and got work she could do right in her shed, sipping warm beers; she proofread for a magazine called *Fighting Knives.*

Somehow Anne always managed to save enough money monthly for permanent waves. Laura and I would buy hot coffee and perch on the curb outside the low-end salon and watch her hair get twirled into corkscrews. When she emerged we'd stroke them and tell her how gorgeous she was. "No, you're gorgeous!" she'd scream, dancing around.

It seems that whenever we were not at our jobs and not sweltering over typewriters we were together, feeling demoralized and acting insane. We'd laugh so hard we had to lie down in pain. It was not menial employment that had us so giddily depressed; in fact we felt very lucky to have work at all. It was more the quality of our lives that alarmed us; we had been old-fashioned, imaginative children, and we'd reached our twenties. We realized we were no longer that young.

But looking back, I see we were young. Young enough to think that unexpected good things would happen; despite our pessimistic and skeptical natures, I see now that we persisted in this idea, that somewhere along the line this became the myth of our friendship: like the misfit-heroines of a fairy tale we had come together, our beings aligned in a strange dissonant tune, and we'd end up just fine and the same.

"WE'RE THE SAME!" was still the sparkling theme even a decade later when we lived in different places and would steal from our real lives to convene. We had grimaces, murmurs— expressionistic codes no one else understood, not even the men whom we loved. In that way too we were similar: by this time, we loved three excellent people. One tall, one less tall, one less tall than that, each with a different propensity for bathing. Each with dark hair, dark eyes, and kindness. I think there was a certain understanding all along that we would not accept a lover for any one of us who was not as passionate about our friend as we were.

And so there would be three lovers for us (though we never really dreamed about marriage) and of course, three babies born close together. This was the enchanted story we told. "When we have children," we'd say. "When our babies grow up together." "When we get pregnant." Once, over pancakes at Laura's favorite diner (where Anne always insisted on getting a fruit cup and being miserable when it would contain mainly an abundance of maraschino cherries), we even imagined that two of them would marry. Oh, how we fretted for the one who would be left out!

As it turned out, that would be me.

LIKE THE MIDDLE girl in a fairy tale I went first; my husband and I tried to have children. Of course, I was afraid I wouldn't get pregnant; this is what I'd been taught to fear. Yet that proved to be no problem: I got pregnant three times in a row. And all three pregnancies failed. My pregnancies began to end during the first trimester; each one the very day before a first scheduled ultrasound, in fact. By the third pregnancy I was thinking not about the future, but rather about the end.

The shock of grieving was bad enough, but as I had always had a tentative relationship with my own body the losses also deepened another fear I always had harbored: that I, unlike other women, wasn't quite whole. Since we were so very the same, Laura and Anne shared similar shadows; and I knew my experience only terrified them.

I had ruined our story.

By this time, we already knew in other ways that things could go wrong, because we were no longer so young; we'd lost other things by then—a father, a lover, religion, the hearing in one of our ears. That is, we had gotten old enough to know the question was not *whether* but rather *in what way* we would suffer. There was a grace to it, then, but what happened still deeply alarmed us. Nothing had prepared us for the dark grief that would accompany a pregnancy loss. And another, and another.

For my part, I felt comforted by a magical belief that I had taken care of the bad reproductive fortune for us all. Bad luck comes in threes, does it not? But still. The spell of we three was tainted; something was different, was changed. That thing, that wildness of being the same. It was gone.

IT HAD STARTED to go with the first miscarriage, which shocked me enough for a lifetime.

I was young, I didn't expect it, no one had told me to expect it, certainly none of the books which relegate "pregnancy loss" to a few paragraphs as if information about it is too horrid to reveal, giving the experience about as much space as a child-rearing manual would a misplaced favorite doll. And my husband and I had planned everything. In a matter of two months I was pregnant. Ten weeks later, I was not. I knew all of a sudden. I called down the stairs for my husband to come up. Something's wrong, I told him, as I lay in bed. He said, I'm sure everything's fine. (He badly wanted it so.) Something's wrong, something's wrong, something's wrong, I repeated. And then there was blood.

I was hiding in the bedroom because Laura was visiting. The day before, we had shopped for clothing; my body had begun to expand, and I was ecstatic! I bought a pleasingly unfashionable pair of blue pants with an elastic waist. Slacks, my friend called them. I had, on this excursion, felt guilty because she and I had shared many tender conversations over the years about wanting to be mothers. She was going through a difficult time, choosing between two fine suitors. One who inspired in her a fierce passion wanted a child; the other who was like a kindly woodsman with whom she felt entirely safe, did not. Now she had a decision to make. Both seemed paths of needles. To have the one, she had to give up the other. So in my pregnancy, with my good husband, I felt embarrassed by good fortune.

Yet in all the years of our friendship, she had been the one with the men, with the future. When we lived together she had two suitors as well, who came and went on different evenings.

One rode her about town on a motorcycle; I'd watch her leave, hair streaming back in the wind, her demure legs showing above knee-high boots. And when the other man visited at night, I would have to play music to cover their noises.

That day, the day I lost my first baby, I felt no passion for life, nor for any friendship or love other than love of the baby who died. Distantly, inside my head, I heard my friend and my husband. Together they paced downstairs. They felt trouble, the walls conveyed. I lay like a dull doll. I could not speak. Laura came in the room; she took my hand. What can I do, she asked, or perhaps she said, Do you want me to leave? I don't recall.

I soon found myself padding downstairs and making home fries for breakfast. I don't like home fries. I served them to my husband and friend and sat wordlessly at the table while they tried gamely to eat. Potatoes had significance for me and Laura: once we had cooked one of her suitors a six-course meal entirely made of potatoes as a joke. We watched him eat, waiting for him to mention the perverse menu, but he just ate and ate and ate, grunting like a giant.

After a while, I got back into bed. I don't remember anything else about the day except that it took a long time, months and months, before I could bear the thought of getting pregnant again.

Laura and I have not spoken of that day since, and sometimes I even forget she was there. I guess it's a strange form of grieving-amnesia, but I have no recollection of when I told Anne about the loss, or how she reacted. Certainly it was in a phone call, since we lived far apart, and certainly it was immediately, since that's how things work with the three of us. But I have no memory of the details. Perhaps I recall the phrase "I'm so sorry," but that's all, and I'm not even sure that's what she said, or how often, or what the lengths of her sympathies were.

What I do remember is that both Laura and Anne said little after being told of the loss until I announced, many months later, my husband and I were "trying again." Of course, they were thrilled, as if the new hoped-for baby would do away with the loss. I'm not saying this is how they intended to sound—or even felt—but I did feel it like that.

THE SECOND MISCARRIAGE is a blur; I remember nothing of that time. Am I the only woman to forget the particulars of my losses? Is it a forgetting I am choosing to do? Why, then, do I so easily remember the slights, the diminishments of closeness with the loved ones in my life?

Again, I certainly called Anne and Laura to tell them about this second miscarriage, and they certainly expressed sorrow and fear. I do remember sensing, in my conversations with them at this time, a pulling back, a drawing away, from what they were told. That is, the news inspired not only sadness for me but anxiety in them, anxiety about their own future as potential mothers.

Also, I probably seemed so depressed and so frightened myself that I was difficult to talk to, to reason with, to bear. The worst part of it was that I knew somewhere in myself that even if they were near, instead of many miles away, we would not feel close. Closeness with anyone was something I was not capable of then. So I burrowed into my depression; at least it was reliable and would not leave me alone.

After a few mildly degrading appointments with specialists, my husband and I moved three thousand miles away from where it happened, to a new place in the country, near where I had grown up, hoping to start over again. "New house, new baby," as the old wives' tale goes. And near there we had access to doctors my mother had researched for me, and to appointments for which she was willing to pay.

But the drive cross-country was sober. The backseat, where for years we had imagined a child, was empty, or worse: filled with two actual, lost souls.

AND THEN THERE was a third. Within three years, I had lost three pregnancies. For some reason, my husband and I were so delicately made that it took us nine months to recover from each pregnancy loss. (I've since heard this is not unusual—one often grieves throughout the time the pregnancy would have taken, had it held.)

Three babies, three years.

What did I tell Laura and Anne this time? I have no idea. Hardly anything, I think. I could barely manage to type the electronic message to the two of them letting them know. Such important news, imparted so impersonally.

I felt less than human.

OF COURSE, PEOPLE are different, and we have different problems dealing with things like birth and death, love and loss. And certainly most fertile Americans don't grieve much for other people's children lost in utero. (Some other countries do have rituals for grieving; most famously, in Korea there is a heavily visited shrine for unborn children.) Neither Anne nor Laura sent me flowers, or even a card, to commemorate my losses, and it's not the lack of flowers that troubles me, it's not so much what they didn't do but what we don't acknowledge, we deathless Americans.

Of course, immediate, heartfelt condolences were expressed and sympathies offered, but a couple of weeks would pass after each loss without it being mentioned again, unless I brought "it" up. It was as if, rather than having had a child die inside me, I had suffered from a particularly shameful bout of the flu. As time progressed, I did discuss my condition with Laura and Anne in medical terms, mainly the lack of treatment available to me. I had been told I was a recurrent miscarrier, a habitual aborter—whatever you want to call it, none of the terms are pleasant—one doctor even wrote "elderly pregnancy loser" on my chart. I guess he thought I would not see it, but for some reason the page was Xeroxed and mailed to me in an envelope, with no cover letter.

But after all the tests and doctors, the cause of my losses remained unexplained. "You have to decide how much loss you can bear," the doctor said. "Maybe six or seven pregnancies down the line, you'll be successful.

"It could happen," she added in a rather weak tone.

My husband, ever the optimist, did not read much hope into these statements, and neither did I.

I explained all of this to Laura and Anne, but our discussions rarely lighted on my grieving. Sometimes I tried to speak of it, but inevitably I regretted it, feeling too exposed when I did.

I once read that sometimes when elephants have stillborn calves, they dig ditches to lie in, and other elephants stand watch nearby, occasionally batting at the grieving mothers to offer them comfort. I have never felt more animal than in my grieving.

I was grieving not just the loss of my pregnancies but also the loss of biology. In my grieving, I felt more kinship with other species than with other women, especially my friends. I felt peculiarly close to strangers I had never met who posted their miscarriage tales online. I voraciously read their stories and the ones about animals (elephants lying in ditches, sea horses becoming transparent and drifting away, monkeys climbing into trees and starving themselves). I watched nature documentaries and wept. I read fairy tales about Bottomless Grief.

And I discovered, from a friend who is a scholar of folklore (and who tearfully shared with me at our first meeting—a professional one—the story of her own pregnancy loss), the saddest of Grimm fairy tales. It is also one of the briefest, which makes sense to me in its alignment with my fleeting times with child.

"Once upon a time there was a child who would not do what

his mother wanted. The child became ill, and then died. He was lowered into a grave and covered with earth, but his little arm suddenly emerged and reached up, and though fresh dirt was shoveled over it, that little arm always came out again. So the mother herself had to go to the grave and beat the little arm with a switch, and as soon as she had done that, it disappeared into the ground and the child finally came to rest there."

This fairy tale serves as a striking metaphor for the long grieving of a pregnancy loss. And also for the shape of the friendships after: each time my grieving died down, something emerged to remind me again, and sometimes it was Laura or Anne.

The myth of my friendship with Laura and Anne had been that we understood each other in an incomprehensible world. But now that myth was gone.

Whatever the reason—because of who I am, because I am American, because I was too sad, I learned to hide my grieving from Laura and Anne, in part to protect them. I also hid from them my disappointment that they seemed unable to recognize the depth of my grieving; or if they did recognize it, all they could do was wish it away (out of fear, out of kindness). Any anger I felt toward them had nowhere to go because it was far less important than grief. Also, I knew that the anger would pass, while the losses would be with me forever. Yet the hiding of anger and sadness had a cost, which was distance.

Sometimes when I was on the telephone with Anne, for example, I'd find myself steering the conversation toward the various native flowers we were both trying to propagate from seed, or toward an exuberant exchange of recipes we considered romantic—beet-dyed boiled eggs, layered coconut cake, Bloody Mary aspic salad. The subject of reproduction never came up, though it hung there between us.

But what could I do? I felt it was up to my friends to speak to me however they could, to rally around that mournful elephant who had fallen silent in her ditch.

But they did not do this; they did not. They recognized I was struggling, but I am sure they thought it was just with the grieving (which was bad enough). They did not know that I also struggled with how they were handling me. I believe they would say they were respecting my needs as they perceived them, and I could not argue with that. And yet, at times, it almost seemed as if they were angry at me for my pregnancies failing, and for my grieving so long.

I was angry at myself too. I was angry at nature, that I was a stupid, helpless animal who could lose my child. And Laura and Anne had lost something as well. Often I told them I wasn't myself. They just wanted me back, I suppose.

None of this was perfectly rational. We all were and were not mad at each other and at my body, at what it had done to our hope.

Because besides worrying about me and my sadness, Laura and Anne were worried for themselves. Both of them, newly married, were about to begin trying to have biological babies. They needed compassion as well; they needed me. But I became very tired trying to navigate all this.

I did not want their pity; when I told them I did not want the pity, they gave me quiet instead. Surrounded by this terrible silence, for which I had asked, I felt abandoned. And when I told them I felt abandoned, they cried; and then I apologized for making them so sad. Making *them* sad? I would think. I was the one who had suffered. And so it began again, a miserable cycle.

For some reason, Anne and I have had the worst time of it. I'm not sure why, but perhaps it is that we are both used to Laura being evasive; I guess I see her failures in grieving as relating to that, to her strange shyness, which I understand. But with Anne, there is sometimes a hardness toward me that I don't understand, and she seems not to want to recognize my vulnerability in this. She will acknowledge it, but she dislikes it. I know this because I know that weakness deeply disturbs her, particularly in those whom she loves, for she desires to protect them so severely.

A mere two months after my third loss, and thirteen weeks into Anne's first pregnancy, we attended Laura's wedding. I had been nervous about seeing her—our recent phone conversations had been strained. She would complain about gaining weight or being tired, and I would retort how lucky she was to gain weight and be tired. She would say how miraculous pregnancy was, and I would say drily, "Not for me." It was not that I was not happy for her; it was that I wanted her to censor herself. But, then again, if she censored herself, I felt out of the loop. It was a nightmare for us both.

So there I was in a motel with a newly pregnant Anne. In that bleak room in a bleak western town, we prepared for Laura's wedding. What a happy occasion, especially because it meant Laura would soon begin to try to have a baby, something she had desperately wanted for years.

But poor Anne was very ill—everything made her sick, even the smell of me, of my rosemary shampoo—and I imagined it was me making her sick.

Outside a motorcycle convention caused great noise and commotion. Anne was pale, panicking about the mutual animosity between us, as was I. The room we were in had just one window, with a half-broken screen peeling back from the frame. I had not slept well the night before. For some reason that now strikes me as perverse, we had decided to wear matching outfits in reverse, so I had on a pink blouse and a black skirt and Anne had on a black shirt and a pink skirt. We were opposites. My black was a pencil skirt; her pink one flowed.

And there was no denying her pregnant condition even at such an early stage. She is voluptuous to begin with, and to many she would have looked the very portrait of womanliness that day; whereas my large breasts, still inflated from a pregnancy that had so recently ended, merely gave me a slatternly look.

(For some reason, with each pregnancy my chest got larger and larger and finally forgot to shrink back.)

When we had been discussing our outfits on the phone before we came, Anne had exclaimed, "I am dreading standing next to you, you with your svelte figure and me with my pregnant breasts." She had not seen me in months, and had no way of knowing I was still swollen from what I had lost. I hesitated that night, then told her that I strongly preferred her to make no further comparisons—however envious—between her pregnant body and my own. (I have not bothered pointing out things like this to other well-meaning friends who say they envy me not having to go through a whole pregnancy because of the havoc it wreaks on a body; most people are not worth the trouble, they'd take too much offense.) I had expected Anne to be different, to understand that I was pleading with her to take note of my grief, to not make light of it ever.

But the repercussions from what I had said were worse than I expected. A situation like this had never before arisen between us. The very beauty of our friendship was a gigantic freedom to be ourselves, and a foolish tenderness we never dreamed we deserved. As we stood beside one another, looking into the hotel mirror, Anne said she could no longer feel natural with me. I had a hot iron in my hand and was straightening my curls to better resemble her lank mane. I was devastated by her words. But I am still like you, I thought. Am I not? Panic rose, winged inside me. "I don't know what to say to you," she told me, her voice rising. "I feel like you're angry I'm pregnant!" I tried not to let her see the terror that overcame me. Angry she's pregnant? Angry? Expletives entered my mind. Never once have I felt angry at her. But I did not say this. Instead, I pleaded desperately with her to leave the room. I felt like a wild caged bird. She left, and I later found out she was horrified that I had banished her from the room. It took us both a long time to forgive each other for that day.

I don't know if Anne told Laura about any of this. We did agree not to speak about it to her at that time, since it was, after all, her wedding day.

A month after the wedding, Laura was pregnant. She told Anne first. Of course, they would share with each other the magical glee, and not with me. They each were pregnant within three weeks of a marriage! And I, who had been married the longest, was still grieving my third loss. Again, three.

THROUGH AN ERROR (an electronic message mistakenly sent to me), I found out Laura was pregnant before she had told me herself. When I called her, Anne claimed that Laura had been waiting to tell me because they'd wanted to protect me, keep me from fearing for her, prevent *me* from having to worry. This strikes me as impossible, though it is not impossible that this is what they believed. Surely, Laura was protecting her-self—warding off my bad fairy charm. Or perhaps Anne was protecting Laura from me, since I had caused Anne such distress during her own early days?

To make matters more confusing, Laura claims that she was always going to tell me right away, that in fact, she did tell me the very same day she told Anne.

I can't even begin to decipher the confusion.

AND SO BOTH Laura and Anne are pregnant now. I never again will be. They've been lucky and are doing well, and though I am very happy for them, herein lies the problem: they cannot be happy for me.

When I talk to my friends about their growing babies, I brim with excitement and pride, and then when I am alone, I cry, or sometimes, much to my shame, become angry. I once told my husband a terrible thing, that I wished it hadn't been so easy for them because then they'd understand me. As soon as I said this,

I burst into tears, knowing it was utterly wrong. I did not really wish it, but I thought it, I did.

Sometimes, I still punish myself for such an inappropriate wish. If I were in a fairy tale, with my second wish I'd reverse it, and with the third, I'd send myself down to the bog to live forever, my feet buried in mud with only a witch and some flies for company.

For, of course, they should not consider that I am still sad—not right now, not during their time. But still, it mystifies me that they seem to have completely forgotten my dead babies.

So I float from it. And from them.

PERHAPS THEY FEEL it is I who am absent. Laura tries to be painstakingly kind to me. In her voice on the phone, I hear caution, and carefully phrased compassion. She fears offending me, I suppose. I feel terrible guilt about this, for I don't like being the cause of this newfound hesitation, but I am also deeply grateful to her, and touched. Still, I know there are things she tells Anne about her pregnancy—most things, in fact—that she doesn't tell me, and I feel awfully left out because of it.

As for Anne, she seems affronted by the whole situation. She claims there is nothing special about being pregnant, that it's sheer biological luck. Of course, she's right, but that she is indifferent to her pregnancy (or claims to be) embitters me somehow, and makes me jealous of her. Of all human emotions I despise jealousy most, and my guilt and jealousy make me lonelier than I already am.

Perhaps it is just that in the end, we all grieve alone for whatever it is we are grieving.

Because of this, I am sure to express my happiness about their own good fortune; it seems more important to me than ever to share happiness whenever we can. But with a thud in my stomach where lack resides, I realize that just as they cannot have shared in the private knowledge of my losses, I cannot share in the mixed emotions of their pregnancies.

That I do not know what they are feeling, and that they do not know what I feel: all this causes unease. One on occasion each, they wept in my presence, saying how awful they felt about the changes between us, but mainly we all pretend there is not unease. We don't address what has happened directly.

Of course the happier I am, or the more distant the pain, the more relaxed they become, so I show lots of cheerfulness to them about their pregnancies. I ask questions, I send gifts, I comfort, I indulge. Perhaps this is not just, or perhaps it is. Anyway, this is how it has been. It is my happiness for them that grows, not their sadness for me, and I accept that. I'm in the thick of my grieving, not them. They have other things on their mind, as well they should. They suffer pregnancy hormones, they say. And because I remember those, I am sympathetic. So I understand some of what they are feeling, I suppose, but I cannot expect the same of them.

My own due dates have all passed unnoticed; on one of them, a photograph of Anne's pregnant belly arrived in the mail. And in the four months since she found out she was pregnant, Laura has called me just once, to announce the conception. Recently, Anne remarked to me that she would have a second biological child because "bearing children prevents breast cancer." My mother had breast cancer this year; I do not bear children. Did she simply forget? I think it is that both of them are so desperate for me to be fine, that in their desperation they make mistakes.

IT'S DECEMBER NOW, and snowing. We've put up a Christmas tree, a kind I've never heard of before, a concolor. I planted them to please my wife, the farmer tells us, kneeling down. When cut, the concolor smells like orange and pine. The farmer broke off a small branch and held it up to me. As he slid the blade between its lowest branches, he said he'd grown the pine from a cutting off a larger tree. He gestured toward it. How humiliating when tears came to my eyes.

The whole thing just seemed sad to me, as so many things do now. I find myself thinking the tree we have cut down is the age my first child would have been; the tree we just killed was older than my second child would have been; and the last one, I'd have carried her out to that snowy field this very day. She'd be an infant, just three months of age. I know that thinking this way is not good for me, and I try to stop myself, but I can't always. And so I conceal what I am thinking from my husband and my brother and his beautiful wife who are standing in the snowy field with me and the farmer. We are bundled up, we are surrounded by oaks and maples and pines. The chickadees sing. That they survive such harsh winters: this seems a miracle to me.

I remind myself of the things living and breathing around me and that they are good. And I remind myself of something my mother told me, which she had recently learned from her rabbi. He told her that in Jewish tradition, the cultural tradition of my family, it is discouraged for a woman who has had miscarriages to think of her children's lives as being shortened by death. In fact, he added, a woman who has lost a child in pregnancy is considered to be extremely wise. For inside of herself she has contained the very circle of life.

I don't believe I know more than other women who have not been pregnant, but the rabbi's advice did allow me to stop calculating absent days, absent days, absent days. I could try to explain this to Laura and Anne, but I don't know where to begin. In the end, I will not admit to them how terribly angry I am at what came to pass this year, at the distance growing inside me from them. Part of the reason is that I truly believe that, when I do become a mother somehow, all the anger I have felt will dissolve into kindness.

And to be honest, I am fearful that if I did express how upset I have been—how traumatized, really—and something went wrong with one of their babies, wouldn't I be to blame? Wouldn't someone, somewhere, think it? Wouldn't I?

What I want most now is to protect Laura and Anne from my misfortune. And so I am careful of what I say. I am even careful of what I think. I stave off my bad fairy charm and make a wish that someday we will be three again.

HOW I LOST HER

Ann Hood

WE TALKED. In whispers during class. Behind closed bedroom doors on the telephone. On double dates. At the mall as we picked out new 45s, lip gloss, miniskirts. Over ice cream sundaes, cheeseburgers, onion rings. During movies. Over tarot cards and Ouija boards. In home ec. At play rehearsals, during study hall, in the library. Lying on the beach, bodysurfing, climbing rocks. Riding in cars and on buses and trains and planes. In London, Manhattan, Honolulu, Rio de Janeiro. While we drank wine and beer and good strong coffee. At parties. At bars. At the junior prom. At my wedding. At her wedding. Breast feeding. Looking at Monet, Matisse, Degas paintings. In bookstores. In her apartment. In my apartment. Long distance. Late at night. On our cell phones. For thirty-five years we talked. And then we were silent.

I did not believe my life would be defined by tragedy even though tragedy always hovered at its borders. An aunt dead at age twenty-three during surgery to remove her wisdom teeth. A grandfather dying young from a mosquito infected with equine encephalitis on a trip to Block Island. An uncle dropping dead at thirty-five while he danced with his wife on Valentine's Day.

These stories, these tragedies, made my grandmother wail and pull her hair and carry huge pots of geraniums, poinsettias, chrysanthemums to cemeteries across Rhode Island. They made my mother sad, marking her losses by sleeping all day, crying at night, staring off in the distance as if she might actually find her sister or brother or father there.

Our family had had its share. That's what I believed. Those dead people, those sad stories, seemed far away from my life in 1968. That's when I met Amelia. Seventh grade. Mrs. Junker's math class. New math. I didn't like it, the math. I wrote haikus in the margins. I daydreamed about meeting Dino Danelli, the drummer for the Young Rascals. I had found his name in a Manhattan telephone book in the basement of the town library, and I saved my dimes until I had enough to call him from a pay phone, also in the library basement. I called him and listened to him saying, "Who is this? Hello?" Then I hung up and saved more dimes.

While Mrs. Junker wrote equations on the board, Amelia took careful notes. She furrowed her brow. She erased and rewrote and tried harder. I wrote down the words to "Sounds of Silence" from memory. No one understood new math. Not even Steven Smeal, the math whiz.

Then one day, Amelia's face brightened while Mrs. Junker explained something. Amelia nodded. She understood new math! I watched her understanding and I was impressed. Amelia had black hair already turning gray. Also impressive for a twelve-year-old. She had big, round brown eyes and still wore handmade dresses. I wore black armbands to protest the Vietnam War and could almost sit on my long, dirty blond hair. I had just acquired a pair of round wire-rimmed glasses, like John Lennon's.

But I leaned over and whispered, "Show me how to do it." She didn't want to get in trouble, but she explained, nervously glancing up to be sure Mrs. Junker wasn't looking at us. After class I asked her for her phone number: 821-1952. I asked her to go to the mall on Saturday. She wasn't sure her father would let her. We walked to class together. That is how I found her.

But this is how I lost her.

Thirty-five years later. We are finally living in the same state again, Rhode Island. She never left it. I never wanted to come back. But I did. She was married and had a daughter and lived about as far away from me as two people in such a small state can. I was married and had a son and a daughter. It was hard to get Amelia out with me. I called her every week. We tried to make plans. Sometimes we actually saw each other.

This week, mid-April 2002, her husband was going away. My husband was going away. We got babysitters. Chose a movie and a restaurant. Girls' night out. Then, my five-year-old daughter, Grace, spiked a 105-degree fever and died thirty-six hours later from a virulent form of strep. Friends started arriving at my house, where I sat numb and horrified at what had happened, at what we had lost. "Call Amelia," I told someone. And someone did.

I said I did not think my life would be one marked by tragedy. But it is. In 1982, when I was working as a flight attendant, I went out for Mexican food in L.A. with the crew on a layover. As I walked down the hall toward my hotel room, I heard the telephone ringing. And in that way that we know somehow there is bad news on the line, I did not want to answer that phone. But it kept ringing, as I turned my key in the lock, and walked inside, and kicked off my shoes, it would not stop. It was 9:00 P.M., midnight on the East Coast. Finally, I picked it up. A man I had just broken up with said, "I have bad news," and I hung up on him and started to cry before I even knew what he was going to tell me; there was disaster in his voice. He called back and I hung up again. But the third time he told me not to hang up. "There's been an accident and your brother is dead. There's an eleven o'clock flight to Boston and you have to take it. You have to get home." I wrote down the flight information on the hotel pad by the phone. Then I told him, "Call Amelia."

I don't remember that flight. But I remember walking out of Logan Airport into the early morning light of the first day of July, and seeing Amelia waiting there for me in her Subaru. Amelia always bought reliable cars, things that lasted. She was sensible and steadfast. She had a retirement fund. She clipped coupons.

That day she drove me the hour to my parents' house, and although I don't remember them exactly, she said all the right things. When we got there, she walked me inside and waited until I told her it was okay to go. For the rest of that summer, as I watched my mother unravel and my father struggle and my brother's seven-year-old daughter's confused face, Amelia brought me beers and sat in the heat of the long nights with me, drinking them.

When I moved to New York City a few months later, I tried to take her with me. But Amelia was firmly rooted in Rhode Island. She did not like change. I went off to do the exploring for both us. And frequently she came to stay with me in my tiny apartments. I would draw her maps of the subway with careful notes on where to get off. I would point her toward Canal Jeans and the good magazine store. Then we would have Chinese food delivered and eat it with cheap wine and talk about love and sex. We would giggle just like we did when were twelve and wondered what love and sex were all about. With a best friend, an old friend, one word can send you into fits of laughter. Plums! Wood chips! Zinfandel! We would whisper these to each other in bed, and laugh, and keep talking until talk turned to sleep, unnoticed.

In this time of most enormous grief after Grace died, there is no day or night. There is just loss. People put food on a plate and hand it to you to eat. They fill your glass with good strong scotch. They arrive at your house with shopping bags filled with

Kleenex, new tablecloths, salads. Things you don't even know you need because the only thing you really need—your daughter's hug, her sleepy body curled into your lap, her voice calling out to you—is gone and will never come back. You can't sleep; you can only sleep. You cry. You scream. You look for her in the corners of each room, search the pockets of her backpack for something left behind, lift her coat to your nose to find her smell, hold her brush to the light to marvel at her pale blond hair still tangled there. A week passes. A month. It grows hot and then cold and then hot again.

Friends take your son to school, pack him a lunch, keep him for hours while you sit in your bed and cry. Friends go over and over and over with you those thirty-six hours that have changed your life. They bring you coffee and ginger scones. They drive from New York City just to hold your hand for a few hours. They climb into bed with you and hug you. They water the plants that keep arriving, and make fun of the bad ones because they know you have a wicked sense of humor. They send their own children with babysitters so that they can sit with you and watch Mario Batali make pudding out of bologna and pizza topped with pork fat. They take you for walks. They take you to the movies. They do your laundry. And time is somehow passing, unbelievably. The world keeps moving even without Grace in it.

But among these faces, this endless flow of friends who never let you be alone because that is the worst thing of all, Amelia's is absent. A note came through the mail slot, delivered by hand. It did not say anything different than all the other notes that arrived those first days expressing love and sadness. A glimpse of her at the memorial service where hundreds of people filled the church while my son sang "Eight Days a Week" for his sister. But in the crush of hugs and tears afterward, I could not find her face.

Then it happens. I find myself alone one morning. There are so many people I can call. I know that. But it is her number I dial. When I hear her voice, I start to cry. I say her name. My loss is still new, a few weeks at most. "Can you come?" I ask her. I can hear the desperation in my voice. She is at work. She hesitates. She tosses out reasons why she cannot come right this minute. A mammogram appointment. Her daughter needs a ride some-where. I can't keep talking because panic is rising in my throat. The panic of grief, of being alone with it. My house has become a minefield. Grace's glittery nail polish, the MOM she shaped into a crown out of pipe cleaners, the shoehorn she used dramat-ically to put on her sneakers, her ballet tights tossed under the bed.

I can't go out there alone, I want to say to Amelia. But I am having trouble forming words, except the most basic ones: Why? Help. Grace. Amelia says she will come another day. Her voice is appropriately somber. "Okay," I say. "Tomorrow?" I am desper-ate. All I can see ahead are hours and days like the ones I am having. "Not tomorrow. But soon. I'll call you."

And she never did. Almost two years have passed and I have never seen her again. That day I called another friend, and she came. They kept on coming, my friends. They still do. But Amelia is gone.

I HAVE LOST her before.

In ninth grade, I was smitten with a different friend. She wore halter tops and French-kissed boys and spent the after-noons alone while her parents worked, making cookies and call-ing boys and doing the Ouija board. When my mother let me choose a friend to come to the beach, I chose Marie and broke Amelia's heart. She never let me forget it, the wound never healed. Years later she would remind me of that summer when I spent my days with Marie instead of her.

But by September—tenth grade! high school finally!—it was Amelia and I again. We auditioned for *Fiddler on the Roof* and spent every afternoon in the high school auditorium singing "Anatevka" and "Matchmaker." We got boyfriends by asking them to the school's Sadie Hawkins dance, our first official double date. The boys were neighbors and best friends, and every Saturday night the four of us went to the movies and then for strawberry pie or steak sandwiches before parking by the golf course and kissing until our curfews.

We went to different colleges. She stayed put and I kept moving away. She had real jobs where she had to be Monday through Friday, all day. I drifted and drifted. But when we came together, there were no differences. We took trips together, always agreeing on where to go and what to do there. We saw plays and movies and went to museums. Our talk about these things was endless.

Other people saw only our differences. Our lives kept moving away from each other, and to outsiders it was hard to see what kept our friendship going. Our husbands had nothing in common. Our kids' ages were far apart. Our tastes in superficial things—houses, cocktails, pets—were completely different. And larger issues—our futures, our dreams—diverged as well. Our teenage selves had fantasized about becoming a painter (Amelia) and a writer (me). The world had seemed both vast and small enough for us to hold in our hands. But our adult selves did not want the same romantic things. One day Amelia told me that when her daughter went to college, she wanted to sell her house and move into a trailer in the woods. I laughed until I saw she meant it. How had she arrived there? I wondered.

But still we met somewhere rooted in history and girlish dreams. When a newer friend asked me one night why I still stayed friends with Amelia—"You two have nothing in common!"—I got angry. Amelia, I told her, was my best friend, and always would be. We could still sing all the words to "Matchmaker" and resurrect our own version of "Tiny Bubbles"; we could sit together after a Chagall show and talk for hours about what we'd just seen. She'd held my hand after my brother died. We'd helped each other through the death of each of our fathers. How dare anyone question us, Amelia and me?

The last time I saw Amelia—not the glimpse of her through my tears at Grace's memorial service but really saw her, was Oscar night 2002. Amelia and I watched the Oscars together whenever we could. We discussed who would be nominated, called each other after the nominations were announced, went together to see as many movies as we could before the big night.

Sometimes I gave elaborate Oscar parties, with trivia games and prizes and costumes. But this year, I invited only a small group of people and made dinner to eat while the stars walked down the red carpet. Amelia arrived with a small Oscar statue. "You can take it out every year on Oscar night," she said. We debated whether to use it as a prize if we played a game or to keep it as the one standard for our own Academy Awards.

Grace wanted to go to bed early that night. So she crawled into a sleeping bag and went to sleep right by the television. I remember Amelia saying good night to Grace before she left for her hour's ride back home. She didn't wait to hear who won Best Movie. She was worried about the time, and the long drive. "Good night, Grace," she said, and she was gone.

"Why don't you call her?" my husband asks me when I tell him Amelia has left me for good.

He doesn't understand the complexities of women's friendships, how hurts sometimes cannot be forgotten, or forgiven. How three decades later, Amelia could still get teary remembering the summer I spent with Marie instead of her. It is the ultimate betrayal to abandon your good friend—for a man, for another woman, or when she needs you desperately.

"What would I say if I called her?" I ask my husband, and my throat burns even thinking of her voice on the other end of the telephone.

"Say whatever you want," he says, shaking his head.

But all I want is to know how she could have left me. I am confused and angry and hurt.

"Perhaps losing Grace scared her," a friend told me. "If it can happen to you, it can happen to her."

It is true that some people bend their heads when I pass by, as if what has happened is contagious. It is true that there are not the right words to say. A breezy "How are you doing?" can make me angry because the answer is I'm terrible, I'm paralyzed, I'm broken.

I am told that some people don't know what to do, what to say, how to approach me. Is it possible that Amelia is among those women who avoid me because it's easier? Or because they are incompetent in the face of tragedy? She was always someone who held back emotionally. When her father died, I couldn't get her to talk about it. She'd hang up quickly, her voice muffled. One day I demanded she tell me just how bad she felt, and she did, forcefully. But only that once.

I was the friend who called more, who got tickets to a play or made a point of seeing movies together. She would go months without talking to friends of hers, I know that. Sometimes circumstances overwhelmed her, like too much work or parenting or simply a difficult week. Still, I believed that I—we—were immune to that. Distance, lifestyles, careers, none of it had kept us apart before.

In my grief, casual friends have become good friends; good friends have become family. Women keep surprising me. The mother from my son's school, the one I hardly know, sends me a card every month. A woman who I met just a few weeks before Grace died didn't retreat but instead emerged with humor and strength to become one of my dearest friends. But my best friend, my oldest friend has left me, as easily as we found each other over a confusing equation thirty-five years ago.

My son, Sam, is a member of an all-children's theater ensemble. One night, after a play, he came up to me, excited and confused.

"You'll never guess who was here," he said. "Amelia and her daughter."

I looked around the crowded lobby.

"No, they left," he said. "I saw them in the audience and then afterward I came out to say hello, and I saw them walking out."

"Did she talk to you?" I asked him. My heart pounded as if an old lover had shown up.

Sam shook his head. He described her in great detail, and her daughter, who looked older now, he said, and wore glasses. He led me to the book where people signed up to be on the mailing list, and there was her name, in a penmanship I know as well as my own.

Had she seen me? I wondered. Surely she had recognized Sam's name in the program. Had she left to avoid me? To avoid us?

Before Grace died, I always invited her to Sam's plays— *Oliver!* and *Stuart Little* and *A Midsummer Night's Dream*. But she could never make it. Now she shows up at every one of Sam's plays. But she does not stay long enough to say hello.

I wonder what I would say if I cornered her one night, if I could even find the words to express what I have endured these two long years without her. She held my hand senior year in high school when an older boy, a college boy, broke my heart. She sat next to me at my father's funeral. She kneeled beside me when I threw up in the snow after too many kamikaze shots. I wonder if she would tell me why she deserted me now, when I needed her more than ever. As time passes, it gets harder to believe that I will let her back into my life and harder to believe she would try.

She does not slip a note through our door, or call to see how we are faring, this wobbly three-person family of mine. I wonder if she remembers the night we took Sam and her daughter to see *The Fantasticks* at the little theater on Sullivan Street, and how during intermission Sam got on the stage and reenacted the Man Who Would Not Die. "He's going to be onstage someday," she said, in the wise voice she sometimes used. "I just know it." Does she remember that I cried that night when they sang "Try to remember the kind of September, when life was slow, and oh, so mellow . . ."? She teased me for crying, but I always was the sentimental one. Does she remember why we used to laugh when one of us said "Plums!" or "Wood chips!" or "Zinfandel!"? Or is all of it, all the threads of our friendship, lost too?

My husband brings home the list of names of people who sent in donations to the scholarship fund we started in Grace's name. He points to one, and I look down and see Amelia's name and a generous contribution. So she is out there, she is thinking of me. But she remains silent, as if in this, there is nothing, nothing, she can say. Her silence is so loud, it breaks my heart.

THE OTHER FACE

Mary Morris

O N T H E F I R S T of every month, when I sit down to pay my bills, I think of Lauren. Or when I am relaxing in my living room, a cup of coffee or glass of wine in hand, and I look across the room and see the lithograph. I can't help but think of her then—whether I want to or not.

It is a picture of a naked woman, sitting almost in the position of Rodin's *The Thinker*. Slightly hunched over, pensive, a hand resting on her fleshy thigh. Except that this "thinker" is looking out of the print, over her shoulder, away past the viewer. She appears to have nothing to hide. Not her nakedness. Not even her sadness.

This print is called *Nude, Seated* and it is signed "Renoir." It was a gift to my mother from Lauren's father over forty years ago. Mort knew how much my mother loved Renoir. In suburban Illinois, my mother named our first dog Renoir, and Mort would laugh at our Sunday barbecues, as my mother ran around the neighborhood, calling after that dog, "Renoir, Renoir."

When things were flush and everyone was alive and well, when our families grilled steaks and drank cocktails on the patio, Mort made a gift of this print to my mother.

The print does not have tremendous value, not in monetary terms. But it is a reminder to me of what once was. I have loved this image for years—as a girl growing up when it hung in our dining room, and later as woman myself. Though I have been drawn to the voluptuous figure, not unlike my own, to the pensive woman who looks longingly out of the frame, what pulls me most into the picture is the other face.

This small face floats like an afterthought in the upper-left-hand corner of the print. A desert of blank space exists between the central image and this smaller one. It is suspended off to the side, as if the naked woman is dreaming this face. It is difficult to tell if it is the face of a man or a woman, and I have often wondered.

Is this a portrait of longing for someone the nude will never see again? Perhaps. And yet at the same time the other face is not unlike her own. This is the part that strikes me as curious. It appears as if what she longs for—the person who is missing—is somehow identical to herself.

"LET'S GO DOWN to the beach," Lauren said. Or "Let's drive to the Rialto and listen to the blues." Muddy Waters was in town. Or Martin Luther King was speaking at Orchestra Hall. These were her rebellious days. Or later, when she was in college and I trailed three years behind, "Let's drive to St. Louis." Sure, why not? I'd go to the beach. I'd go down to the South Side, where she knew I wasn't allowed. I'd drive with her across the whole state, beer cans clutched between our thighs.

We grew up together. In the same Illinois town just miles apart. I spent Sundays at her house or she spent Sundays at mine. We swam in her pool. She got me drunk, taught me about boys. We went skinny-dipping. She was older than I and she was wild. She drove me across the Mississippi River in her convertible on a sunny day, laughing. I can still see her golden hair blowing in the wind as she stands up at the wheel.

She wasn't at all like me. Or rather I wasn't at all like her. She was lighthearted and funny. She never took things seriously—not school or boys or her mother's drinking or her father's rages. I was bookish, thoughtful. When I laughed, it was from a slightly pained place, but not Lauren. She laughed with her whole body as if she were shaking something out of herself. She smoked cigarette after cigarette and dated boys who wore real leather jackets.

Our fathers were business partners. But they were more than that. They were boyhood friends. They grew up together as well, except they lived in the same house—my grandmother's. When Mort's mother died, his father remarried, but as if in a fairy tale the stepmother was evil. When Mort was sixteen, he moved into my father's house. When Mort was twenty-two, he made his first million on the stock market. He brought my father into his business. They were partners in real estate for forty-five years.

Our lives were intimately entwined. We shared holidays. The only discussion in the matter was their house or ours. But there were jealousies too. My mother resented their house on the lake, their swimming pool. Mort made more money than my father, and he had invested it wisely. They had done better than we had. My mother resented this, but mostly she resented my father's friendship with Mort. It was more important, she said, than she was—than we were. "Whatever Mort wants, he gets," she said bitterly. And she was right.

But Lauren was the sister I never had. My confidante. The bad girl I wanted to be. She took chances. When she graduated from college, she moved to New York City—a basement apartment on the East Side. I went to visit her. When she was at work, I accidentally flooded it. I left the water running in the sink while I went out sightseeing. I returned to find two inches of water and spent the rest of the day, bailing out. When she got home, her apartment was dry and very clean. I never told her until years later, and then she laughed and laughed. She thought it was the funniest thing she'd ever heard.

She had a boyfriend named Dan, who was blond like she was and rode a motorcycle with a motorcycle jacket. When I slept on her sofa, he slept next to her on the floor. I remember his dark shadow slipping in at night, out in the morning. After years of dating, she married Dan and stayed in New York. I was her maid of honor. She threw her bouquet right at me. All I had to do was reach out my hands and grab it.

"YOU'RE COMING FOR Thanksgiving, right? And Christmas too? You can't not come," she'd say after I moved to New York. I was single then and she was married. She seemed to have shed the rebellious ways I'd always envied. Now she had other things I wanted. She had a house, a baby, a husband who was doing well. It was as if we'd switched roles.

I was living in an L-shaped room, doing odd jobs, trying to make ends meet. While I struggled to earn a living, Lauren glided through life. She lived in Mount Vernon and drove a new Volvo. I had a set of mismatched plates and furniture from street sales. But I could cook.

On holidays I cooked a Butterball turkey, homemade cranberry sauce, candied yams, and chestnut stuffing while Lauren sat in her breakfast nook, making floral arrangements and smoking. The TV was always on, and she kept one eye on the parade or the football game. While rooting for the Bears, we chatted about our lives. She'd shout between snippets of talk, "Come on! Let go of that ball!"

We were still fundamentally different. She with her cigarettes, football games, and PTA. Me with my books and single ways and financial woes. But Lauren had been there when Steve Korchask threw me into the pool with a giant fish. And when I'd hidden our beers under the seat when the cops stopped us on the Edens Expressway.

We joked about our mothers, who'd never gotten along. The stories of their rivalry were astonishing. The time her mother cornered mine in a powder room at the Empire Room and said, "I just want you to know the money is mine and it's going to stay mine," as my mother put her lipstick on.

Money was a big thing with my mother. As well as with Lauren's. Once my mother made me a Halloween costume. I was a money tree. She spent weeks on that costume. A brown bodysuit trunk. A headdress of branches with paper money taped to them. At the party at school the boys tore my money off. I walked home through the woods, my bare branches blowing in the wind.

But as we sat at Lauren's kitchen table, peeling yams and slicing onions for Thanksgiving, we found these stories funny. We joked about etiquette, imitating our mothers in their elegant dresses, cigarette holders in hand. "So nice of you to come," "So good to see you again," as if Jewish girls from Illinois could morph into English aristocracy.

We made jokes about men as well—mostly the men in my life, who seemed to come and go with the seasons. The one I'd met at Easter would be gone by the Fourth of July. Lauren loved hearing about these men. The one who made me dinner but hid the extra pieces of chicken so I wouldn't ask for more. The one who broke up with me because of the way I washed dishes. The one who asked me to pay him back for the theater seats. These were all hilarious to her.

Dan found them funny as well. He'd break out the wine early, bottles and bottles of it. It just seemed to flow and flow, and Lauren would say, "Oh, tell him about the guy who didn't like your cat." We'd be roaring with laughter and pretty much drunk by the time dinner was done.

HER PARENTS DIED young. Her mother—a mean, forbidding woman who once told me I was stupid when I asked her what existentialism meant—died of lung cancer. Mort of a heart attack, on the toilet. An undignified death my father could not believe.

But my parents lived on. And on. Not that I didn't want them to. They just did. There was my father's seventy-fifth. His eightieth. There were parties at the Standard Club. Sit-down dinners, family gatherings, reunions. In all of them Lauren and Dan sit at the family table— their family blended into ours, our arms wrapped around one another, mugging for the camera. "The two-headed monster," Dan would quip.

When my father turned eighty-five, his financial adviser gave him a piece of advice. "You may as well invade principal, Sol. How long've you got? Have a good time." They lived high. Winter rentals in Palm Beach. Money slipped to their children for down payments on homes. Expensive dinners with friends where my dad always picked up the check. No use fighting over that one. Trips to China. When my mother redecorated her apartment, she redecorated the corridor as well.

Then, as if in some weird Dickensian saga, their fortunes began to change. It was a slippery slope, and they didn't see it coming. I certainly didn't. My father kept expecting to die as he dipped further into his savings, but instead he lived on. And there were the mistakes. Property sold that should have been kept. An investment eaten up by taxes.

I was too busy to notice. I had married by then and had a child. With a down payment from my father, we bought a home in a good school district. But we were artists, writing, teaching. My husband was a journalist. Money wasn't growing on trees.

But my mother with a stroke of bravado I have learned to regret told me to send our daughter to private school. "I don't want her going to that public school up the block." When I hesitated, she said, "Don't worry about Kate's education. I'll take care of it."

Our fortunes improved. My husband got a better job. When I went to Lauren's, we shared child-rearing secrets, hints about home repair. One Christmas, Dan gave my husband a toolbox. We hardly noticed the obvious. My mother's checks came less often. Sometimes not at all. Or they were diminished. There was always some reason—an unexpected doctor's bill, a credit card come due. And finally she told me that there was no more money for Kate's education. In fact there was no more money at all. I was dumbstruck as they told me. Then they sold their apartment on Lake Shore Drive, invested the proceeds, and moved into a retirement home in Wisconsin near my brother.

One day a moving van pulled up in front of my house. Thirteen boxes were unloaded. They contained my mother's china, her silver, her jewelry and art. My inheritance. All that she had divested herself of. For weeks those boxes sat on my basement floor. My brother had sent no inventory, so I had no idea what was inside. But slowly I began to pick through them. I opened one or two. They held buried treasure. A silver chafing dish and silver tray, porcelain made by the House of Limoges. A gold bracelet with my grandmother's diamonds in it. All these my mother had given to me when she moved to a retirement home in a middle-class suburb on the outskirts of Milwaukee—a fall from grace as far as she was concerned. I found myself surrounded with all the accoutrements of an affluent life—all of which I had inherited or had been given to me or divested or passed down from my family. But no cash. We could not meet our obligations; we could not pay our daughter's tuition.

I discussed this turn of events with no one, except my husband. But we discussed it endlessly, obsessively. We made lists.

We could save money doing this; we could sell that. I would work harder, earn more. My husband's was a plan of attrition. No Florida vacation, dinners at home. My main concern was seeing my daughter through high school into college, and we had literally nothing saved for this.

I began thinking more about those boxes in the basement. Could I sell my mother's silver? My grandmother's diamonds? Could I sell my own engagement ring? What could I part with? What would I keep?

LAUREN'S HUSBAND, DAN, is a gemologist. I have seen him squint over a diamond, fondle misshapen pearls. He has a touch for beauty. And money. It's no secret he's done well. Given that my father was the executor of Mort's estate, I knew Lauren had done well too. Though it wasn't an easy call to make, I decided to ask Dan to help me sell some of the jewels.

I would begin with my own engagement ring, which Dan had sold to me when Larry and I got engaged. I would move on to the diamond bracelet my mother had made of my grandmother's wedding stones. If I could sell these two objects, I could pay for the next year of Kate's school. Then I would sell a few more things and begin to put the money away for college.

I gave Dan a call. "Hey, Dan," I said, "how're you doing?" Tried to make the normal chitchat.

We talked for a few moments. He asked after Kate and my folks. I asked how the kids were doing. Then I told him I had some diamonds I wanted to sell. I wondered if he'd help me find someone who might want to buy them. Or better, perhaps he'd want to buy them from me. He knew the stones. He had had them set himself.

"Which diamonds?" he asked, sounding surprised.

"Well, I thought I'd begin with my engagement ring. And there's a bracelet with diamonds. It's not really something I'd wear . . ."

"Oh," he said. "Don't do that. Think of Kate. They'll be hers someday . . ."

"Well, that's right, but I think I'd rather have her go to college."

There was silence on the other end. "I don't understand . . ."

"Dan, I've known you almost thirty years so I guess I can tell you. We need the money. I wouldn't be selling these if I didn't . . ."

Dan was stunned. He could not imagine how we could need money. "Well, ask your folks," he said.

"That's the problem. They don't have anything."

"That's not possible." He didn't believe me. No one really did. Hadn't we all danced to that swing band combo at my dad's ninetieth? And there had been all those winters in Palm Beach, where we'd all meet up for brunch at the Breakers.

"No, it's not. But it's true."

Dan was reluctant to talk about this further with me. I may as well have been discussing the intimacies of my sex life—some S and M practice I'd gotten myself into. Debt was deviant—the fiscal equivalent of bondage. The scarcity of cash flow a sexually transmitted disease. I had trod into an area where he would not go. Even as I write this, talk of money—filthy lucre, Shakespeare said—feels vaguely lurid. As if we're talking whips and chains.

IN THE BASEMENT I began the methodical process of going through my mother's things. On a yellow pad I wrote down an inventory. And the value of what we had. Running the numbers in my head, I needed so much for next year—for the mortgage, for the school bill. I was trying to figure out how to pay for all of it when I saw it.

It lay in Bubble Wrap at the bottom of an unmarked box, but I recognized it right away. It was neatly packed, wedged inside. The *Nude, Seated* which had hung throughout my childhood in my parents' dining room. A room I had not eaten in in thirty years. Carefully I unwrapped it, then held it up. Dusted it off. My eyes drifted over it. The naked body of the woman and, floating above, overhead, the other face.

"Hello, Lauren," I said one Monday morning. "It's me."

"Oh, my god, you must have read my mind. I was just thinking of you . . ."

"And you were going to call me, right?"

She laughed at this joke as she always did. I was always the one to call her. "Right. Let's see, what's the date? Is there a holiday soon?"

"No, not for six months. I was just thinking of you." We spoke for a few minutes about this and that. Then I said, "You know my parents moved. Did you hear?"

"No, I didn't. Where did they move to?"

To Milwaukee, I told her. To be nearer my brother. "My mother sent me some of her things. Her silver and china. Did Dan mention this to you?"

"No," she said slowly, sounding a bit confused. "No, I don't think so."

"Oh, I called him . . . for appraisals." I was relieved. I didn't think he would. "You know, I was just going through them and I came upon that Renoir print—the one your father gave my mother—the naked woman."

Lauren was quiet, and I could tell she was trying to visualize this image. "Yes, I always loved that print."

"Yes, I know you did. I always loved it too."

There was another pause. "So . . ." Lauren waited for me to go on.

"I'm going to sell it. I thought I'd ask you first before I do . . . To see if you'd like to have it." I paused and realized she may have thought I intended to give it to her. "I mean if you would like to buy it."

She cleared her throat, and I heard her light a cigarette. "Yes, I always loved it . . . Actually I would, but why?"

"Well, this is awkward for me . . ." And then I told her. It all poured out. My parents' change of fortune, the fact that we could not meet our obligations. My concerns over Kate's education.

Lauren listened quietly and then said, "I think I understand." She took a drag from her cigarette. She began to talk about our fathers, who had loved one another. How we've known one another all our lives. "Kate's a special girl," she said. "Money shouldn't be an issue for her education. You know our fathers were in business all those years. It's all the same pot in a sense, isn't it?"

"I'm not sure I—"

"The money is there, so I don't think you should worry about it. In fact, I don't want you to worry about it."

"Well, but I am worried . . ."

Lauren's voice got very serious. "I want you to hear what I am saying. I want you to listen carefully . . . I don't want you to worry about money when it comes to your daughter's education. Do you understand?"

I was silent for a moment. I thought I understood. "Are you saying—"

"I'm saying we'll take care of it. You'll get what you get from loans or scholarships or whatever, and the rest, you don't have to worry about." She took another drag. I could hear her exhale. Once we had smoked together. "Do you understand now?"

I did understand. Lauren was saying something to me that was unbelievable. A true act of generosity. She and Dan would take care of Kate's education. Whatever the shortfall, she'd be there. "I don't want you to concern yourself about this again."

We set a price for the Renoir, which she said she'd send right away. Then I thanked her. I couldn't believe it. I didn't know what else to say. I told my husband. I told my daughter. I told our friends. Lauren had said I did not have to worry about my daughter's education.

But I was nervous, and rightly so. Mark Twain wrote in *Pudd'nhead Wilson,* "The holy passion of Friendship is of so sweet and steady and loyal and enduring a nature that it will last through a whole lifetime, if not asked to lend money." I knew that money was the root of all evil. I'd seen families, including my own, split over inheritance. Lifelong relationships devoured.

My grandfather once stopped speaking to his son-in-law who hadn't made good on a debt. My mother no longer speaks to any of her first cousins over an estate. I have a friend named Carol who once borrowed seventy-five dollars from me at a time when seventy-five dollars meant something. I never anticipated seeing that money again, but she sent me a check as soon as she had it and we've been friends ever since.

Another friend tried to sell me her car. My husband and I paid over a hundred dollars for an inspector who declared the car junk. Which is what she sold it for. When she told us proudly that she'd made seven hundred dollars on the deal, she couldn't understand why we were miffed.

But somehow with Lauren I knew we were immune. We had danced in the dark to Johnny Mathis. Cried at weddings and funerals. I could not remember my life without her in it. In dozens of photos from the time we were small, didn't we sit huddled together, our arms entwined?

LAUREN SENT ME the check for the print, and I paid Kate's outstanding tuition. Then she left for Europe with her family. When she returned, we went away. I told her I'd deliver the Renoir at the end of the summer, when we were all back in town. Two months after Lauren sent me the money, I called to make a plan to drive up and see her and drop off the print.

Kate's school bill for the following year had also come in. I thought I'd use the occasion to kill two birds with one stone. I wondered how much she'd be willing to contribute for the coming year.

There was silence at the other end, and immediately I knew it was wrong. "Oh, I think you've misunderstood . . . I was offering to buy the art from you. Not help you out . . ."

I found myself shaking. The calm I'd experienced for the past couple months was suddenly gone. "But you said it all came from the same pot."

Again there was silence, except for her heavy drag. "I said I'd help you out this one time . . ."

How had I misheard this conversation? How had I gotten it so wrong? I had heard her distinctly tell me never to worry about my daughter's education again. That our families and our lives were intertwined. Had I only heard what I wanted to hear? I began to doubt myself and my own perceptions.

FOR WEEKS, THEN months, the Renoir sat on the floor in Bubble Wrap, waiting to be delivered. During those same weeks and months, Lauren never called. Each time I was close to bringing the print to her something occurred. My parents took falls, broke bones, were hospitalized. My husband went into a tailspin over his job. Our daughter got a tattoo; our dog had to have its teeth pulled. Serious things, stupid things—all of which added up to the fact that the Renoir which I owed my oldest friend in the world went nowhere.

And I did not hear a word from her. Not a word. I started thinking, Why do I have to deliver it? Why can't Lauren come and get it? Why am I the one who always has to pick up the phone, come to her house? Why can't she come to mine?

I began to think about my mother, who loved Renoir so much that she'd named our first dog after the artist. How my mother savored the streets of Paris. How she'd stroll into a museum and start pointing at the paintings she admired and people followed her as if on a guided tour.

And she had loved this print. She loved it for its quick study, bold strokes, for the lush female form. This picture reminded me of my home in Illinois and what little remained of it. One day, a rainy day, I was sitting in my living room, looking at what life had brought me, thinking about the good and the bad, what was there and what was missing. I had not seen the Renoir for a long time. I missed the naked woman and her dream of another person who floats above her head. Or a memory, a thought that slips in and out of her mind.

I wanted to see that painting again, so I unwrapped it, and then I wanted to see it on the wall as it had once hung in my parents' house in its green frame. I put it on its hook, back on the wall. Then I looked at it closely for the first time perhaps in years. As I looked at it, I missed Lauren. Or perhaps it was not Lauren I was missing exactly but rather something in me that once was and now is gone. Now I saw what I had never seen before. That the face floating above the nude's head is not some man or woman she longs for. Rather it is a younger version of herself.

It took me weeks to compose the letter. The gist of it said that I was keeping the Renoir. It was a piece of the past, and there was so little of that left. But I would make good on my debt. I would pay her back monthly all that I owed her with interest. I knew she would be upset by this and I would be happy to talk. I didn't want this to come between us. Let's forget the whole thing, I said, and just start afresh.

I never heard from her again. She never responded to my letter. Birthdays have passed without a word. Holidays are cobbled together without her. At Christmas I wait for a card. Sometimes I think I should just take the *Nude, Seated* and send it off to her. But I know it is hanging where it belongs. There are moments when I long to talk to her. I have picked up the phone, started to dial. But for whatever reason I still want her to call me. One day I will call and Lauren will be on the other end. And we'll laugh about this as we've laughed about so many things. She'll think it was the funniest thing. How we didn't talk for so long.

For the time being, I am paying off my debt. Each month I dutifully send a check. I wait for her to cash them. But she never does.

EMILY

Heather Abel

HERE'S THE IMAGE: The hallway of Willets, a typical dorm built in the late fifties, when cinder block was appreciated, was quiet that late afternoon. The eight doors were closed; the shared hall phone—this was before cell phones or even room phones—dangled off the hook. Then, some life. Two pretty girls dragged out a CD player, its electrical cord stuck like a tail under the door. While Sinéad O'Connor sang, they began flailing their arms around, leaping and shimmying under the flickering fluorescent lights. This was a liberal arts school. These were liberal girls. Both bodies had taken ballet lessons; both bodies pushed to be sexy, and the result was somewhere between awkwardness and delight. The hall was narrow and long, and they ran the length of it. The song was on repeat.

That freshman fall, they danced often in this flailing, wafting way. They could do all sorts of things together that they would never have done alone. Once they danced shirtless and outside. They were singing a song, maybe the same Sinéad song, and it was raining. They'd been taking a walk and ended up in the college's wooded amphitheater, where years later, hardly speaking to each other, they would receive diplomas and graduate. It would rain then as well. This is the story of what happened in between.

Sometime during the first week of college, I don't remember when, I met Emily. I liked her because she was sweet to me. Midwestern sweet. And she was funny and impeccably pretty, but not in a way that would dampen me.

What I mean is that Emily and I were different in specific and obvious ways. I'd brought vintage dresses and velvet skirts to college. She wore pale blue shirts tucked into jeans. I already knew about Foucault. She could draw, write poetry, and sing like a starlet. The child of lefty academics, I was more worldly. The daughter of genuinely friendly people, she was kinder. As I saw it, she was the sparkly, shimmery skim of water. I sunk deeper, where the seaweed grows.

Perhaps as a result of growing up with two sisters—and sharing my mother with them—I had at a young age found a way to compete without competing. I would decide that certain things were mine and that I alone could claim them. In return, I'd abstain from other things. Early on, the color red was mine. Blue was my sister's, even though I quite liked it, so I would not choose the sweet blue sweater at the store. Later, Nicaragua was mine. Marxism was also mine. Doc Martens were mine. Having best friends was mine. Having boyfriends was not mine. (This got confusing because I actually had a boyfriend through much of high school and into college, but I still didn't identify as someone with a boyfriend.) Discussing was mine. Making out was not mine. Apartheid was mine. Athleticism was not mine. Deep, difficult things were mine; I wasn't actually depressed, but I liked to talk animatedly about depression. Drinking games, TV, and one-liners were not mine. The environment was mine, both the outdoors (yes, I claimed the wide world) and the defense of the outdoors.

This is the thinking, I can say in retrospect, of a scared girl.

BECAUSE EMILY AND I had separate talents, I wasn't afraid we'd have to compete over something I cared about. Without this fear, we attained something I can only call equanimity, and it allowed us, at times, the buoyancy of a soap bubble. That's how I see it now, two girls dancing and singing and drawing and learning Foucault and talking about boys in code, all inside a soap bubble.

With our differences frozen in place, Emily and I could be practically the same. We were both girlie girls. Girlie like first-graders, trading stickers. We picked music, boys, shirts, and posters that were pretty as strawflowers. And we both wistfully and vehemently missed our moms. If college is a railroad away from your mother, we had both hopped the slow train. They'd been our first friends, our models of just how close you could get to someone.

The term *boyfriend* is coy, hiding all implications of intimacy or raunchiness. "Sure he's my boyfriend," you retort in eighth grade. "He's a boy and he's my friend." The term *best friend* is not coy. It puts the competition implicit in friendship right out there for everyone to see. It says that some friends are good, some are better, but all of these girls are left standing on the second step wearing silver medals, while only one girl wins first. Everything is in its understood place. That's why I liked having a best friend.

Of course, gaining a boyfriend is much more straightforward than winning a best friend: there's a first kiss. But becoming a best friend is also physical. Maybe you trade clothes. Maybe, with your fingers, you scoop white frosting off of a row of yellow cakes after everyone has left the dining hall. Maybe you describe in detail how you feel about giving blow jobs.

Or maybe, you lie on the grass, and with four feet in the air and your hips aligned, you compare the length of your legs. There's no way to describe an eighteen-year-old body fourteen years later, because at the time I thought mine was large and ungainly, and now I'm sure it was adorable. (My capacity for jealousy is huge; I am jealous of myself then.) And I don't remember Emily's body either, except that she's about four inches shorter than I and was comparably smaller, and we could wear some of the same clothes but not most. And at times I minded that. So, it's not that I thought that we had the same body exactly. Or that we didn't ever feel envious. It's just that I liked them both together.

I'm not talking sex. I'm talking familiarity and ownership. Sometimes when I saw her and she was beautiful, I thought I was seeing myself.

BY THE FIRST snowfall, Emily was my best and I was hers. We walked on the thin crust to the faraway part of campus that held a frat-house-turned-feminist-center. I'd never lived in winter, and Emily taught me to wear tights and mittens and what chipmunks looked like. She also taught me to sing in tune. *We are self-sufficient, self-empowered women*, we sang. *But sometimes we get a little horny*. We didn't date boys that year, and this is one reason I think our own romance bloomed. Instead, we both had high school boyfriends who sent us letters. Instead, we rewrote a song from *Les Mis*, rhyming *horny* with *Californ-y*, and performed it to boys in a perverse flirtation.

A week later I was home for winter break. It was a day like a flirt, when Los Angeles flaunts its distance from the East. Bright blue sky behind feathery palm fronds. Robins alit on scarlet bougainvillea, the purple tips of jacaranda. I was lying next to my mom, on my parents' bed, trying to bring the coasts together by conjuring up snow and bare branches and every tiny thought I'd had since I last saw her. That's when the phone rang. I didn't pick it up right away. The world felt too full: somewhere there were mittens and here was my mother and outside, aloe plants; but perhaps we just remember fullness before emptiness. I sat cross-legged on the edge of the bed. *Is this Heather?* It was Emily. She was calling to tell me that her mother had a headache, and it turned out to be a brain tumor.

Emily's mother started dying for real in the beginning of sophomore year, and I took on the death like a project, with the self-importance and fervor I brought to protest the Gulf War: My job would be to carry Emily through this. When she returned home, I offered to audit her classes and take notes. I spoke to her teachers and the deans. I called her nightly. But mostly I spent a lot of time telling myself: Pretend it's your mom. How would you feel?

At the funeral, I sat next to Emily in the front row. I have no memory of her boyfriend or other friends. My job felt enormous, but I believed I would succeed. I did dishes all afternoon, staring out the window that had been cut out of the wall for Emily's mother, so that she could look at the woods while working.

Emily and I shared a room in a quad, and when she didn't return to school, my concern grew until it filled the space of her. In early December, my parents visited me for the first time, and we were walking through a portrait-lined lounge when my mother told me that her mother was very sick with cancer. *I'm sorry*, I said, not looking at my parents; I was staring at the faces of Swarthmore's founders, lovely pacifist ladies, full of sympathy I couldn't muster. *But I can't think about it now. I'm full up.* My grandmother had played favorites (it's a tradition in our family); my sister was hers. I was not. So, I reversed the equation. Emily's mother's death was mine. My grandmother's death was not.

This, as they said throughout college, was problematic. Emily's mother's death was hers. Or, perhaps, her mother's.

When the spring semester began and Emily returned, I developed a hierarchy of suffering among our roommates. I was at the bottom; my grandmother's cancer was an age-appropriate tragedy. Molly, who had just begun grappling with a history of sexual abuse, entered a claustrophobic and demoralizing relationship with a guy; she was easily several rungs above me. That winter, Tina learned that her father was HIV positive, and her high school boyfriend overdosed. She surpassed Molly. Emily was on top, the queen with the true, visceral horror. Her mother had gone, in a few short months, from being lovely and nurturing to bald and strange to dead. Since happiness was denied our quad that year, I decided that the person with the most suffering would likely receive the most love. I knew how pathetic and cruel this hierarchy was, but I also knew that, according to its rules, I'd lost, and it was up to me to take care of everybody.

I have to admit: for a while this gave me an incredible sense of resolve. I liked being busy all day in class, and then, the rush ended, I liked knowing I was needed. Most of all, I liked the time in between, the long, purposeful march to our dorm. I could see it, pretentious in stone and turrets but somehow still looking like an Elks' lodge, as I crossed the train tracks and then the vast lawn used by sports teams in the spring, now brown as tundra. One day, I carried ice cream, which made me hopeful. It was crucial to come home with a plan.

Up in our room, the afternoon light hit like a beacon, the slant call of a lighthouse.

In the center of the room were two single beds, pushed together. And on them, only a small part of Emily was visible to me: one arm and black shoes. The rest was hidden by her bedspread. On our windowsill were her sea green vases, and there were my Nicaragua posters hung on the wall, vestiges of the girls we were the year before, which seemed so silly now.

Also seeming silly: the ice cream. A pathetic gesture against grief so giant that you would wear shoes to bed. Still, I gingerly set it down on our two desks, also pushed together. I stood there. I wouldn't wake her.

What are you doing? She was annoyed, not asleep. *Um, I got some ice cream. Do you want it?*

No. Of course not. It was a stupid plan.

Should we take a walk to the creek?

No. I thought how in two years I'd grown to like this winter light, but I didn't say that. Emily didn't like it now.

Want to go to dinner? No. Order pizza? No. Emily! Tell me what's going on. Tell me how you feel. I don't know. Should I leave? No.

The sun slipped west. *Can I turn on the lights? Is that okay?* Emily made an unsure noise. When the room was totally dark I switched on the overhead, and she pulled a pillow over her head. Sometimes, this was all there was all night.

But this evening, our friend came by. During the hours I'd spent trying to get Emily out of bed, she'd gone for a run, eaten dinner, put on a dress with cowboy boots. She told us about a party and said, *Please come, Emily, please come, sweetie.* Emily sat up. *I want to go.*

At the mirror, she pulled her hair back and loosed the one curl that would corkscrew the length of her forehead. It was her new hairstyle. I believed that after what she'd seen of her mother's body, after she'd bathed it and smelled it, Emily changed her own. She developed an attentiveness to her beauty that I lacked and that took all her energy. I didn't touch my hair; looking put-together was now Emily's. I thought: I need to study; I need dinner. But really, I was jealous. I had wanted to be the one who got her out of bed. I wanted her to wake up from depression because of me, because of how much I loved her.

On the way out the door, *Aren't you coming, Heather?*

I said no, so I can't say what happened at the party, how she suddenly unspun from her cocoon in our bed and became multisyllabic and conversant, but I can describe how guys looked at her those days. We were no longer noticed together, those two pretty girls singing their smug song. She was noticed alone. I told myself I didn't care. I had one crush. He was an outdoorsy guy named Greg, and he seemed as untroubled and beautiful as a boy could be. I didn't flirt, exactly. Instead, I searched for Greg on campus and then ignored him or, if I felt brave, talked about plants. This was no time for frivolity: In L.A. people were rioting, burning stores; in New York, my grandmother was hurrying to finish her eighteenth mystery novel before dying; and in our room, Emily's sorrow shot up, tall, narrow, and awkward as a palm tree. But still, I had plans for him. After all, the outdoors were mine and, in my hopeful heart, the outdoorsy guy as well.

I'd been asleep for a while when Emily returned. First I heard her giggling in the hall, then she slammed the door behind her.

The next day, Emily and I walked at noon to the campus store. She'd said yes to gummi fish. She'd said no to lunch. All the way across the lawn she was telling me what she hated. Apparently she hated a lot. Her stupid classes, for one. How tired she was. She was so amazingly tired. This was obvious; her voice dragged and stalled, like a screen door on a foggy day, squeaking open, inching closed. She hated the stupid people at this school. The guys looked at her as tragic. The teachers treated her delicately. But she also hated how some people ignored it. How they blithely talked about their mothers. Like she wanted to hear about their mothers.

Before we reached the store, a guy from Emily's English class came scurrying up the hill, laden down like a hermit crab with the paraphernalia of a poet: an army satchel presumably chockfull of verse on one shoulder, a hat, an oversize suede jacket. All of him coffee-stained, but his face was lavish, dark featured and eyelashed like a girl's. He needed to talk to Emily about some poem he'd written. Only she would understand it.

Me? Smiling. She touched her curl. She looked radiant. *Sure,*

I'd love to. For one flushed second, I hated her. Then I stopped myself.

Over the past ten years, this memory has calcified, so it's almost all I have from that time. I know that she started to be mean to me, to say sarcastic, cutting things, but I can't recite them. I know that she seemed angry at me for having so many things to do, but I can't describe how she showed this. I remember only the sense of failing at my job and not knowing why. I remember only that there were two Emilys. There was the drowning one, who turned to me, and there was the illuminated one, who everyone else saw.

This made me furious, but I turned the fury on myself, deciding the disparity was my fault. That past Thanksgiving, a few weeks after the funeral, I had sat between my aunt and mother on a sage green couch in my grandmother's elegant brownstone on the Upper West Side. I'd rarely felt so safe as then, sitting between these women. The aunt was a psychiatrist, and she was talking to me—in that intense, biannually intimate way of my family—about the death of my best friend's mother. She wanted me to know that, in mourning, Emily might come to despise me, not only because I had seen her at her most vulnerable but also because I'd participated in the event that was most hateful to her. So, as Emily walked with the poet to the dining hall, I held on to what my aunt had said, believing Emily shunned me because of my beneficence.

But I began to suspect Emily had another reason: My mom was alive. She was in London, in fact, and I memorized the calling card number and used it daily. She talked to me about concentric circles of grief. I always pictured the surface of a stump after the tree falls. The dead person is in the middle. The people close to the dead person are the first ring. The people close to the people close to the dead person are the second ring. My mother, presumably, was the third ring. The lesson was: We're all in this together.

Perhaps I wanted to join Emily in the center of the stump, because I spent that afternoon, like many others, nervously trying to imagine that I had lost my mother. And I could barely handle it. I didn't want my mother to die.

It's hard to write about this year because I'm embarrassed by it. Not because I couldn't save Emily but because I chose to do so by rushing up next to her, trying on her loss. Because I understood, on some level, that the equanimity of our perfect friendship relied on us having set things in common—like mothers—and I dared to think that I could equalize our experiences. These days I figure that the only way I could have assuaged Emily's sorrow would have been to go dancing with her, to distract her with guys or *90210* or drugs, joining her in the idiocy of grief rather than in its psychology. But to do that would have been to give up my role as the receptacle for her dark moods, really, to give up my role as best friend. I wasn't able to separate enough from her, just as I couldn't separate from my mother. And now I remind myself that this is what she'd been forced to do, and I'm embarrassed again.

IN MID-FEBRUARY, I came home and the windows were open and she was listening to music. This wasn't normal. Greg had stopped by to ask me to help him organize an environmental conference. Finding Emily instead, he offered her the job. *We're meeting Thursday,* she said, smiling. *Probably you could help out, too.* I walked out the door.

Sometime the next week, Greg asked her out. Our roommates had helped set it up, and everyone was excited about Emily getting out, having a date. This time, I didn't just leave the room, I left the state, taking the bus to Connecticut for the weekend.

What drove me away was unspeakable: I felt competitive with someone whose mother died. I was jealous of how loss had changed her, making her more attractive, almost foreign. I wondered, was grief black and murky for her, or did she take some

pleasure in the fact that men were adoring her and our roommates babying her? I was supposed to be the deep, dark one.
Despair was my terrain. I'd believed we were going to get
through this together by hunkering down and being sad and
feeling things, all sorts of things, flushing them out of us. Then,
if there was a party, we would go together, we would perform
those public displays of secrecy that make having a best friend
so thrilling: *We are self-sufficient, self-empowered women…*

God, I was angry. I was so angry I wrote in my journal what a
foul person I was. *I am a BAD best friend,* I wrote in large letters
across two pages of the book. *I am a BAD daughter. I am a BAD
girlfriend.* None of this was true, of course. I was a very good
daughter and a devoted friend and nice enough to my boyfriend
across the country. I only *wanted* desperately to feel free enough
to be bad, to say: Fuck you, Emily, I need things too.

Of course the date didn't happen. Emily wasn't ready to desire
anything. Her charm shone brightly but had an infantile attention span—suddenly, in the middle of a sentence, she'd be
nowhere near us—and I'd gone to Connecticut for nothing.
Except for this: On the bus ride home through wintered woods,
I decided to stop eating.

This seemed very bad indeed. I believed anorexia to be one of
the meanest things girls could do to each other. If being thin is
a competition, I figured, the anorexics win unfairly. My
approach was anthropological. I joked with my women's studies
professors about the triteness of college eating disorders and
carefully studied the habits of the anorexics in the dining hall. I
interviewed them about exercise. They said: Run.

I didn't think it would last. I'd always harbored a strange terror of running. Athleticism was not mine. But it turned out, to
my great surprise, that losing weight was a job I could handle.

It's untrustworthy to impose a narrative on something so
murky. Why does a girl stop eating? But I'd venture that anorexia
was my way out of all the anger I wouldn't admit to. I had been

obsessing about Emily. I knew where she was at all times during the day. I knew when she might be alone and whether that might be a problem. I knew what time her classes began, and I knew if she wasn't getting out of bed to make them. This was how I cared for her. But she didn't care for my help.

It was simpler for me to starve myself than to tell Emily how pissed off I was about this. Dieting gave me something easier—and blessedly achievable—to obsess about. One week, instead of making sure she arrived at the dining hall, I searched for plain rice to eat. The next week, I stealthily went running even though I knew she was by herself. And while running I couldn't think so much about how my mother's death would feel right then, on a clear, windy day, with the first crocuses out. I thought: Holy shit, I'm running!

I ran and ran until finally, in late March, Tina turned to me and said, not very nicely: *You're starting to look just like Emily.* It's true. I've never, before or since, looked more like her; I shrunk out of my clothes and started wearing hers. But by then our equanimity was off, our friendship staggering like a drunk.

One night around that time, I was sitting in the college coffee shop with Greg, waiting for Emily to come plan the ecology conference. For fifteen lovely minutes I talked to him alone. I knew exactly where she was: listless with the covers up. For months I'd waited for her to get out of bed, and now I wanted her to stay there. Twenty minutes passed. Twenty-five. In came Emily, her hair perfect, her lateness excused by the sight of her.

BY EMILY'S BIRTHDAY, April 19, I'd lost twenty pounds. I promised her we'd do something exquisite. But then Greg asked me to go to a diner along the highway on the night of her birthday, and I told her, vaguely, that something had come up.

I remember listening to a sort of sexy song about a girl kissing a girl as I got dressed. I remember wearing Emily's smallest pants with my Doc Martens. She went to New York City for the night, and the next day I compensated by hosting a picnic on the lawn. It was a lofty spring day, pastel blooms everywhere. I felt the sweet breeze and considered that I'd cheated on my best friend.

IF I HAD to find the moment I stopped trying to understand Emily, it would be this: Two weeks after that first date, I'd returned from my grandmother's funeral late in the evening, and I sat on the wet grass outside our dorm considering Emily and the other girls inside. Then I stood and walked to Greg's room and woke him up. *Take off your dress*, he told me, and I did. I was skinny and kissing Greg, who was huge. My body had nothing to do with Emily's body. It had to do with his body.

For most of my life I've had a rather remarkable memory for the unimportant detail. I would shock my friends by recalling what I wore on the first day of school from kindergarten to senior year. I would list off my activities for a series of fifteen Saturdays. I've recently realized that this was just an insomniac's party trick; I'd been memorizing these mundanities as I lay awake. But in any case, I've never cultivated such near-perfect recall as during the first days of dating Greg. For years I told myself the bedtime story of everything that happened those six weeks before summer. So it's extraordinary that I can't remember how Emily entered this time. I can't remember ever talking to her about my relationship. I've tried over and over again, and I can't.

Mostly I remember this: I was happy. I was so fucking happy.

It felt corrupt to be thrilled when Emily wasn't, as if I'd won this happiness at the fair and she'd lost it. My logic—the reasoning of my entire life then—was that it was cruel to be happier. That if something pleased me, it displeased someone else, and there went the friendship. That's why I don't remember spending time with Emily during those weeks. I wouldn't expose my happiness to her. I was hiding.

WHY DID I guiltily assume that, by dating a cute guy and being thin, I hurt her any more than she was already hurting? As I figure it, I learned some of this from my parents, who suggest that another person's joy can be so sharp it cuts you. Recently, my sister had a baby, and at a celebratory dinner that evening, my father asked if it was hard for me, being babyless and all, as if only one baby exists and she got it. There's something touching about this: the rotten side of each of us—our jealousies and hurts—was always attended to. But it generates a sense of scarcity. And this scarcity made me scared to want something and terrified when someone wanted what I had. (Thus my decision that there was only enough thinness, Nicaragua, joy, Marxism, or blue for one friend.)

It's false, of course. There *is* more than one baby or beauty or boyfriend. There's even, despite its exclusionary title, more than one best friend. The world is crowded and we are easily distracted. But in one crucial respect, this schema is true: There are simply not enough mothers to go around. This is what I learned when her mother died and Emily became furious. It confirmed what I'd been taught, and that frightened me. I worried that having a mother would become my weapon; it could wound. Wanting to give up something in exchange, I made everything scarce. I shrunk the world.

I am not a quick learner, so when, at the end of junior year, my mother was diagnosed with breast cancer, I did it again. I decided to move home and drive her here and there, joining her suffering and compensating for my health. Once again I was surprised when I was miserable. *I should be happy*, I wrote in my journal. *I have all this free time at home! I should learn something. Guitar lessons? Pottery classes? I should start my thesis.* I don't remember Emily calling or writing.

My mother lived, and in the years since her illness, I've been able to do all sorts of things with her. I stopped relying on her for reassurance. I started talking about writing with her. I watched her age. I worried about her. I've changed the rules of our friendship so many times she's dizzy. Emily hasn't done any of this with her mother. Unlike me, she didn't call her mom when beginning this essay to ask what she remembered. My mother said: *Honestly, it was disturbing, that fall after her mother died, when you called me so much and that poor girl had nothing.*

There is a dearth of mothers. It's the immovable fact of our friendship and of this essay. I tried to shift the balance, feeling bad for having things, giving up things I wanted, but it didn't work. I hate that helplessness.

THE END OF the story is quick. I spent the fall in Bogotá; she studied in Ireland in the spring. We met once, at New Year's in Ohio, smoking a cigarette out her attic window and kissing at midnight. It was a relief, both the day together and the year apart. We did share a house during senior year, along with three other girls, but we didn't have much of a friendship. Frankly, I don't know which it was: either she was elusive and unknowable, or I felt that to really know her would be to relinquish the happiness I'd scrounged. I'd feel guilty when she complained, angry when she was caustic after my mother's chemo ended. Then suddenly she would be delightful, and I grew tired of watching out for her moods.

I already had a new best friend. Luckily, I never competed with her like I did with Emily. But neither did I ever mistake her beauty for my own or take such a personal pleasure in her physical presence.

It wasn't like we never talked again; it wasn't that kind of breakup. It was just that sometimes she'd be sitting across from me at dinner, when she made it to dinner, and I'd miss her terribly. I missed my vision of her as buoyant, and I missed her vision of me as brilliant. It was a kind of heartbreak, the kind that makes you wish someone never existed, the kind that is entirely uncharitable. I was—and remain—puzzled by how soon I felt done with being charitable.

Except, I would never really be through caring for Emily. I remember one shining fall day during senior year. Greg, who had graduated, was visiting for the last time before we broke up. He'd just arrived on campus, and we'd barely talked, when Emily walked across the lawn. As she approached, his face lit up. *Hey lovely*, he said. I didn't feel mad or jealous. I just looked at her and thought, Why yes, she's the loveliest. That is hers.

HEATHER

Emily Chenoweth

M Y MOTHER WAS my first best friend. We were each other's great confidantes, advocates, and allies, bound by a deep and sometimes ferocious love.

When my mother was dying, my best friend was Heather. There had been other intimates over the years, but Heather had eclipsed them. When she came to Ohio for my mother's funeral, she sat with me in the first pew—the royalty of the grieving—and held my hand through the eulogy and the hymns. My boyfriend sat somewhere in the back of the church, another indistinguishable mourner. It was November 1991, and Heather and I were nineteen.

I met Heather at Swarthmore College, when we were assigned rooms on the same freshman hall. My first impression of her centered on her hair, which was coppery brown and fell in uncombed but shiny waves almost to her waist. To me, it was a striking style: in the Midwest, girls wore their hair long only until their mothers let them cut, perm, and feather it into lacquered crests. Heather's hair made her look younger, more approachable; she was the kind of girl boys at my high school called a granola.

My father, in between unloading suitcases, was charming the new arrivals: You came from California all by yourself? he asked Heather. Heather smiled brightly: she had. My mother proclaimed her very brave—and her parents, too, she said, for letting her come so far alone. We stood for a moment in Heather's doorway and watched the other students filing past. Someone had set up a stereo already; *Rico Suave* poured into the hall.

Later, after all the families had waved good-bye, I went back to Heather's room, where she sat me down amidst the mess of her unpacking—the space would never fully recover from it—and pulled out a fat photo album. Here was Santa Monica High, she said, and here was the beach; here she was getting ready to go to a party, and there was her boyfriend with the grape boycott sign. She had dozens of friends, and a story for each—that one had joined the cheerleading squad as a joke; this one spent her summers in India; that one wrote passionate editorials for the school newspaper. Like currency, she counted the friends up; they were beloved and she missed them already. Then she told me that her high school best friend and her mother were both named Emily.

She closed the album and turned to face me. "Emilys have always been very important to me," she said.

I was shy and uncertain; Heather could not have crafted a more gentle invitation to friendship.

In those first days, smitten already, I watched her use this gift of instantaneous and effortless connection. "Oh, I was at the Greek Theatre when Jerry played 'Dark Star,'" she said to a hippie with bells jingling on her wrists. "I took campers all over the Sierra Madre," she might say to a boy wearing hiking boots. To the political, she was an activist; to the athletic, a dancer; to the academic, a straight-A student who'd decided, at the last possible minute, not to go to Harvard.

None of this was disingenuous—she was all those things. She was also the daughter of distinguished professors and the proud progeny of, as she put it, "a long line of atheist intellectual Jews," the girlfriend of Cesar Chavez's godson, and a family friend of Jackson Browne. She had been arrested while protesting at the nuclear testing site in Nevada and had given her name, at the police station, as Mother Jones. She had once cooked dinner with Jerry Garcia.

Meanwhile I'd been playing the violin, getting good grades, and lettering in sports in a shabbily picturesque small town, part of a family that had been blue-collar until a generation ago; I had nothing to compare to her range of experience. Perhaps this is why she offered as our bond the simple fact of my name. But, like me, Heather was also somewhat of an innocent. Neither of us had been allowed to watch TV, or stay out very late, or eat sugar cereal. Our teachers had loved us; our parents had enjoyed the relative ease of our raising. We had not done any real drugs or had any real sex to speak of.

THE EARLY WEEKS of college were marked by shifting alliances; coalitions were made, briefly nurtured, and then abandoned. Who knows exactly why Heather and I stuck? There is only to say that we did, and that we were, for the most part, inseparable from the beginning. Thanks to Heather, I became a vegetarian, hennaed my hair, boycotted Gillette products, bought Birkenstocks, stopped shaving my legs, joined the student environmental group, and spent long afternoons drinking tea at the Women's Center. Thanks to me, Heather drank at a few fraternity parties, occasionally wore lipstick, and began chewing with her mouth closed. Heather and I wore each other's clothes and jewelry; we cowrote a paper on Nicaragua; we fasted for Oxfam. We listened to Edie Brickell and bands with girls in them and the Philadelphia public radio station. When studying bored us, we wrote songs about the Swarthmore boys, and how none of them was handsome enough, and with the casual heartlessness of pretty eighteen-year-olds, we sang our favorites in front of them.

That first semester, we waited for the cold weather and then for the snow, I with a midwesterner's resignation to the months of gray skies, Heather with the voluble anxiety of a Southern Californian: women in L.A., she told me, shake out their minks the minute it drops below sixty. Her parents sent her her first ever winter coat in the mail—we made an appropriately big deal over this green woolen novelty, with its big fur-lined hood—but for the rest of her gear we went to the mall. We lifted sweaters and scarves off their hangers, holding them up: What do you think? Would I wear this? Would you?

By then we had gained the fifteen pounds everyone said we would, and there was only one pair of jeans (Heather's) between us that fit; most mornings involved a decision about who got to wear them. We'll eat better next semester, we promised ourselves.

I left Heather at the sweaters and wandered off to look at shoes. When I came back, bored, unable to find anything and reluctant to spend the money anyway, Heather was still flipping through the racks some fifteen feet away. Because there were mirrors everywhere around us, I saw her, in the yellow fluorescence of the juniors' section, from many angles at once. For one thrilling, vertiginous moment, I stared at her and I thought: What am I doing over there?

THAT WINTER, ON New Year's Eve, my father walked into the kitchen for coffee and found my mother unconscious on the floor. He called an ambulance but told my younger brother and me that we shouldn't worry, that she had probably fallen and hit her head. At the hospital, before the nurses had even asked my father her name, she had a terrible seizure.

The subsequent MRIs were fuzzy—it was a portable machine—and the phrase "neurological problem" was proffered and repeated in low tones of concern. My mother woke aphasic and confused, which I insisted was a result of the drugs they'd given her to prevent further seizures, the first of which had laid her out on the kitchen tile and the second of which, in the ER, had almost killed her.

In the hospital gift shop, I bought her a little yellow chick; it peeped when squeezed. "Oh," my mother said, "look at the . . ." She turned it over in her hands. "Cat?" she asked me.

She had a biopsy when I was back at Swarthmore: it was an astrocytoma. Named for the star-shaped glial cells from which it grows, the astrocytoma is one of the most common types of brain tumors. Some are operable. My mother's was not.

Heather's empathy was immediate and genuine. She vowed to take care of me, and in those early months of my mother's illness, I still knew how to be grateful.

Had my mother remained healthy, I still might have lost my energy for activism—in protesting and do-gooding. My social conscience was not, by nature or nurture, highly developed, and I'd done what I could to encourage it. But after her diagnosis I abandoned all interest, except what remained as a guilt-inflected afterimage. Heather, on the other hand, had grown up playing games about world peace—of course she retained her commitment.

In February 1991, a few weeks after the United States invaded Iraq for the first time, Heather and some older students from the Swarthmore Political Action Committee decided that they should hang antiwar banners on the I-95 overpasses. Since this was illegal, they were going to do it at night—the night, as it happened, of a big college dance. My date, with whom I'd been set up, was ardent and eager, and because I did not return his affections I wanted Heather to grab a boy and come with us. I knew I ought to protest too—if not to express my outrage and fear then at least to preserve some of Heather's regard—but I couldn't summon either the decisiveness or the desire. I thought that the other students, whom I held in some thrall for their righteous passions and senior status, would be able to see right through the PEACE NOW T-shirt to the provincial moderate I feared I was. And anyway, there was a *chance* I'd have fun dancing.

When I saw that Heather wouldn't be swayed, I half hoped that she would encourage me to come along. But she was focused on the protest—not my participation in it—and her impatience was clear. "Why don't you just borrow my dress?" she said.

I knew which one she meant. It was a steely blue velvet minidress with a shirred empire waist, and I had long coveted it. "Thanks," I said. I opened her closet with a mixture of shame and relief.

When Heather left in someone's car, I put the dress on and admired myself in the mirror; I'd gotten thin again since my mother's diagnosis. I'd started borrowing a different pair of Heather's jeans—ripped, faded Levi's—which only I could fit into. (Before she became too impaired to kid around, my mother used to say, "Cancer—it's a great way to lose weight.")

Then I went and drank half a bottle of Southern Comfort with a girl from Tampa Bay. In a dining hall transformed by strobe lights and a rented sound system, I left my bewildered date standing on the dance floor as I ran outside and ducked into the bushes, where, weeping with humiliation, I threw up everything.

The night was clear and cold. Couples streamed in and out of the dance; the pale clouds of my breath formed and then vanished. I wiped my eyes and looked down—I'd vomited all over the snow and my shoes, all over the beautiful velvet and shiny lacquer buttons of Heather's perfect dress.

SPRING CAME WITH a profusion of flowers. Magnolias blossomed all over campus, blood-red tulips bloomed outside the library, and the stately oaks that lined the path to the main administration building waved their green fingers. On the Beach, a soft, sloping lawn bordered by daffodils, students lay about and sunbathed, the adventurous girls topless. Someone was always playing music out a nearby dorm window, and we were young enough to still be moved: Van Morrison wanted to rock our Gypsy souls.

Heather and I sat with friends on the Beach to relax but took our tanning down to Swarthmore's little slice of woods, where on the edge of the forest, small-breasted and modest, we sunned in our bras. We put flowers in our hair and took pictures; in them we are wild-haired and smiling.

WHEN I TALKED to my mother on the phone, there were long silences in which she groped for words. In the notes she sent me, her handwriting was uncertain, childish. P's became B's, and Z's were C's. The tumor was growing, branching out, but no one told her. This was a kindness—she truly didn't want to know. Probably I didn't want to know either, and for a while, I didn't. I wrote her back: "Hey, Mom, how are the radiation and chemo things treating you? Are you having any fun?" Really I wrote that.

Heather accepted the rhythm of my moods; she was giddy with me when I wanted to forget and sympathetic when I couldn't. Her responsiveness stood in marked contrast to that of others I confided in. A college administrator whose daughter had died of a brain tumor sat me down in his office and told me to quit wasting my emotional reserves. "Don't let yourself feel too bad right now," he said. "You have no idea the shit you're in for." When I went to the school counselor, she blew her nose through-out the session—she had a wet, nasty cold—and rolled her eyes at most of what I said. Only when it came time to book my next appointment did she show any sign of human warmth: Next Tuesday then, she said with a thin, wan smile. These people are supposed to make me feel better? I asked Heather one day at lunch.

That night she begged the keys to someone's car. She put me behind the wheel (she didn't have her driver's license), turned on the radio, and pointed me toward town: we went to McDonald's and CVS, and maybe an ice cream shop or a grocery store, and we stuffed ourselves senseless on french fries and Milky Ways and mint chocolate chip. We laughed because we were such disgusting pigs and because Heather had gotten food in her hair again. Drowning out the radio, we sang along to R.E.M.'s "Shiny Happy People." With Heather, I could remember what it was like to be happy.

IN MAY, AFTER classes ended, she came to Ohio to visit. I know this not because I recall the week itself but because my mother made a sign for her. She used colored pencils for the script; with a marker she drew three blue, wobbly hearts. "Welcome Home (ours is yours)," it said. "We're glad you're here Heather + Emily. Welcome Welcom. Be 'combel.'" She meant "comfortable."

I didn't want to go back to school sophomore year. The only consolation was that I was living with Heather. We'd gotten a suite with two D.C. girls, Tina and Molly—friends Heather had made for us—while Rebecca and Sasha, with whom we'd also become close, had found rooms down the hall. Flush with the excitement of co-ownership, Heather and I went to South Street and got pretty postcards and a Maxfield Parrish poster to pin up. We bought incense, and a red vase for flowers. Back in our room, we pushed three single beds together to make a giant, creaky raft. We slept on the outer two while the middle one accumulated papers, books, shirts, and socks—a precarious heap that we whispered over at night beneath the high ceilings, with the lights from the parking lot shining down on us.

Heather had a wonderful laugh, silly and infectious; it was one of the many things that drew people to her. She couldn't take a class without bonding with someone in it, couldn't join a group without stealing someone away to have dinner. She chummed around with a Colombian girl from New York City, a pretty military brat she'd met in the environmentalists' organization, a blond sophomore who was questioning her sexuality. In working on a video project for one of her courses, she became fast friends with not only the other students but the young and exotically hip professor.

I couldn't understand this at all. The way I saw it, I'd made my choice in the first few days of college; I was happy to know and love other people, but at some level, Heather would have been enough. And I was afraid—now that I spent so many of my days tearful and furious—that one of the new friends would replace me.

What distinguished me from these other girls, besides the fact that I was first, I wondered. I could not pretend to be as worldly or ambitious or comparatively untroubled as surely they were. College meant almost nothing to me then—my mother was *dying*, who cared about recycling, or sexism, or Literature of Conscience? I was convinced that every single connection Heather made cheapened the one she had made with me.

There is nothing more primitive and ordinary than the mating instinct, no easier social transaction than one of desire. I went a little boy crazy: I made lists of the ones who liked me; I dissected significant glances; I parsed casual conversations into snippets of promise. These activities passed beyond minor distractions into a carefully nurtured project to help me avoid thoughts of my mother's heartbreaking decline. I encouraged the affections of a poet and a lacrosse player; I went to parties. There, through a superficial smiling prettiness, an ability to charm and be charming, I felt relief.

One night at a party there were two boys circling, moving in and out of my orbit. Heather sighed volubly. "This is getting boring," she said. Maybe she found flirting hard, or a waste of time, or maybe she wondered why I wasn't thinking of my boyfriend in Chicago. But more likely I think she couldn't understand why, when I had so few moments of vivacity, I would waste them in banter, in guile.

The answer was simple, if impossible, then, to explain. I could feel her sliding away from me—to a new year, a new leaf, and new, happier friends—and I could not see how to prevent it. In the neat equation of our gleeful early friendship, what we needed from each other, what we gave and got in return, had been, it seemed, precisely balanced. But that had changed with my grief: the companionship, the sympathy, the energy and affection that I demanded were far greater in quantity than what I was able to give back. In every interaction with Heather, I felt my own insufficiency.

With the boys, though, the reckoning was elementary. "I think of you / and your eyes of a saint," the poet wrote. The lacrosse player was blond and wholesome, a good son; he planned to become a doctor. The inarticulate ache and resentment I felt around Heather vanished when I was with one of them. They didn't need me either, necessarily, but they thought they did, and that was something.

When I went home in October to be with my mother in her final weeks, Heather called me almost every day, and it seemed then that our friendship had regained its original force. For her to call that often was harder than it sounds: Swarthmore had been founded by Quakers, and due to the peculiar but egalitarian logic of the Friends, there weren't phones in dorm rooms since not all students could afford to make long-distance calls.

So Heather had to find a pay phone in the library, or wait in line for one in a dorm hallway.

My mother lay in a hospital bed in what had been my brother's bedroom. She couldn't communicate anymore, but sometimes when we moved her to change her sheets, she cried out *Hail Mary, Mother of God.* The neighbors brought us soups and casseroles, and I was cruel to them: I snatched the dishes from their hands and shut the doors in their faces. I had a strange twitching in my eye.

Heather was the only person I wanted to talk to, and talking to her was pretty much the only time I didn't wish that I were dying instead, or also.

She skipped classes to fly to Ohio for my mother's service. When I couldn't seem to fix my hair that morning—the problem to which I clung to avoid the unspeakable other—she told me I looked beautiful. I wore my mother's too-large dress; it was navy blue with a white lace collar. An old family friend reached for me, weeping. "You look exactly like her," she cried.

Maybe Heather went to the florist with me to buy the funeral flowers, a giant bouquet of freesia and delphinium. Maybe my father told her to take care of me, and maybe she had to tell me to eat. She may have stood beside me in the receiving line, greeting a church full of people she had never seen before. Who knows, in our blind grief, how much we asked of her?

Afterward, at my house, Heather and I sat together on the living room couch (my boyfriend had been kissed at the church and then banished) while my aunts and uncles and all the friends of my parents wandered from room to room, holding drinks and plates of cold cuts. There were flowers perfuming every corner; on the mantel leaned a giant photograph of my smiling mother. People came together in mournful knots, lingered, and then moved on. I knew what they were thinking: We're so young still, we barely have gray hair—how could we be dying?

Margot, my mother's cousin from Palo Alto, sat down next to

us, smoothed her silky blouse, and introduced herself. Heather's social graces held; Hey, I'm from California too, she said. Margot and Heather traded West Coast moments, and then Margot told us a little about the yoga book she'd written, and the lifestyle consultant who'd advised her to wear only loose, flowing fabrics.

Then she told us that she went to an eminent palmist—$150 a reading, she said, and he's so good he'll only reveal what he knows you can bear to hear—and that in her many sessions, she had learned how to read palms too.

Margot took Heather's hand first, and then mine. She was earnest and careful. Amidst the swirl of the extended family, she ran her fingers over our palms, reading our characters. She told Heather that she was creative and strong-willed; she told me that I was ambitious, and had unreasonably high expectations of myself. She said that we ought to look at the shapes of our thumb pads—the ideal shape, she said, was full and rounded, and it signified joy and self-actualization. We didn't have thumbs like this, but Margot assured us that we could work toward them. Heather and I privately doubted, but everything else Margot said felt precisely and uncannily true, as if the secrets to our temperaments were written in script on the pink of our skin.

Then, because she had to go back to her hotel, Margot summed everything up. "You," she said to Heather, "were put on this world to use your voice."

That was perfect, I thought—with her intelligence, her drive, and her fierce dedication to social justice, Heather was going to change the world. What, then, would Margot say to me? What bright promise did my future hold?

"You," she said, her voice quieter now, and sugared with sympathy, "were put on this earth to work on relationships."

THE LOSS OF hope brings a whole new and terrible mourning. Even in those final weeks before my mother died, I could still—barely, but still—imagine a happy ending, a miracle. But back at school the following semester, there was no more pretending that my life was not forever changed. I missed my mother with a wordless and wild desperation. Like an infant, I slept, ate, cried, and slept again.

Heather tried to get me out of bed—for weeks. I don't remember this, but I have the evidence: on a Xeroxed page from a Dr. Seuss book ("Look at me, look at me, look at me NOW! It is fun to have fun BUT you have to know how"), Heather wrote: "This is a note to try and fill your mailbox and let you know that even during my most intense moments of study in the library I am thinking only of you. Love your long-lost roommate and spiritual adviser, H."

I considered how hard she worked for her classes; I counted up all her other smiling friends. Thinking only of me? Impossible, I thought. A nice thing to write—but unquestionably a lie.

Tina found out that her father had HIV that spring. Molly's relationship with her boyfriend had become complicated and unhappy, and she was also, though I didn't know it then, struggling with memories of past sexual abuse. When the four of us ate together in the dining hall, we helped ourselves to tiny portions of salad dressed only with balsamic vinegar and looked suspiciously at one another's trays. In the evenings the air in our suite crackled with tension. Throughout these weeks, nothing knocked me from my carefully guarded reign as the queen of sorrow. All of this was bad news, okay? but it wasn't like anyone else was dead yet.

And when someone did die, still I defended my position. Heather's grandmother, with whom she was close, passed away in April of that year. She had been a mystery novelist, and the *New York Times* had run an obituary. That was a big deal, Heather told me, because it was a validation of her career. I remember looking at Heather—it was sunny outside, and we

were in our bedroom—and wondering why she was telling me
this. My mother's death was horrible, but her grandmother's
death was newsworthy—was that what she was trying to say?

"And before she died," Heather said, "she dictated the last
chapter of her book to my aunt from her hospital bed."

I thought of my mother, and of how by the end, sight, movement, speech, understanding—*everything*—had been taken away
from her. Dying elderly and sharp-witted? That seemed like a
luxury.

ONE AFTERNOON THAT spring Heather and I walked into
town and bought a pint of Ben & Jerry's, which we took to a
bench alongside the field that lay between our dorm and the
main campus. The forsythia bushes had exploded into a riot of
yellow blossoms, and though we were miles from water, seagulls
dotted the grass, calling to one another in their shrill, hard
voices. To a passerby, we would have made a lovely picture—two
coeds leaning over a tub of ice cream as the girls' soccer team
jogged onto the field, sending the birds wheeling away into the
sky.

It had been a while since we'd spent any time alone together,
and I was tense and nervous, but hopeful. We would bond, I
thought—we could laugh and gossip and it would feel a little
like freshman year again. At some point, after we'd sat there for
a while, I noticed that I was the only one eating the ice cream.
Heather made small, random stabs at it with her plastic spoon
but barely took any.

"Eat more," I told her. She demurred; she wasn't hungry.

One doesn't eat ice cream because one is hungry, I thought.
One eats ice cream because it is ice cream and it is delicious.

I pressed her; she shook her head and looked away. In front of
us, the girls passed soccer balls back and forth, kicking them low
across the field and then in high arcs through the air. But this
was Heather's idea, I thought. This hour—this shared indul-

gence—was supposed to bring us together, or at least a few halting steps closer.

I did not then think longingly of our past—of how we used to have such an appetite for everything, be it food or talk or indignation at what we saw as an inequitable society. Nor did I think of this moment as more evidence of Heather's eating disorder, which on some level I knew she had developed. Every girl starved or gagged herself at one point or another in college, didn't she? Eating was what we controlled when we thought we couldn't control anything else—it just seemed so tiresome. All I could think about then was how angry I was at her. I just wanted to her to do this one small thing with me, eat this ice cream, and she couldn't, or wouldn't, do it.

The truth was that Heather and I hardly knew what to do with each other anymore. We had both grown snappish—though I was worse. When, in the mornings, Heather turned on public radio, I demanded to know why we couldn't have a little silence for once. When she rewound a tape in my stereo without pressing the Stop button first, I yelled that she was going to break the machine. Sometimes when she wanted to use my computer, I lied and told her that I just getting ready to use it myself.

Heather began to avoid me and started palling around with other girls in the dorm. At some point that semester, the decision was made to pull our beds apart.

As the weather got warmer, Heather was around less and less—"I'm out enjoying the spring," she would say, and it wasn't until later that I found out why. His name was Greg.

I, along with most of the other Swarthmore girls, had taken note of Greg that fall, when he returned, after a year off, to join the junior class. It was impossible not to notice him: he was an extraordinary physical specimen. He had brown, slightly unkempt hair and blue, blue eyes; it seemed possible that he might, at any moment, climb up and then rappel down something.

He was in my ecology class spring semester. I was too shy to talk to him, but sometimes, in the computer lab, we found ourselves sitting near each other, working on the same assignment. Hey, he might drawl, smiling—he always smiled—did you figure out that problem yet?

The problem was why the species of trees on one side of a small hill were so markedly different from the species on the other side. What explained it: sunlight? drainage? cultivation? I thought about it, though not very hard, and when I got a D on the paper, I called the dean and had her withdraw me from the class.

"We're both heavenly bodies," began the note Greg sent me in campus mail. What else it said I don't remember, only that it culminated in a question: Would I like to go out sometime?

I would, but it wasn't to be. When I couldn't go to the dance he'd asked me to, he went alone; there he met someone named Peggy and started dating her. I was sorely disappointed, but Heather was blasé, philosophical: Boys are stupid, she said.

Heather and Greg's first date took place a few months later, not long after Greg and Peggy's breakup. I don't remember hearing about it, or about their subsequent courtship. I only remember the night I found them together.

It was late at night, and I was alone in my room, working on a paper about the Gospel of John and drinking instant coffee brewed with Folgers crystals and warm water from the sink. At some point, I got up to go to the bathroom, which was through Tina and Molly's bedroom. I opened their door; a thin sliver of light from my desk lamp pushed feebly against the dark. I took a few steps, and then I froze; there were people in the room. I couldn't see them, but I heard the sheets rustle, caught the faint sibilance of their whispers.

The air was warm and close and humid. My body felt giant to me, immovable, and for a moment I didn't breathe. When I did, the thing that tightened my throat, the thing that buckled my knees, was the dusky, faintly rank smell of sex.

The hurt I felt then came not from the knowledge that it was Heather and Greg. It came, instead, from a sudden, flinty understanding of my own ignorance. A year ago, Heather would have told me everything about her relationship with Greg. I would have known what it felt like to kiss him, and the ways in which he professed his affections, and how much she thought about him. I would have known *this night* was going to happen—but now I was left to stumble on it, like a trespasser.

No one spoke in that room. I simply turned around, closed the door behind me, and went to the public bathrooms down the hall.

FOR THE FEW weeks that remained of sophomore year, Heather and I circled each other as warily as cats. The following year we were going abroad in different semesters; we wouldn't be together at college again until we were seniors.

In deference to all we'd been through, we still called ourselves friends. But the world, for me, had shifted on its axis; I could no more be a part of Heather's active, engaged college life than she could be a part of my despair. We talked on the phone that summer, and we sent the occasional letter; we made promises to visit each other that we didn't keep. We had had that first semester—five perfect months—and then a year and a half of struggle. For a long time after that, my love for Heather was a piece of glass in my heart; it hurt every time I moved.

In-Betweens

Diana Abu-Jaber

WHEN WE FIRST move to Jordan, our new house is actually a big ground-floor flat inside a larger building. It's circled by a courtyard, and running along the inner courtyard is a garden thick with nodding sunflowers, and marigolds, and mint plants, and now it's my duty to go pick the leaves to steep in the teapot. I'm eight and I know how to do this; my sisters, on the other hand, are two and three, and utterly hopeless. There are also furious-looking cats that moan and skulk all over the garden. The night comes at a new time, and the moon looks sideways like a silver cup. There's so much to look at that for a while I feel that all I can do is stand in one place and stare. This is one of the first times that alone-ness, the state and sense of being isolate in the world, presents itself to me with such a clear face. My parents have each other, my sisters are in their separate hemisphere of the very young, and it seems that the world itself has turned a strange face to me: everything I thought I knew has changed—the people, the food, the words, the water, the earth.

The morning after we move, a gang of grinning, dirty-kneed kids pounds on our front door and pulls me outside. The gang expands and diminishes like a flock of starlings. We run everywhere, up stairs and down alleys. Are these my friends? I don't understand anything that they're saying, but this doesn't matter because I know how to run.

In a matter of days, I am familiar with the complex, labyrinthine windings of our neighborhoods. There are buildings here so rickety and narrow they look as if they're built on stilts; there are marble staircases leading into murky darkness that I refuse to ascend; there are apartments—many apartments—that smell powerfully of babies and dinner; and there are even more feral cats clattering out of the garbage, glaring at you. One day my gang takes me to the roof of our building and I discover yet another world of children running around, women gossiping, clotheslines flapping gaily as sails. I lean over the precariously low edge looking down five flights to the ground and someone gives me a play-shove from behind that swipes the breath from my lungs and makes stars pop in my head. I swing around and lay eyes on Hisham for the very first time. I can tell right away that he is the one I like best of all: he is about my age, small and thin and dark with close-cropped hair, soft, myopic eyes, and full, round, almost feminine lips. Of all the children, his sweet, soft face is the most appealing to me.

Hisham and Hisham's seven or so younger brothers and sisters as well as a number of neighborhood children play in the streets and courtyards around my building. I'm not completely sure which of these buildings they actually live in. I only know that no matter what time of day I step into the street, one or more likely all of them will be out there singing, skipping, throwing things, running. Hisham and I hang on the balustrades of the swinging iron gate of my house's courtyard railing and ride it shut, the rusted hinges shrieking as it goes. Then we get off, open it, and ride it shut again. Then we play our talking game.

Sometimes I go first, sometimes he does, but frequently we go at the same time. I say:

"Idon'tknowwhatyou'resayingbutIwishIknewwhatyouweresayingIwishsomuchyouknewwhatIwassayingreallytrulyIdobecause it'ssoweirdit'sreallycrazybutyoudon't . . ."

And he is saying, "Yabaainteesadeekatibessintimajnoonashway moomkimbazunbessanamishakeddleeanoabensamabafimtwainteematfimtkaaamoolaishhathamabafimtculshi . . ."

It seems we spend whole afternoons in this way, talking and swimming through our private thoughts. In the distance, the calls to prayers rise overlapping from the eight neighboring mosques and quaver through the streets, overlaid with musical threads like silk carpets. We spy on Hamouda the gardener as he washes his hands, face, feet, and neck with the garden hose behind my house. He lays out a few sheets of newspaper and uses that as his rug to pray upon.

Eventually our game starts to change, slowly at first, with meaning creeping in around the edges of what Hisham is saying to me, like a slow burn eating at the edges of a page. And one day, after weeks of running around in the streets, for some reason, I am speaking my father's language. It's the language we spoke in specks and pieces back home, a confetti language that Dad saved for his brothers or for getting angry or for driving in crazy traffic. Suddenly, all of it is there in my head. My mother is the first to notice—she interrupts as I'm chattering with the Bedouin woman who works for us. "Since when do you speak Arabic?" she says to me.

I look at her, and I see there is something in her eyes when she says this that I feel immediately in the center of my chest, just under the bone. Instantly, I don't want those words in my mouth anymore.

EVEN THE CHEWING gum tastes different in Jordan. They sell it in knobby gray nuggets, a handful for one fil, at the *dukana*—corner shop. (The first complete sentence I learn in Arabic is: *Atini nosher beyda,* "Gimme a dozen eggs," which the dukana keeper puts loose into a brown paper bag. Then I dutifully run home and deliver up a bag of squashed egg mess.) The gum is dry, tacky, unsweetened, and tastes like tree bark, but it's still gum. There are many things about Jordan that I find rough and disappointing, and I learn that here one must make do with items like chewing gum. We take compensation in higher pursuits like running and babbling.

So we all stand on the corner, chewing till our jaws ache. Me and Hisham, Mai, Talal, Dalia, Rana, Rafat, Nadia, Hussein, Hind, Azzam, Nazri, and Belal. But sometimes a pile of real bubble gum turns up in the dukana—hard, pink, sugary compressions, valuable as gold. I buy it with the pennies my father gives me, then we take turns chewing the one piece, sharing it around until the last modicum of sweetness runs out and then chewing it till it turns tacky and stiff. I show them how to blow a bubble—only I don't know how to do it inside my mouth. I have to use my fingers to press and hold it pasted flat against the outside of my lips, and then I blow and a bubble comes. Almost instantly, as if by magic, Hisham understands how to blow a bubble starting from inside his mouth, the way some kids are born with a special aptitude for math or languages or knowing how to whistle with their fingers, and then there is no getting the gum away from him.

While the other children dart around like sparrows, hunch over, laugh into their hands, stand on one foot, stagger like madmen, there is a stillness and a wholeness about Hisham. The look in his eye suggests that, for him, being a child takes great concentration, self-possession, and presence of mind. He does not confuse being a child with being an adult. He simply takes it all very seriously, so the other children tend naturally to look at Hisham whenever there is a decision to be made, a high wall to be climbed, or a dark corridor to be looked into. When I first start tearing around with this gang, I notice that Hisham watches me with a particular sweetness, a solicitousness, as if somehow it's been given to him to understand how strange and solitary it is to awaken one morning on the other side of the world. He has an older brother in the Jordanian army whose curled military photo he keeps in his back pocket. He watches me with his lush, heavy-lidded eyes and guarantees that he will grow up to look like his brother. He brings me to their house for lunch, and his mother serves a luxurious buttermilk soup with strips of onion floating in it. When I finish mine, Hisham gives me the rest of his. He and his mother watch dotingly as I gulp it all down.

I am not used to this style of friendship—one without any of the reserve of the American suburbs we just left. These children don't own a thing beyond the clothes they are wearing. There is nothing between us but running and shouting; they demand my presence; they're as affectionate with each other as maiden aunts—we walk together, ten or twelve abreast, our arms around each other's shoulders.

But then one day Bennett appears in the courtyard and everything changes. My first months in Jordan are like that—I attach to various people, toys, foods willy-nilly: for an entire week, I listen to the same record, *Music for Belly Dancers*, over and over. It's as if I've lost my coordinates, and until I can adjust to this new place, I have to take everything in small, intense fragments.

Bennett is a powerful distraction. I suppose he has parents, but I see no sign of them. They're like a legend that he speaks of but that never quite materializes. Nor does he seem to have any aunts, uncles, grandparents, cousins telling him what to do, nor any troubling little sisters to watch over! His life is a paradise. Bennett has see-through skin and eyes, and hair that rises and falls like corn silk; he wears impossible woolen shorts from God-knows-where and gray kneesocks, and his pinkened knees knock together with every step he takes. He is the first person I meet in Jordan with eyes the same ocean color as my mother's. And perhaps it is just the fact that he is a native speaker of English, but after weeks of encounters with startling new flavors and sights, I find there is something comforting to me about this boy, something familiar. And his way of speaking is wonderful! It sounds like the voice that would come out of a little baby doll, so clipped and perfect that I listen raptly. When Hisham shows up, wanting to babble our talking game and swing on the shrieking gate, Bennett sniffs scornfully and gazes off. Horrified, I shrug one shoulder at Hisham as if I barely know him and say, "Maybe you should go home now," not daring to look at his face.

Because Bennett happens to possess even more powerful enticements: a fire-engine red scooter with two wheels, a steering bar, and a platform to push from or to stand on once you get going. I know about bicycles, ice skates, sleds, Big Wheels, and roller skates. But I've never seen a scooter before, and once I do, I know that it's perfect, just perfect.

At first, Bennett refuses even to leave the courtyard, which he says his invisible parents have confined him to. That gives us a meager twenty or so feet of marble walkway to roll around. I assure him that the courtyard rule must only apply to England. When he still purses his lips, I yawn in the manner of Munira, who yawns every time a shop owner offers her a special price.

"Oh well," I say, sighing indolently, "I guess I'll just go play with all my other friends then." To my great pleasure, he turns a bright purplish, eggplanty color; then he says, Well perhaps then we could go just a bit outside the gates, just for a bit.

And for a while, Bennett is my best friend. I forget all about my previous life—those days are gone! As if by some tacit agreement, perhaps in acknowledgment of the superiority of the scooter, Hisham and the others start playing with the rooftop children instead of down in the courtyard. At times I'll guiltily sense a shadow cast from high overhead. But when I look up, all I see are the carrier pigeons flapping from the cornices, or the edge of a drying bedsheet. There is a feeling of disorientation that comes over me at such moments, a form of vertigo: where should I be? Tearing across the dust-white rooftops and hidden, winding alleys, or bold in the street as a European motorist, bright, noisy, and taking up all the space that I desire? Occasionally, I feel darts of remorse—I miss Hisham and my old companions—yet the scooter is so fast, so pretty, how can I resist it? It seems I would be a fool to turn down such riches, so freely offered.

Bennett and I ride and ride in the street in front of the courtyard: sometimes there are cars, sometimes not—we scarcely notice. We trade the scooter back and forth, then we ride together—I crowd in behind Bennett, balancing and hugging his waist for dear life, each of us pushing like crazy with one foot. We crash this way several times, and then after a while we can ride together without crashing, like we were made to do this.

BENNETT REFERS TO his invisible parents as "Mother and Father." He quotes all sorts of rules from this Father pertaining to what he calls "the Natives," as in "Don't talk to the Natives," and "Don't eat the Native Food." But this, I believe, is just one of the many mysteries of Bennett's world—I don't know what these Native Foods might be. I can hardly imagine they have anything to do with the whole baby goat that Madame Haddadin roasts on a spit behind her flat or the lovely, ceremonial lunches of stuffed squash and hummus and tabbouli that my father prepares for us every weekend.

His father, Bennett says, works as some sort of horrid diplomat, whatever that is. His father and mother give "horrid, dreadful, just frightful parties," Bennett says, at which he is required to wear a suit and tie and to play piano. I learn that even though he says he's from England, Bennett has never actually been to "the Motherland," not even for a visit. His family has been moving around Jordan for over a year now and he finds it "unbearable" but rather prefers it to Singapore or Guyana. He doesn't like the weather in Jordan—"it burns," he says, rubbing his red-tipped ears, the skin ragged and peeling from his nose and cheeks. He doesn't like the food, it's dirty. "I only like clotted cream and crumpets or nothing," he says. And he doesn't like the Jordanians. "They're much too loud and hairy."

Early one morning, a sound wakes me and I discover a little basket filled with sugar-powdered cookies propped on the wide marble windowsill of my room. Underneath the cookies is a scrap of paper with a heart and a tremulous letter H written in pencil—probably the first letter in English he has ever written. I look upon these cookies with nostalgic tenderness, as if it has been years since I've seen Hisham. Sambusik cookies are among my favorites and a specialty of Hisham's mother. I offer one to Bennett, who takes it, inspects it, then replaces it daintily, saying, "I never eat Native Food. Neither should you."

I look at him out of the corner of my eye. I notice that no matter how much he swats at himself, there is always a fog of dust on his face and clothes. And he's forever drinking tall glasses of something he calls Nutritious Horlicks—both words, every time. It seems to be milk mixed with something musty and fussy and vitaminy and which leaves a white mustache on his upper lip, which I stare at pitilessly as if it were further proof of something terrible about him.

After three weeks of the scooter, Bennett puts one hand on his hip and one hand on the steering bar and says to me, "So we're best friends, then?"

I scowl and don't answer, even as I recognize that this is very bad behavior. I eye the scooter, calculating how much longer I can stand being best friends with Bennett. It seems I no longer want to be nice to him at all. Suddenly I have a question. "What does a crumpet taste like?" I ask in a surly, skeptical voice.

"Oh!" Bennett's eyes flutter. "They're lovely! Lovely, lovely things." Then he sniffs a little and kicks a pebble and adds, "Course, they're not available here."

"Why not?" I ask, even surlier. "We can get pancakes here."

"Pancakes are entirely different," Bennett says. Then, as if reciting an inscription on a stone tablet, he says: "One cannot get a proper crumpet in a land like Jordan. Father says. Not now and *not ever.*"

I glare at the scooter, and it occurs to me for the first time that when Bennett talks about Native Foods, he is talking about exactly the sort of foods my father prepares. A sick, disloyal feeling floats in my center.

After four weeks of Bennett and the scooter, our across-the-courtyard neighbor Madame Haddadin stops me as I walk in the front gate. Madame Haddadin has a kindly voice and a grieving, ancient expression that makes her look decades older than her forty years. She is Palestinian, but she came to Jordan long ago when she says she and her whole village were driven out by the Israelis.

Madame Haddadin says that she was meant to have a son—he would be eighteen by now and his name would be Herve. He would be in the air force—not yet a captain. She knows this, she says, because she has dreamed it, very vividly, on several occasions. But her destiny was tampered with: the Israelis frightened her so badly that everyone could see the mark of that fear on her and no man would ever marry her. "They smell it on my skin," she says, pressing the tips of her knobby fingers together, as if she keeps the scent pressed between her fingertips. I inhale but smell only the cardamom pods she arranges on her windowsill, the smudge of turmeric she sifts over her pastries, and the fresh peppermint in her tea. Every morning she brings out a pot and two cups and gives one to me, then she stares into the steam above her cup and sighs two great damp sighs.

Later in the afternoon, she will patrol up and down behind our courtyard gate, on the lookout for the day the Israeli army will come pouring into the streets of Amman. As a result, she sees absolutely everything that happens in the neighborhood. She stoops to look in my eyes and says, "Why aren't you playing with your other friends anymore?"

I mull this over, desperate for a good reason. Finally I have to surrender. "They don't have scooters," I mumble.

She straightens up, her mouth a taut line, her eyes fogged over. I watch her expression, horrified. I ask her in a tiny voice, "Don't you like Bennett?"

She looks down at me, eyes glittering. "That boy is a bitter melon."

ONE NIGHT AFTER my sisters and I are in bed and the baby cats have ceased their crying, my parents come to our room, whispering and nudging each other, their smiles sly, as if they shared a private joke. They shake us out of sleep and say, "C'mon, we're going to do something!"

We yawn, slide out of the warm caves of our beds; our parents are gesturing us out the front door, their laughter lowered and mesmerizing. Then we are running across the stone courtyard— my sisters and I barefooted in cotton pajamas, the stones waxy beneath our feet. The neighbors and the street are all asleep, the buildings shut up, rose-tinted under a brassy, round moon. In one corner of the courtyard, tilted under the staircase to the upper floors, is the scooter, its red gleam muted now, private and soft. For a moment I think of my grandmother back in New Jersey, who wears a lipstick in the same fluid tones: red shot through with an undercurrent of blue. I look back at it as my parents open the car.

We drive through parts of the city that I've never seen before, where the lights glow like melted butter and the girls on the sidewalks are wearing brimmed hats and high heels. Men smile and turn to watch our car passing: I watch back, hands pressed to the window. Then we race beyond the glowing streets—they dwindle to a star—and the road ahead of us is long and dusty blue and smells like a warm, blue must, like the heat of a sheep's back.

When we finally get out of the car, there's a gravel lot, an expanse of folding chairs, patios, sparkly restaurants wedged in a long crescent along a flat blackness like gleaming enamel. Dad holds his hand out toward the gleam. "And what did I promise you kids?" he asks, though I recall no promises related to anything like this. "It's the Dead Sea!"

We've come, as usual, with no preparation, so my parents let us run into the water in our underpants—like the Jordanian kids around us. The salt water is satiny, so soft and dense it seems to bend beneath our arms. My father, who is generally afraid of the water, comes out and shows us how you can sit in this sea. He lazes back in it, and my sister tows him around by his hair while he makes boat sounds.

One of the restaurants on the lip of the water has a string of red lights that drop their reflections in the moonlit water; they make me think of the lonely red scooter. After a while, I straggle out of the water, yanking up my soggy underpants with their sprung elastic waistband. Mom is stretched out on a canvas chaise longue, holding a drink with a little parasol on the side. She wraps me shivering into a beach towel and makes room for me beside her on the lounge.

I blink out of my towel cave at this new place around us, then touch my mother's ribs through her cotton shirt. "Mom, how long do you have to be best friends with someone if you're best friends?"

She flitters at my bangs; they're drying stiff with salt. "Well, honey, I don't think there's any rules about that. I guess you can be best friends with someone your whole life if you're lucky."

"Are you and Dad best friends?"

It's hard to make out her expression under the cherry lights.

She seems to be thinking about it, staring out to where Dad is still drifting around, piping and tooting like a tugboat.

"You have to do whatever your best friend says, right?"

Now I can see her face—amused and wary. "Why do you say that?"

"Dad said to come to Jordan, right?"

There is even less sound now than before, if that is possible, just a slip of waves on the shore, a sighing wash like the sound of someone saying *hush, hush,* or the rustle of the palm fronds arching over the sand. "Your father . . . needed us to come here, he needed to see—what it felt like."

"What does it feel like?" I ask quietly, not quite knowing what I'm asking, just following the path of the questions.

"I don't think—" she starts, then stops. My father is climbing out of the dark wash of the sea. "I don't think it feels the way he remembers it."

I put my hands on her waist—something that feels a little like a spark of alarm bounces through me. "Does he know that? That it doesn't feel the same?"

She looks over her shoulder, my father's shadow falling toward us in a long, cool slip as he walks beneath the neon lights. "He's still finding out."

The medicinal waters of the Dead Sea roll behind us, and the wild, heavy scent of honey, rocks, and thyme tempers the air. People come to dip themselves in these waters, to be cured of everything from skin ailments to spiritual wasting. I breathe it in deeply and sense a sort of dawning sweetness—of loss and nostalgia. Mom must feel some of this as well because she draws her hand around a ripple of sand beneath her beach chair and says dreamily, "It's lovely here. Just lovely."

I touch the liquid sand as well. It turns from beige to amber. It is just that simple. Just lovely.

———

THE MORNING AFTER the Dead Sea, I wake with a wonderful hankering for gray gum. I feel as if I've been away on a monthlong vacation to a cooler, distant country, and it's great to be home again. I run to the dukana and buy a piece. As I stand on the corner and start to chew, my old friends begin to saunter over—Mai and Rafat, Belal and Hisham; they greet me as cordially as if I hadn't been away at all. We spend the day on foot, running along the alleys in our old style. I am set free; I am back again. At the end of the day, Hisham and I race to my house. I have flying hair, a skinned knee, and grubby nails—I look like every other child in the streets of this neighborhood. Hisham, as usual, gets there first, but then he pulls up short. Bennett is standing just inside the courtyard, still as stone, his face fixed as if all the light had fallen straight out of it.

Suddenly the door to a steep place that I didn't know was inside me has been thrown open. I know I've done something wrong, though I can't put a name to it. "Hi," I say, guilty and angry. Hisham looks as shocked as if Bennett were a stone idol come to life. He takes a step back and bumps into me. "Don't touch her!" Bennett snaps at him. He shakes a finger at Hisham. "Do you live here? I don't believe so! I don't ever remember inviting you to our courtyard." Bennett's face is a streaked, liverish color, as if he'd just been slapped. He shrieks at Hisham, his voice leaping into the highest registers, his body rigid and doll-like. "I think you'd just better get out of here. I think you'd just better be gone!"

Hisham's mouth opens and closes, as if he can barely get enough air. I grab Hisham's wrist and am about to suggest we go play in another courtyard, but Hisham turns to me and whispers in Arabic, "Something is wrong with this boy—I'll go get my mother!"

"No," I answer, though I'm frightened of the sharp, thin line of Bennett's mouth. "I'll stay here. I'll talk to him."

After Hisham has gone, for a long moment, Bennett doesn't

speak and doesn't even give the impression of seeing me there. Then quickly he says, "You know that isn't proper. It isn't proper and it isn't done. It isn't done at all."

I take hold of the iron spikes of the courtyard railing; they feel good and cold and rough in my hands. I wish that Hisham hadn't gone away. "What isn't?"

The color starts to subside in his face and I can see him recollecting himself. He purses and unpurses his tidy red lips, he crosses his arms in a business fashion. Finally he slits his eyes at me as if admitting to himself, at last, that I really don't know much of anything. "You don't belong with them! You *know* that. You know that. The sort you are belongs with the sort I am. Like belongs with like. Father says. No in-betweens. The world isn't meant for in-betweens, it isn't done. You know that."

He speaks as if this is a conversation we've had countless times and he's very tired of going over it with me. I lean back and swing on the iron railing while he stands like a stake in the ground, glaring just past the top of my head. I've started attending a private school run by the French nuns, and what Bennett says reminds me of something in the way the nuns speak. We are forbidden to speak Arabic in school because, according to Sister Hélène-Thérèse, "Arabic is the language of animals." She taps the list of three languages on the blackboard, explaining that English "is the language of mortals," and French, she says with a soft, glossy smile, "is the language of the angels."

"No in-betweens." My voice a pale vapor.

"They belong with their own kind. You with me, they with them," Bennett sums up. "No in-betweens. It's not allowed."

I squint at Bennett; his face is blotted out by the fiery sunset behind his back. I don't know what these in-betweens are exactly, but I feel sorry for them. They might look like the embroideries of the sad-eyed sheep—the solitary ones, apart from their flock, trapped inside the circle of Munira's embroidery hoop, stitched eternally apart. I imagine them walking the

earth, friendless, lonely and improper, *not allowed*, lost somewhere in the corners between the animals, the mortals, and the
angels.

"How do you know it?" I press. "How do you know that I
belong with you?"

He rolls his eyes. "Well, it's obvious, isn't it?" He thrusts out
his arm. "Look at the color you are!" He presses his arm to mine:
his is a gleaming, nearly bone white, dotted with freckles and a
faint sheen of burn. Mine is grimy and golden with a telltale
greenish cast I'd never noticed before, not till I'd compared
myself to someone like this.

I'm not like Bennett, and he yanks his arm away as if I'd just
done something unexpectedly disgraceful. But in that moment I
realize I'm not like Hisham, either. Not nearly as dark. I think
about the way the relatives come to visit, standing in our bedroom doorway, appraising me and my sisters, the way their
words float through the air, dividing blood from blood. "There's
the dark one," they say. "And she—she's the light one....That
one is American, that one is Arab ..." I'd never before thought
to wonder which of us was which.

BUT DESPITE BENNETT'S decree, I no longer want to be
with him—I no longer feel myself to be *of* him. And my interest in the red scooter has miraculously dried up and gone. I'm
once again running up and down the steps with Hisham and my
old group of friends. But something is changed—nothing feels
simply, truly right anymore. Every game I play, every race I run
with these children feels a bit like something I'm seeing from a
distance, something set upon a stage.

When Bennett approaches me in the courtyard pushing the
red scooter before him like a sacrifice, offering to let me ride it
alone for the entire day, I walk past him without a word. Is it
possible that I am this heartless? But isn't that what they say
about children: *Children can be so cruel.* The borderlands of our

worlds are nettled, uncertain, unknown. Other people exist as if figments of our dreams. Our friendship, it seems, was based on a toy—an exciting, bewitching toy—and that was all. Or perhaps that isn't correct—perhaps there is the slightest pang when I turn and see the way he lowers his ghostly eyes. It seems that, if I had wanted, I could have stayed with him in his world apart— like the Americans and Europeans I saw in Jordan, living in their fine Western hotels, their rooms rising ten stories above the dust of Amman. But at that moment, I only know that Bennett turns into a shadow, and then, as suddenly as he appeared, he disappears. He slips completely out of my mind and imagination, as do his Native Foods, his Nutritious Horlicks, and his In-Betweens. I forget him so quickly that his memory now seems grainy, half-dissolved, like an image made of powder.

Weeks after forgetting him, I am swinging on the iron railing when Madame Haddadin calls me over to her wrought-iron chair near the flowering mint plants. She swirls her cup of tea and informs me that "my little English friend" and his mythical parents have moved back to Singapore. It takes me a minute to remember who she is talking about. Then she gestures toward the staircase, and there it is, where it has been all along, ever since I abandoned him, yet somehow completely invisible—the red scooter.

The breath goes out of me in a gust. It waits like a mute accusation, an unblinking eye.

She watches me, frowns. "Do you know why he did that?" she asks, very curious. "Why didn't he take his English toy?"

I shake my head, astounded. I don't know the answer, not inside my head. But I sense it somehow, the truth prickling, a thing that will take a long, long time for me to bring into words: he left it so I wouldn't forget him.

Madame Haddadin stands over me, squinting into my eyes, taking my measure. Her eyes are orange-inflected and amber, too light for her cinnamon skin. She gazes down at me and I look up; I can almost see the thoughts moving within her eyes, dark and illuminated as a jinn's; I can tell she is wondering about me as I sometimes wonder about myself—what sort of person I am; where are my loyalties; and whom will I remember when I grow up.

Madame Haddadin, who remembers everything and everyone—even a son she has never had—cannot fathom how deeply, powerfully forgetful I have already become. Though I am only eight, I too have already had to leave behind entire countries and lifetimes. A friend is a small sacrifice in such a context. And Bennett himself is the one who spelled things out for me: no in-betweens. If Jordan is now my country, then Hisham must now be my friend.

At eight, friendship was still a blunt instrument to me, crude, unfaceted, immensely practical. I'd pick up each tool as I needed it, then lay it down when I was done. Now that I am an adult, it seems to me that friendship, like love, is a thing that should swamp us, overtake and never leave us. It must run much deeper and truer than what is practical or useful. But my eight-year-old self showed me the clean, honest possibilities of friendship as well: a diversion; a hedge against isolation; a looking glass. I'd like to think I didn't lose Bennett's friendship so much as set it down. But then I think—that isn't quite true, is it? I traded it in. An English scooter for a bowl of soup; blue eyes for brown ones; a loyalty to one friend, one country, for a wider way of being in the big, unknowable world.

THE NEW GIRL

Nicole Keeter

I WANT TO INSIST that when Gina came to town, she changed everything. She was African American, which made her an oddity in our insular little community. I'd like to cast her as the star of an integration saga, one in which the brown newcomer alarms the white folks but ultimately endows them with a deeper appreciation of all humanity. But the truth is I beat Gina to that role. I am black, too, and I was there a few years before she was.

There, I understand now, was an ideal specimen of small-town Iowa. Norman Rockwell himself couldn't have asked for a more picturesque collection of well-kept Victorian homes, tidy lawns, and lofty church steeples. Gina arrived in the early 1980s, when across the state rural communities were withering in tandem with the old independent farms surrounding them. But our town thrived, thanks, in no small part, to the highway that linked us to two good-size, job-rich cities nearby, and to the minor but stately-looking college that capped the hill around which the town was arranged.

Along the highway, atop the hill, waves of people steadily came and went. The same process of regeneration was largely absent elsewhere in our town, however, since only a handful of new families folded themselves into the native German-Swedish stock each year. This meant that there was little movement in the school's social rankings, and so almost from day one, you knew and were bound to your standing among the sixty or so people in your grade. While puberty might boost the status of a few, mostly you were resigned to staying in your place until you were old enough to leave town for good.

Before Gina came, my place in this equation was special. I was in the third grade when my family moved to our picturesque town from a suburb of Indianapolis, lured by the same qualities that must have later called to Gina's parents. At first there were stares, then the usual questions: Why did you call it perming your hair when it's really making it straighter? Does it hurt how your legs are so dry? But I'd heard comments like that before at my old school and I was used to them.

To be the lone black kid around was to be about as unique as you could get in my town. Perhaps the school's two or three Asian students would not agree, but to me, these girls—they all happened to be adopted girls, and they all had ratted masses of Sun-In-baked hair and bouncy midwestern lilts and male admirers to camouflage their foreignness—seemed to blend in seamlessly. Other kids who were different, who were too fat or thin or were handicapped in some way, were ridiculed, but my special status protected me.

Special, I found, meant that the other kids, and their parents and the teachers, were always nice to you. I had never been as in demand as I was shortly after I began school there. There were invitations to sit with the popular girls in the cafeteria at school or at the soda shop on the town's main street; it really was that kind of quaint, soda-shop place. There were many slumber parties, sometimes hosted by girls I barely knew, at which the adults would address me by name and say that they were delighted to have me in their homes.

But my status was not perfect. From the beginning, I sensed that the dimensions were still to be determined, that special was shaky and its boundaries were best not tested. So I did not complain that none of the boys would ask me to couple-skate at the roller rink, and I did not try to approach any of them. I laughed through games of Truth or Dare, though I never got the juicy, interactive dares, the ones that sent my friends squealing into dark closets with red-faced boys. Once, someone invited every other girl in our grade to her birthday party except me. My friends swore that they attended only because their parents made them go, and they pledged their solidarity and offered assurances that the offender was indeed stuck up, but we never probed too deeply into why I was left out in the first place.

I was aware of a distance between myself and my classmates, but I saw no real advantage in letting myself be angry about it. Though blackness stared back at me when I looked in a mirror, the rest of the time I pretended that I was the same as the other kids, and I did not ask for anything more than what they wanted to give me. I see now that this was where Gina and I differed. She was not willing to play along.

Gina came during the fall of our fifth-grade year, late October. The walls were still haunted with mini orange-construction-paper pumpkins and diminutive ghosts of all colors. Midmorning, the face of Mr. Johnson, the elementary school principal, appeared through the glass of our classroom door. He beckoned our teacher, Mr. Acker, to join him in the hall. A minute later, they marched back into the room in single file, Mr. Johnson, Mr. Acker, and Gina.

Mr. Johnson introduced her and told us that she was from Chicago, and that the next Monday she would join Mrs. Marshall's class, one of the other fifth-grade sections. Mr. Johnson's gaze kept settling on me as he spoke, so I took her in with a few gulps and then stared at my desk. She was tall for our grade, and had one plump black plait poised on either side of her head. I wondered how she had gotten her braids so even and neat. She was not thin or fat, but her green jumper was swelled by a hint of developing breasts, which I would have killed for. She had creamy brown skin, a shade lighter than mine, and a smooth stretch of it peeped from between the hem of that jumper and the long, white socks she wore ending in brown leather loafers.

My mind filled in the rest of Gina, unironically casting her as something bigger and badder than she could possibly have been. Her face was attractive but also hard, and she gave off the tough confidence of coming from somewhere better, more exciting and more alive than this. I imagined that she was amused by our childish decorations and tedious outfits. Beneath our skirts almost all the girls wore thick wool tights that were scratchy and too warm for that particular fall day.

When I sat down at my usual table at lunchtime, Anna Johnson, a blonde with green-grape eyes, studied me for a bit. "Is she a relative of yours?" she asked, then glanced around the table as if to gather support. "Because if she is related to you, you should have told us she was coming." Most of the other girls pumped their heads in agreement. Perhaps Anna's theory had not occurred to them, but they eagerly acknowledged that it made sense. They all seemed a little disappointed when I told them that she was not a relative, and that of course I would have told them if a relative were coming.

Anna considered the situation. She had, with a child's logic, taken the available information and constructed a reasonable explanation: I was there, Gina came, and since she looked like me and no one else around, we must be related; if Gina were a redheaded kid with a ton of freckles, maybe she would have put a similar question to Sally Lewis. And Anna was secure enough not to be ruffled by her mistake. "Well, she seems nice," she said, serenely handing down her verdict. "And it's really great that you have someone else now." She focused on her tray, and we all began to eat.

Sometimes, I get Anna's voice that day confused with other voices over the years. The one that comes through the strongest is that of a girl from my first-grade class. I still lived in Indianapolis then and attended a fairly exclusive private school. This girl, another prepubescent queen bee, had neglected to assign me a boy's name while pairing the members of our clique into imaginary couples, and when I asked why, the puzzlement in her voice was sharp and absolute. "You'll be with Warren, of course, Niki," she said. "Who else would you be with?"

Warren was a smart boy with a bushy little Afro and a tendency to dress in stiff corduroys and dorky sweater-vests, and he was, of course, the only option for me because he was the only black boy in our grade. I smiled gratefully at my friend's explanation. I think that I even affirmed her choice. And I ignored Warren for days.

The weekend after she arrived, I told my parents that we had a new girl in our grade, that her name was Gina, and that she was black. Their utensils paused briefly over their plates; a quick look passed between them across the table. "Where is she from?" my mother said, chewing thoughtfully. "What is she like?"

"Chicago," I said. "And I don't really know. Mr. Johnson only brought her to our classroom for a little while, and she doesn't officially start until Monday." My own chewing was brisk, determined. "We think she seems nice."

"Maybe you should invite her over sometime," my stepfather said, setting down his fork. He seemed undecided as to how gentle or firm his encouragement should be. "Only if you want, honey. Maybe we could get a pizza."

I nodded okay, through a mouthful of food. My parents exchanged glances, then one of them prodded the conversation elsewhere. In the weeks after, they would occasionally ask how school was, what my friends were up to, with a bit more emphasis than before, but they did not specifically mention Gina again.

For the first few weeks after she officially entered our grade, my impressions of Gina were mostly fragmentary. Our classes rarely mingled, but I was always acutely aware of her if she were in the vicinity, and I furtively charted her course through the school. At lunchtime, I would scan the room as I waited in line for food. Once I spotted Gina in a blue-and-red dress, a springy ebony pom-pom of a ponytail instead of her usual braided pigtails. She was sitting at the end of a table of fourth graders, near them but with her body hunched forward and her head down as she ate, so that it was clear she was not actually a part of their group.

At midday recess, my friends would burst outside when the bell rang, flinging mounds of thick parkas and colorful moon boots and bundled scarves toward the tetherball courts or the kickball field. But I began to take my time putting on my outerwear, and to drag my feet through the school doors so that I could spy on the new girl. Here is Gina on a winter day: Face uncovered above her lemon coat, which fit her well but did not look very warm. On her legs stiff new wool tights, ending in her usual dainty brown loafers. She was positioned near the pile of giant stacked tires, watching the boys and girls who wriggled across the structure or hid within the rings, not caring that if you stayed inside for very long you came out smelling like rubber. After school, I would hang back while walking home with my friends to monitor her until she disappeared in the other direction, alone and headed toward the highway and the new and not very fancy housing developments that were cropping up beside it.

Once or twice, my gaze stumbled across Gina's, and our eyes would lock until I looked away. It seemed clear that I was not, to her, just another classmate. Her expression, at these times, was curious, appraising, but it was not what I would call friendly or welcoming. If she had smiled at me, I probably would have smiled back, but she did not. If she had walked up to me and started talking, I would have responded, but she never approached me.

She didn't really connect with anyone for a while. Then she made the potentially irreversible mistake of taking on Marsha Lane as her first friend. Marsha was our grade's awesomely instructive example of different: She had cerebral palsy; her legs were encased in metal leg braces that creaked when she walked; and, most damningly, she trailed the odor of stale urine in her wake. Marsha granted the rest of us the huge favor of also having an unvaryingly pissed-off-at-the-world disposition. She rejected our weak gestures at camaraderie, but she accepted Gina immediately. For weeks, they were inseparable, at lunch, at recess, after school.

It wasn't that the other kids were mean to Gina or purposely ignored her, just that no one went out of the way to befriend her initially. Maybe it was because she appeared guarded, closed off, different, of course, but not in a way that was entirely satisfying for me. And so I kept tabs on Gina. I studied her to see if she would try to crowd my turf. I had worked hard to adapt, first at the Indianapolis private school and then even more so in this town that I was ready to defend as mine. It was a relief to me when Gina aligned herself with the easily ignored Marsha. She was off the stage now, where she wouldn't matter. The threat, stripped bare, was that Gina's presence might expose me as one of "them," not special just different. Back then I clung shamefully to the idea that there was something unique about me that made me worthy of my town's affections, that distinguished me from the faceless masses, despite the fact that black and white were so divisive in the rest of the world.

Then, unexpectedly, Gina's situation at school began to improve. In early November, I was sure to locate her on a bench with Marsha during recess, at the far end of the school yard. Their bodies would be angled together, and they would usually be playing hand-clap games. This basic setup was the same through mid-November, but at some point there was a shift. Gina would face forward and dig the toes of her new bubble-gum pink moon boots into the first snow we'd had that year, several inches distancing her from where Marsha talked desperately into her ear.

One recess, just before Thanksgiving, I could not find Gina. I knew that she wasn't sick, because I had seen her pushing food around her tray as she sat beside Marsha at lunch. I circled the playground, the intensity of the search warming me against the cold day. She was not at the tetherball court or at the kickball field or the tire pile. Marsha was perched alone and forlorn on their usual bench. I considered betraying my panic by pumping her for information, but as I neared Marsha her eyes widened fleetingly in hope, then clouded.

I almost didn't see her. I just happened to glance in Mrs. Marshall's window as I passed by. Gina was inside, cutting out brown and green turkeys and pilgrim hats with Cathy Miller, nice and cute and socially acceptable Cathy Miller, their heads bobbing together as they worked. Gina was smiling, then her teeth flashed very white against her face, and her cheeks and eyes scrunched with laughter; it was the first time I had seen a look of pleasure on her face, and she was transformed by it.

I observed them for several minutes, shivering from a corner of the window. When I finally moved to leave, I glimpsed my reaction in the glass. Glowering back at me was a dark little girl with glasses and uneven pigtails, wasting another recess to spy on a stranger.

By the time we returned from Thanksgiving, Gina had been inducted into Cathy's circle. The more comfortable she became, the more that smile appeared and the more her face opened and softened. She no longer hunched over but stood straight for all to see. She was lovely, inviting. I am sure that I was not the only one who noticed the changes in her, who began to consider from afar strategies for getting closer to her.

Our grade's star boy, Travis Burns, who was lean and dark haired and to whom only Anna Johnson could speak in complete sentences, missed the kickball one afternoon, and it soared from the field over to the tetherball court, where Gina was waiting her turn. The red rubber ball, wet and dirty from being in the snow, looked as if it might have bruised her cheek as it landed. Her hands flew up to her face, and the game stopped as her new friends crowded around to console her. They stepped back when Travis ran up to her. I could tell that he was apologizing and promising her that it was an accident. I could see that he put his arm around her and patted her cheek. He gave her his remarkable smile, the effects of which had been praised and analyzed at numerous slumber parties over the years, and walked backward, slowly, as he left, to make sure that she was okay. When he was gone, the other girls circled her in confusion and awe.

Watching her and Travis from across the school yard, I felt a twinge of envy and vague panic, but these were drowned out by a sudden flood of warmth for her, and sense of hope for us both. Someday, I, too, would ditch my glasses for contacts and get my hair under control, and then we would see what could happen. The way Gina waved good-bye as Travis returned to his game, but really seemed to call him back to her, that was something that I could learn to do. It was not just about boys, it was about new possibilities. Gina was stronger than I was, braver, and I wanted to learn to be different like her.

A few days after Gina's inspiring display with Travis on the playground, I stayed after music class to help the teacher clean up. Christmas vacation would begin the next day, two whole weeks of freedom then the start of a bright new year, and as I returned to Mr. Acker's room the halls seemed to be empty except for the green, red, and white paper trees and snowmen and snowflakes covering the otherwise cheerless concrete walls. The entire school was somewhat obsessive about saluting the holidays; the classrooms didn't need calendars, you could just mark the seasons by the miniature figures the students were forced to churn out month after month. I was taking my time getting back to our classroom, because the next subject for the day was math, my least favorite, and as I walked, I remember thinking that one of the best things about advancing to middle school in September was that we would escape that sort of silly task forever.

I almost passed right by her. She was slumped on the floor in the doorway of the girls' bathroom, only the loafers and the ends of her red pants stuck out. I knew those shoes, I must have known that it was Gina, and while the prospect of our first meeting was daunting, I kept walking toward her. As I drew closer, I saw that her arms were wrapped around her knees, and although her face was hidden, the way her braids quivered softly indicated that she was crying.

I did hesitate then, but she had heard my footsteps and peered up. Tears had left twin trails on her cheeks, each slightly darker than her skin. She rubbed her eyes and swallowed hard, as if preparing to speak. I wanted her to tell me what was wrong, but then with sudden panic I knew that she was going to demand to know why I was always watching her. Maybe she would tell me to keep going and not look back because she didn't need help from a traitor like me.

"How do you . . . ," Gina began, but then she lost out to the tears and had to swab her forearm back and forth across her eyes, until her creamy white sweater was also darkened and dampened. Her voice was faint, so I knelt down beside her, and this act seemed to encourage her to try again. "How do you," she said, then paused and gathered herself. "How do you do it here, Niki, with only them all the time?"

Even cracked and faltering, her voice, now that I was finally hearing it, was pleasant, low and rich. The tenor was a bit thicker and the cadence a bit looser than what was customary in the town, but if I had expected something akin to the sloppy voices I'd heard on television, voices that reeked of ghettos and ignorance and made me cringe whenever I heard them in the presence of my friends, Gina's was far from that. I was so caught up in mining the sound that it took me a few seconds to take in what she was saying. "I'm sorry, I don't know what you mean," I said, which was true in that instant. "Them?" I continued, and as I spoke I recognized that my own term had been not only reversed but transformed, made somehow potentially dangerous when Gina used it as she did. I felt my body stiffen, just a bit.

She studied my face for a few seconds and then breathed in and out slowly. She hugged her arms tighter around herself. "These kids, when they are mean to you," she said. "Some of them, the boys, when I was walking back to class before, these boys said all these mean things." She stopped. The tears came back into her eyes, and she snapped her gaze over to the opposite wall, where a string of large red letters wished us Merry Christmas.

"They were laughing and talking about how gross it would be to kiss a little nigger bitch," she said, and now her voice was almost inaudible. "I didn't really see them, they kind of came up behind me and I was afraid to turn around, but I think I know who it was."

Nothing like this had ever happened to me at school, but wasn't Gina's experience exactly what I had been waiting for? What she said was strangely thrilling, the great, sweeping relief that comes when your deepest fears and suspicions are proven true. More exhilarating still was the very fact of sharing that moment with Gina. What she had said, in a language that I immediately comprehended, was this: How do you survive when you're not like everyone else? How do you survive someone calling you a little nigger bitch and saying how disgusting it would be to press his lips against yours? Because it was one of the boys you saw every day who said those things, who reminded you once again that you were different. Not in some obvious way like Marsha, so that the other kids felt free to tease you, but a different so bad that no one even talked about it to your face.

I wonder now why it took me so long to connect with Gina. I think I worried that if I did she might see how terrified I had become of blackness. No one else in town would have suspected this about me. My friends did not need to look closely at these questions, and if they had correctly identified my fear of blackness, then they might have had to address the same repugnant truths about themselves. But what if Gina, the only person at school who looked like me and might understand some of the secret things I felt, saw the truth and turned away? What if the things that made me so contentedly "special" there, an ideal citizen of my town, would make me alien to all the other people who looked like me?

But Gina showed no signs of finding me alien. She was there in the hallway beside me, accepting me, even asking for my help. I took her hand and squeezed it, groping for words to comfort her. Gina shifted at that point; she swayed forward a bit, away from the protective doorway, and stretched her legs out in front of her into the hall. As she did, a white envelope with a festive gold border fell to the floor. She retrieved it swiftly and set it face down on her lap, but before she did I read the name "Travis" on it.

The reassurances I was preparing died in my throat. The affection I was feeling for her, the soothing sense of harmony and of our invincibility, together, turned into hot, vivid anger. I wanted to shake Gina and make her see, if there was any way, that by doing this she had ruined this place for both of us. I pictured Gina and Travis on the playground, the way he'd lingered in her presence. I could imagine Gina as she must have been earlier that day, giddy with the same memory, at once eager and scared to deliver a Christmas card to her crush. I did not dwell on what Travis's reaction would have been if she had completed her mission without anyone catching them. Instead, his friends must have seen the card, and what they said to her in the hallway stopped her from giving it to him. It served her right, I thought, for daring to assume, for asking for too much from them. I wanted to punish her, first for forcing me to look at myself every day, and then for giving me hope and failing to deliver.

When Gina spoke, I flinched and dropped her hand. "What do you think I should do?" she was saying. "I don't want to tell a teacher, but they shouldn't be able to get away with something like that." She sniffled. Tears glistened prettily in her eyes.

I looked up and down the hall, then finally back at her. "I don't know," I said. "I'm sorry, but I can't help you. They are my friends, and I've never had anything like that happen to me." I believe that before I left her sitting there, I said I hoped that she felt better, but I am not certain now. I know that she did not try to stop me as I walked away.

Gina was gone when we returned from Christmas vacation in January. Cathy Miller told us she had called her toward the end of the vacation and said that she would not return to the school. She would begin the next semester at a place in the city, and her family would be moving as soon as possible. Cathy, sounding miffed, said that Gina had not wanted to talk about why she was leaving and would not promise to send her new address. That was the last anyone heard of her.

I assumed that life in the town would go back to normal after Gina left. In most ways, it did. I was special again, all to myself. I never said anything about what Gina told me that day, nor did I hear anything more about it. The town continued as it was. But eventually, I began watching for her again. Not in the town's school yard or cafeteria, but in the city where she now lived.

I started asking my parents to drive me there on the weekends.

Sometimes, I thought I saw her. I'd see a flash of bright yellow coat, or a patch of brown skin between the bottom of a dress and the top of a pair of socks, and I'd twist my neck around and look hard until the girl was gone. It was never Gina, of course, just someone who looked exactly and nothing like her.

First in Her Class

Helen Schulman

YESTERDAY, I SAW Leigh on the street. She was walking up Broadway, pushing a stroller, a newborn boy buckled in and riding, a little fluff-headed girl child in a pink dress toddling by her side, her hair the yellow-white of a baby chick. Leigh was wearing a tank top with some black camisole underneath, cropped army pants, her blond hair dyed even blonder (with purposeful roots) and twisted into braids. There was a tattoo on her left shoulder. She looked happy but tired, and when she noticed that I was staring at her, her blue eyes blazed into mine. "I am here," her eyes said. She was the pretty, picture-perfect, exhausted New York mom that Leigh would have been were she not dead.

But she is dead. She's dead at least nine years now—I've stopped counting. I've even stopped counting these visitations of hers, when she comes to me out of nowhere—on the bus in a chic work outfit, juggling the *Times,* worrying the newsprint off her fingers lest she mar her crisp white blouse; or alone in an

East Village café, nose pressed into a book, notebooks and mugs of tea splayed before her on a banged-up coffee table as some scruffy but cute guy tries to catch her eye; once at the beach in Nice, amidst all those topless French girls, it was Leigh rising out of the water, vital and alive, laughing in the spray.

At first I found these Leigh sightings unnerving—always those eyes, sometimes blue, sometimes green, those chameleon eyes boring into mine, assertively announcing her presence. (It kills me that I can no longer remember their exact shade.) But now these drop-in visits are a part of the fabric of my life. I will always see Leigh, as long as I am alive, from time to time, out and about in the living, breathing world; I will always see Leigh as she was meant to be.

Teacher, student. Mentor, apprentice. Friend.

In a letter dated 2.92, typed on pale blue, unlined paper with handwritten scribblings marring her attempt at professional presentation, Leigh wrote: "Dear Helen, I realize after my confession to you, for lack of a better word, I asked you to invest."

I was thirty years old and teaching fiction in the MFA program at Columbia, a program I had rather recently graduated from, and so I was nervous and insecure—who was I to hold forth from the front of the very same classroom where I had just finished being too afraid to speak in the back row? I had a stomachache before every single class. And afterward, in the afternoon, when it was all over, I'd go home, drink a beer, get into bed, pull the covers over my head, and sleep till morning.

Leigh was a member of a great workshop full of supersmart, supertalented, intimidating students who as often as not were better educated and better dressed than I was. The week before I received the first of her letters, the "investment" letter as I think of it now, she'd met me for an office hour, and because it was a beautiful day we'd sat outside on the marble steps of Butler Library. Leigh was twenty-five—she would die just before her twenty-eighth birthday—with waist-length blond hair and that sort of fresh, earnest American prettiness I've always thought of as "Iowa good looks," and we were discussing her first story submission, the only piece of her writing that I have not kept because it was so lousy. The story had to do with a mother and child, a little kid of some ambiguous age who had some horrible but unidentifiable disease, and there were teddy bears in the foreground and breaking waves in the background; at least that's how I remember it. I remember it "with violins." I also remember that I had had a fight with my boyfriend that morning, and shampoo to buy. Leigh and I weren't really getting anywhere with our discussion—I was insisting she do some research so that the details of her story would feel real. (There's a laugh.)

"What about 'pain meds,'" I said. (Pain meds!) "What about the real truth about the relationship between the mother and her kid? Maybe this mother is ready for her child to die; maybe her child's death would set her free."

It is unbelievable to me now how I went on. But go on I did. "DeLillo says: 'Look at the hard surfaces, the blatant flesh of things.'"

Leigh just stared at me. An appropriate response, I think, looking back. Then, she gave me a heartfelt spiel about why she'd chosen writing school over acting school. If you've talked to as many incoming grad students as I have, you know that this specific conversation and its inevitable permutations (writing school versus law school, writing school versus working for a living, writing school versus doing nothing) is usually the verbal equivalent of students holding up a giant neon sign flashing the words "dilettante" and "afraid of the real world" over their unwrinkled foreheads, and so you can gather how satisfying this conversation felt to both of us.

After the meeting was over, I walked back into the building where I taught and into the cubicle that was my office, closed the door with a sigh of relief, and was just sitting down at my desk when that inevitable knock came. It was Leigh at the door. Polite and determined. Asking me "to invest." Wanting more. More than I'd offered.

But that's not how it happened. Is it? The letter was dated February 1992, but I remember sunshine and undergraduates playing Frisbee on the quad and banging on bongo drums and making out on the grass. February meant cold and snow and me having the flu. How could Leigh have played her trump card that day, knocking on my door and asking me to invest, telling me she had cancer?

As time goes on I lose hold of my memories of her, they swirl in and out, forming weird alternative chronologies, like snapshots tossed in a messy drawer and retrieved at random. So impossible to sort and order. I think now that perhaps mourning and memory go hand in hand. That's why it is so hard to let go of grief. Because when you do, memories begin to fade, too, and you are left with nothing.

Leigh's eyes must have been blue, she was so blond, but if my life depended on it, I'd say they were green. In the only picture I have of her, Leigh's hair is whipping across her face and she is laughing her head off as she runs shrieking down a sandy dune to the water. She loved the beach. Her ashes were scattered somewhere off the coast of Maine. This photo accompanied the invitation to her memorial service. Her mother sent it to me, at the beginning of our friendship. Me and Leigh's mother, our friendship set in motion by Leigh's death. No eye color in that photograph. Just wind-whipped blond hair and a smile that lit up the world. I no longer have her mother's phone number, but I could call information. After all these years, I could call Leigh's mother and ask her: "What color were your daughter's eyes?"

Right.

They must have been blue. Aren't all blondes blue-eyed?

So here's an alternate memory of the day that Leigh told me she was sick, that she had cancer: Leigh was my student for an entire semester and the semester was almost over. I liked Leigh but thought she was a little checked out. (Of course she was checked out; she was on chemo, she was trying her best not to vomit, she kept her head down, eyes focused on the wood grain of the desk. Staring at a fixed object is an antivomiting technique, I'll give you that, although it's also what students do when they are bored and sick of you, high on drugs, or clinically depressed, and I hadn't a clue then as to what was wrong with her.) I liked Leigh, but I wasn't compelled by her. There were other students who seemed more committed, more promising, ringing a closer orbit to the white-hot center of what I felt about fiction writing at the time, which was that it simply was what tethered me to the earth.

Leigh came to see me because she wanted to study with me a second semester, that was it, so it must have been the end of intersession, it must have been winter. I found her interest hard to fathom. I hadn't exactly been an effective instructor. And I didn't like anyone to repeat my class in those days; I frankly didn't want to be responsible for them, for their fellowships and their thesis evaluations; I didn't trust my own instincts enough, my stature in the department, blah, blah, blah, the distance between my students and me, intellectually and emotionally, seemed a hairsbreadth. Too much proximity and my cover would be blown. I looked young. I was young. On absolutely no terms would I let my guard down with a student. I'd told Leigh all about my "professional policy," no second semesters and the allegiances they implied, but she knocked on my door anyway, and there was nothing I could do but let her in.

"I believe in the power of continuity," Leigh said, "but I'm sorry to trouble you."

"It's no trouble," I said. "I just think it's important for you to get as many experiences as possible. You're only here for four semesters."

"I have cancer," she said.

"Oh," I said. "I'm sorry." I said I'm sorry, but I thought, Why did you tell me that! I don't want to know about your cancer. I don't know how to handle this.

"But I don't want you to treat me any differently from anybody else," Leigh said. "I have cancer, but I'm sorry for telling you."

"Are you secretly Jewish?" I asked her, because enough was enough with the apologizing, especially when obviously it was Leigh who was now calling the shots. And she was making me feel so guilty—I'd have to be Genghis Khan at this point to say no to her.

"Take the class," I said—but only if she'd throw out the story with the teddy bears and write something more truthful.

"Write the story you wouldn't want your mother to read," I said, before sending her out into the hall.

I asked her to write a story betraying her mother—it was an assignment I had used on the teenagers I taught in the summers, to free them up, to get them to tell the truth, bend all their internal rules, to get them to "look at the hard surfaces, the blatant flesh of things." Who knew then that it was Leigh's mother and I who would betray her?

After Leigh left my office, I thought: I can embrace this kid or I can leave her to her own life and protect myself.

It was a moment of clarity and decision; I realized this at the time. I decided to utilize every defense mechanism I had and treat her like anyone else, to do my best to forget what she'd told me.

But the next week I found myself chasing her down the hall with an armload of books I thought she might like to read. And then, after that, when I received the first of Leigh's letters, I invited her out for coffee. I pursued her, right after I resolved not to engage with her.

Under the harsh light of day, I suppose now that there was something oddly thrilling about the situation: I was a teacher;

here was someone I could teach. Someone whose life circumstances made it possible for me to make a difference—which is the mandate of teachers everywhere, isn't it? It wasn't the six grand a semester. If I could help this kid at this time with her work, I figured I could establish my own sense of legitimacy. Plus I liked her. I liked her moxie. She'd been polite, but she hadn't taken no for an answer. I guess I thought she'd give Life (with a capital L) the same treatment. That she wouldn't take no for answer.

I just didn't believe that she would die then. My father was a doctor. I believed in modern medicine. Now Leigh is dead, and my father, too. He suffered from advanced dementia and paralysis in the long years before he died. What I believe in at this stage of my life is luck.

Leigh and I began to meet. We began meeting regularly. I looked forward to these meetings. I gave up other students, other friends, other breakfasts, reading the paper, even writing time.

We'd meet at La Rosita's, a Cuban rice and beanery on upper Broadway that made the best eggs and the best coffee. We'd sit there drinking our café con leches and talking about books and Leigh's stories, stories written with painstaking care that, with my red pencil, I ripped to shreds. We went over them sentence by sentence. I was tougher with Leigh than I've ever been with any other student, and she'd come back eager for more. It was as if her disease gave us a mandate to be serious, to work as if our lives depended on it. And isn't that what literature requires, really, for the writer to feel like her life depends upon it? And if you accept that basic tenet, then doesn't it only make sense to embrace the work itself and not focus solely on the product?

"Relax," I told her, when Leigh got frustrated. "Writing takes time, these things take time," I said, trying to be reassuring.

"I don't have time," Leigh said.

"So we'll work like hell," I told her, and we did. We worked hard. And it was fun. It was exciting. She was alive and I was alive and we were embarking on this great adventure, because we were both young enough and idealistic enough and dumb enough to think that art can save your life.

THIS MORNING, I sat down at my desk and for the first time in eight years reread Leigh's short stories, and they were so good, it kind of shocked me. I'd forgotten how good they were—yet another important thing that I've forgotten. She'd needed permission to write about her family and the strain she'd put on them by being ill, so I gave her that permission. And when she still held back, I goaded her. It is with no small amount of vanity that I still think the pieces invested with this emotional truth and pain were her strongest.

I'd hit on something with that "write the story you wouldn't want your mother to read" business that I'd so casually tossed out, reaching into my hat and taking hold of whatever trick I could find. Leigh went to great lengths to preserve the independence she was just beginning to establish as a young adult. She managed her own medical care. She almost never allowed her family to accompany her down to the National Institutes of Health in Maryland, where she was receiving experimental treatments. Later, after she died, her mother told me that when she finally convinced Leigh to allow her to come along, one of the oncology nurses had pulled her mother aside and said: "Thank God. We were wondering if she had any family." Her mother was eager to accompany her daughter, but she had felt compelled to honor Leigh's choices; in truth I doubt she had any alternative, Leigh was so stalwart. She was so private! She believed in a certain stoicism. And yet she wanted to be a writer, and it has to cost a writer something to write anything worth reading. In the story she did not want her mother to read, Leigh explored the havoc she feared her own death would cause to the rest of her family. As a daughter, she felt she was failing her mother by dying before her.

After I reread the stories, I reread Leigh's letters. I'd saved them all; I am convinced that she wanted me to save them. They were very crafted, and as confessional as Leigh would allow herself to be. With no book or publications to leave behind, no thesis completed (which drove her crazy—she wanted so much to graduate, to earn that diploma), the letters along with the stories are the last tangible evidence I have of her singular talent and voice. Once, after a series of CAT scans gave Leigh a brief period of hope, she sent me this in a P.S., a P.S. to a rather mundane note apologizing once again for not having completed some stupid assignment I'd dreamed up, burying the lead as they say, as if this were the only way she could sneak out her own excitement and pleasure: "My mother was there after I got those last x-rays. I usually insist she not come, but she was here that time and I could show her the good news. Even though I think it's a person's right to be healthy and not a privilege, I can't deny that I felt privileged then. I got what I'd asked for."

After that brief window of hope, the protocols were unsuccessful. Leigh got sicker. She did so much chemo I thought the chemo would kill her, and then one day she got pissed at her doctors and she quit. She quit chemo altogether and had six glorious months where she felt great and looked great and she went on trips and stayed up all night and had a terrific time, and by the end of the six months her lungs were full of tumors. She went back on chemo and did protocol after protocol until two days before she died. I remember her calling me and asking me months earlier what she should do—keep at it, which was so hard, the vomiting, the diarrhea, the hair loss, the hope; or give in. I've thought of this conversation many times since. I've thought that I handled it badly, that I was selfish.

I said, "Leigh, you have to fight," even though I knew the fight would get her nowhere.

I said, "You have to try."

I didn't say: It's your choice, I support you, it is your body.

I didn't ask her what she wanted.

I wanted her! So I told her to fight, even though clearly the fight was useless.

There was silence on the line after that, and then she said: "I would feel the same way about you."

Before she died Leigh came to visit me at my apartment on the Upper West Side of Manhattan. I had just had a miscarriage, and I was sad and confused and scared that I would live a life without children. She had been staying with her parents near Boston, too sick to be on her own, which she absolutely hated, the fact that she'd had to move back home, that after giving up school, and her beloved New York City, she now had to relinquish any semblance of an adult life. She was in town to see friends, she said, she'd come with her sister. I didn't realize then that she'd come to say good-bye. In an effort to cheer us both up, I invited her to a small dinner party my husband and I were throwing. She declined but offered to come and watch me cook. That sounded like fun to me, so I bought us a bottle of wine, put some music on, set out some crackers and cheese—I was very eager to see her, and so I guess I was in denial.

When I opened the front door to my apartment, I did not recognize her. Leigh was emaciated, skeletal, but still chic—she had such a terrific sense of style. Her bald head was covered with a little beaded Moroccan cap, and she was wearing these great earrings (earrings that later her mother sent to me as a gift, to remember her by), and she was carrying a purple orchid for me as a present. I led her into our tiny city kitchen, where she helped me to make a mess of fiddlehead ferns; neither of us knew how to fix them.

I received a letter from Leigh the following week. "Sitting in your kitchen doorway, dosing out bad advice about cooking fiddle heads (sorry. I hope your dinner was a success regardless), receiving such helpful advice from you and just being in your presence was so . . . peaceful. Felt safe for the first time in so long. I only wish I could've been some help to you."

Of course she was a help to me! Looking back, I can't remember if I returned the compliment. I hope I did. I hope I called or wrote her back to let her know how comforting she'd been, how she was one of the very few people I confided in about my infertility and the pain it caused me. I know that at the time I really felt she understood how much I wanted to be a parent; it was a loss that she too was feeling deeply for herself. I wonder now if in my own need to express my grief and get reassurance, I wasn't being insensitive to what the discussion may have cost her.

When it was time to say good-bye, Leigh stopped to scratch my cat behind the ears on her way out the door, and I remember thinking, Who will last longer, the orchid? The cat? Leigh? That was the last time I saw her. We threw the orchid away about two weeks later. The cat is still living. He sits on my lap now as I type.

The first time I heard Leigh's mother's voice was on my answering machine. She just stated her name and asked me to call her back, but I knew instantly that my friend had died. Why else would her mother be calling me? At first, I pretended I didn't hear the message. I went about my day—I had an assignment due, I had a meeting, there were groceries to be bought, wine . . . Who remembers? Whatever I had to do seemed so important to me at the time that it scared me to think I might not complete it—only later, when I returned to my apartment, did I listen to the tape again, acting as if I was hearing it for the first time. It was a strange, secret exercise, embarrassing now to recount; I actually thought I could reorder the experience into a sequence that made it possible to endure. Now with my swirling memories, I'm wondering if I'm not doing the very same thing, reordering time and events to make things bearable.

Her mother and I talked that evening for a long time. She shared with me the details of her daughter's death, which I appreciated, which helped me. After we hung up, I wanted to do something to help her too. So I wrote a letter to Leigh's mother, this woman I had never met. I wanted her to recognize the depths of Leigh's gifts as an artist, so I excerpted her stories. I wanted her to know Leigh's capacities as a friend, and so I shared pieces of our correspondence, and then I let my memories and feelings run wild as I tried to impress upon this woman how much her daughter meant to me. I guess I just wasn't ready to let go of Leigh; I wanted to keep contact. Her mother called me after that letter, and then I called her, and before I knew it we were calling each other back and forth. Although we never met in person, we talked regularly on the phone for several years.

Looking back, I am still amazed at how our friendship grew out of this loss and then deepened over time, even though we never set eyes upon one another. At one point she'd sent me a family photo—she looked so much like Leigh that she was instantly familiar, and perhaps that aided the intimacy between us. I found myself looking forward to our talks. Perhaps the fact that the friendship existed outside of the fabric of my life gave me a certain freedom to be open with her. And just listening to Leigh's mother share the way she confronted her pain, the way she turned her grief into something positive by volunteering at a nearby hospice, helped me to learn how to use my own heartache in a way that made it tolerable. Her mother divorced, and I miscarried again and again.

Leigh's mother tried to rebuild her life, I struggled with raising children and caring for ailing parents. We would get on the phone and laugh about our misadventures and confide our fears about our own rapidly diminishing capacities to face our struggles and then gasp in wonderment as we continued anyway, and moved on. My children still sleep under the quilts that Leigh's mother made for them at their births. My daughter Zoe's pattern is entitled "Life in the Time of Craziness." Zoe still plays with the tea set Leigh's mother sent her from the gift shop of the hospital where she does hospice work.

Our friendship was very important to me and yet also somehow illicit, illicit because Leigh would have hated it. Nothing would have been a bigger violation to Leigh than her mother and me swapping stories, especially when we swapped them about her, about Leigh herself. Her mother told me about Leigh's childhood, her adolescence, with a loving perspective that no student would ever want her teacher to hear. I told her about Leigh's style, her power, the young man in our class who had danced his attentions on her—Leigh would have hated all of it.

She was so reserved, she was trying so hard to individuate from her mother, she'd seen her relationship with me as something professional, mature, and somewhat sacred, because I was her teacher, see; and for Leigh, as for so many of us, wisely or not, a teacher was something holy—for all these reasons, Leigh would have hated my friendship with her mother. I knew this, but it didn't stop me. We broke her rules. We talked about her.

"Leigh would have hated this," I said once over the phone.

"I know," said her mother, "but she's dead."

And then we both burst out laughing, the kind of laughter that makes tears irrelevant. She abandoned us, fuck her, we would talk about her.

LEIGH'S MOTHER AND I lost touch a few years back. My father was brain-damaged in a fall and I was distracted and busier than ever in my efforts to help my family. My time at Columbia ended abruptly and, for me, sadly. I had once talked about leaving the department, and Leigh's mother had entreated me to stay on. "You must keep teaching," she said. We'd set up a scholarship in Leigh's name. Who would be left to shepherd it?

I couldn't bear to share the unhappiness of my departure with her mother—I felt like I would be letting Leigh's mother down. As for Leigh's mother, Leigh's death had nearly destroyed her family, and I think after a while survival triumphed over correspondence as a priority.

On some level, I may not have wanted to disappoint Leigh by becoming ever closer with her mother. In some ways it was becoming a more mature friendship then my relationship with Leigh, basically because I was more mature then, because we didn't have the formality of the teacher-student thing, because we'd shared a major loss together. And this may sound really stupid, but I think that, though I expected Leigh to die, I did not expect her to stay dead. When she did stay dead, year after year, still dead, I was astonished by it. Perhaps part of letting go of her mother, finally, was letting go of Leigh; it was as if her mother were holding Leigh's place for me, saving the spot. We'd helped one another and moved on.

I think of Leigh's mother from time to time, and sometimes I move to pick up the phone, but something always stops me. I don't know where to begin with her now. I don't know how to make that first step. If Leigh hadn't died, her mother and I would never have become friends. What can I say to Leigh's mother? I miss you? I miss your daughter? I want her back? I want her back.

I have been teaching for fifteen years now. I've had students publish, students marry, become parents, go into rehab, become millionaires, go crazy. I even had one student who committed murder. But Leigh was the first to enter my heart, the first in her class.

"I cannot promise right now to pay off, but I will try my very best," Leigh wrote in that initial letter in which she asked me to invest.

Pay off? It's such an old story, the one about the student teaching the teacher. About what? Oh, perseverance, suffering, dedication, passion, grief, how to tie a scarf so you look French and not like an old lady—I won't bore you with that story. I loved Leigh. Losing her was terrible.

"Look," I said at Rosita's that day. "This takes time; writing takes time."

"But I don't have time," Leigh said.

And she was right. She didn't.

It Felt Like Love

Vivian Gornick

I HAD A FRIEND once with whom I was certain I would grow old. The reason I was certain was that by the time we were thirty we had already known each other fifteen years, and were just arriving at the starting point. In high school, we passed each other haughtily in the corridors; in college, classmates brought us into wary contact; in our twenties, we sparked belligerently. What a pair we had been: two of those very intelligent, insecure girls whose anxieties make them grow up sharp-tongued, overdirect, equipped with voices that, with hardly any effort at all, generate scorn and judgment. In time, we alienated just about everybody. Which did not mean that we ourselves drew together. To the contrary. For a whole bunch of years we each heard the sound of the other's voice and shrank from it, thinking silently, "Thank God, I'm nothing like *that*." It was only in our early thirties that these formidable defenses began to alter sufficiently that each of us, at last, could recognize herself in the other; whereupon there developed, almost immediately, the kind of connection that soon made it necessary to meet or speak at least three times a week. The open road of the rest of our lives then spread out before us.

In the centuries behind our own, when most marriages were contracted out of economic and social considerations, friendship was written about with the kind of emotional extravagance that we, in our own time, have reserved for an ideal of passionate attachment. Montaigne, for instance, writing in the sixteenth century of his long dead, still mourned for friend Étienne de La Boétie, tells us that between them communion had achieved perfection: they were "one soul in two bodies." Of La Boétie's actions, Montaigne says, not one "could be presented to me . . . that I could not immediately find the motive for it." This shared soul "pulled together in such unison," each half regarding the other with "such ardent affection" that he, Montaigne, would have trusted his well-being to La Boétie more readily than to his own inadequate self. The privilege, for each of the friends, resided in being allowed to love, rather than in being loved. "In this noble relationship, services and benefits, on which other friendships feed, [were not] taken into account. . . . We could neither lend nor give anything to each other," as the one who was receiving a favor was inevitably in debt to the one who was delivering it.

This is language that Montaigne does not apply to his feelings for his wife or his children, his colleagues or his patrons—all relationships that he considers inferior to a friendship that, unlike these other attachments, develops not out of sensual need or worldly obligation but simply because it feeds the spirit; in its presence "the soul grows refined."

My friendship with Emma was not one I would have described as Montaigne describes his with La Boétie, but in some important ways, it is analogous. It was an attachment that, if it did not refine the soul certainly nourished the inquiring spirit so well that in each other's presence we bore witness to our own lives more usefully than I have ever done, before or since. The quotidian became raw material for a developing perspective that acquired narrative drive. In conversation with Emma, I felt the strength of context imposed on the dailiness of life.

To the uninitiated eye, this vitality of connection between me and Emma might have seemed puzzling. No dating service would have matched us up. In none of the ways that gross social profiles accumulate would we have been imagined compatible. Emma had married and stayed married, become a mother, pursued graduate work; I was twice divorced, had remained childless, and lived the marginal existence of a working freelancer. She was a bourgeois through and through, I a radical feminist who owned nothing; she dressed beautifully, I indifferently; she longed for sexual adventure, I didn't know what to do with it; she also thought carefully and spoke slowly, while I ran on heedlessly, the words pouring out of my mouth. More to the point, Emma lived in perpetual struggle with herself as a wife and mother, I with the emotional bewilderment of my increasingly solitary state.

Beneath these separating realities, however, there was a deeper, more compelling influence that drew us toward one another. Together, we seemed always to be puzzling out those parts of the general condition to which our own circumstance applied: the exhaustion of love and the anguish of work; the smell of children and the taste of solitude; the search for the self, and the confusion that came with the mere construction of the phrase—what was it? where was it? how did one pursue it, abandon or betray it? These questions, we soon saw, were the ones that concentrated what felt like our deepest concerns. A growing awareness had begun to take hold in each of us that throughout our lives we had both responded to the same set of anxieties, albeit in diametrically opposite style. Emma had embraced the family, I had rejected the family; she endorsed the middle class, I loathed the middle class; she dreaded loneliness, I endured it.

Yet, the longer we went on meeting and talking, the more clearly we saw that to know who we were, and how we had come to be, had become for both of us the central enterprise. Consciousness as a first value, we each concluded, was everything.

The absorption grew in us day by month by year, fed by the excitement of abstract thought joined to the concreteness of ordinary life. The more we explored the trivial and the immediate in service to the large and the theoretical, the more we seemed to feel "ourselves." The more we felt ourselves, the larger the world grew. Sitting in a living room, eating in a restaurant, walking in the street—the conversation made it seem that we had grasped things whole without ever having had to leave home.

We went on like this for nearly ten years. And then one day the bond between us began to unravel. I had a bad exchange with Emma's husband, Henry, and suddenly, the divisions between us angered her. She read a book by a liberationist writer I prized, and I was stung by her scorn. We each made a new friend whose virtues the other failed to respond to. That winter I could barely pay the rent, and Emma's endless preoccupation with redecorating her apartment got under my skin. Who *is* she? I thought one day. Then I seemed to be registering acutely and persistently—and as though for the first time—that she opened her eyes onto the mob scene of family life, while I opened mine to a landscape that had to be peopled each day anew.

One day Emma's husband and I fell into a real disagreement, harmless at first (it was over a movie, I remember) but gradually escalating into a full-scale argument. I saw Emma then seeing Henry through my eyes—also as though for the first time—as a man for whom facts were the only truth; and she withdrew visibly: from me, not him.

Another time she was visiting my house. I'd just gotten a new piece of furniture, a light-colored velvet armchair of which I was still being careful. Emma carelessly let a pen in her hand run a black line down its side. I became inordinately upset. She immediately went to work with cleaner fluid, erasing the discoloration almost entirely; then she looked slowly around my apartment, which until then I had thought cozy; now, as I followed Emma's eyes, it looked small to me, small and sterile.

Slowly but inexorably, the enterprise of mind and spirit to which our friendship had been devoted began to lose strength before the growing encroachment of the complicated and opposing sympathies out of which our lives were actually fashioned: Emma's husband, my feminism; her security, my marginality; my lack of interest in her children, hers in my loneliness. Like an uncontrollable growth that overtakes a clearing in the forest, the differences began to move in on us. I remembered that once, long ago, I had thought brashly that time would stand still for me and Emma as we were using it so well. I hadn't understood then that what I called "using time well" really meant paying no attention to who we were becoming. It struck me now that it was the sheer hubris of the conceit that was doing us in.

In no time at all, the friendship that had for so long generated excitement, and exerted power, was experienced as a need that had run its course. Overnight, it seemed, it took one long stride and moved from the urgent center to the exhausted margin. Just like sexual infatuation, I remember thinking idly one morning, as I lay in bed staring at the ceiling. And then, somewhat dazedly, I realized, "That's right. That's exactly what this is like. Sexual infatuation."

In the end, my friendship with Emma did prove to bear a striking resemblance to romantic love, its strength of connection ultimately as limited as the one exerted by an attraction of the senses that does not integrate itself organically into the larger body of a lived life. The companionate-ness of mind and spirit between me and Emma became an equivalent of the erotic feeling that flares up, overtakes the territory, then dies of the very intensity that, if isolated from a larger mutuality of will and circumstance, is destined for burnout. The irony was that sexual love usually fails because of an insufficiency of shared sensibility, whereas sensibility was what we had in abundance. Yet in isolation it, too, had proved insufficient.

What do I mean by "insufficient"? For that matter, what do I mean by "in isolation"?

Winston Churchill once said, "There are no permanent friends, there are only permanent interests." The sentiment is usually taken to mean that, inevitably, worldly ambition usurps personal loyalties; but now, as Emma and I began to disintegrate, I saw the provocative statement in a new light and concluded that by "interests" Churchill had meant something deeper than the pursuit of material success. The reference, I now thought, applied to the stability of that organic network of related connections that fosters the illusion, if not the reality, of inner coherence. Take away the *conviction* of an integrated existence, and one is set adrift, floating like a leaf in the wind: a fate most people cannot tolerate. Which is why the world has never been well lost for love.

Coherence was the key word. I saw in the year that Emma and I came apart that the hunger for inner coherence is strong enough to subdue desires of every sort, for the simple reason that in its absence the ability to believe in oneself evaporates. Without self-belief one cannot achieve trust, express affection, act reliably with tender concern—all of which make life worth living, and all of which are engendered by a community of "interests" fed by mutuality of will and circumstance.

In the same moment I saw, too, that people would rather operate in a small, safe sphere than in a larger, more uncertain one if, by remaining in the smaller, they can be assured that they will never feel cut adrift. Exactly what Emma and I had each done: I by remaining alone, she by remaining married. We had made for ourselves a small, safe world, one that our friendship had once promised to enlarge but now threatened to undo. The adventure of knowing one another had metamorphosed into the anxiety of feeling exposed before one another.

Montaigne's friend died young, at a time when it was easy for the two men to imagine themselves joined at the hip for life. What wisdom, I have often wondered, would the great essayist have given us had they lived on together into the maturity that, inevitably, would have produced divisions of taste, experience, and ambition capable of sucking them into the very circumstance of which I have been writing? No doubt, he would have thought longer and harder than I have been able to do about the astonishing antagonism that may obtain between the drive toward self-protection and the need for a soul mate.

For myself, I can only say that the failure of shared sensibility to prevail over all else administered a shock to the nervous system from which I don't think I ever recovered, however much I came to value my hard-earned understanding that fellowship of the spirit alone can no more make terms than can a passion of the senses. I will mourn Emma's friendship as long as I live.

IN A WHIRLWIND

Beverly Gologorsky

ESSICA AND I were comrades the way soldiers are buddies; a sense of do or die was always near. We first met in the Union Station ladies' room in Washington, D.C., on the way to a demonstration. The door to her commode had malfunctioned and she was locked in. I threw over a nail file and talked her through jimmying it open. That day we marched together.

When she came into my life, it was an intense period. A time when sleep was as prohibited as romance novels—1966 through 1975: the movement years. The U.S. government wouldn't get out of Vietnam no matter how many millions wished it. Jessica hated the war as much as I did. We shared tears and frustration as the number of body bags continued to rise. We were gassed, beaten, jailed.

During the bombing of Cambodia, thousands of us angrily circled the U.S. Capitol, while on the steps Vietnam veterans tossed their medals into trash bins. Many were arrested. Jessica and I were taken to a Virginia jail and refused our right to make a phone call. At her suggestion a group of us sang "This Land Is Your Land," loudly and continuously until they relented.

Together we attended endless meetings and analyzed the politics for hours afterward, wrote hundreds of leaflets, traveled often to different cities. We sat in at various institutions, including Columbia University, although neither of us was a student there. Jessica was at Barnard then; I was a typist at a magazine.

The cascading events were bigger than each of us; history needed our participation, and our reward would be a chance to change the future. Had you asked us then we would have said friends for life, come what may, arm in arm. Our backgrounds may have been different, but our worldview was the same.

Having been brought up in a rough New York City neighborhood, I had street smarts. She, raised more delicately in New England, had a sense of self I could only envy. Tall, slim, with a posture so correct it seemed she could shoulder many conflicts at the same time. Fearing no rejection, she rushed to face down anyone: university president, four-star general, or Henry Kissinger for that matter. I may have been fiery, but she was dauntless. Although she could charm people, she was more interested in raising consciousness, a difficult task to achieve with those in power, and she always left the scene angry.

Her father was a corporate giant, so I was surprised to see how small he was when she brought me home for a weekend. Her family lived in a beautiful, large, very white house with landscaping so complex, I remember thinking about Alice in Wonderland's trip through the labyrinth. I would've been glad to lounge there for a while, take it in like some sweet-smelling perfume, but Jessica immediately began fighting with her dad about the war. (Her mother barely said a word.) Too polite, or perhaps too cowed, to put forward my usual antiwar arguments, I saw in her father the steely-eyed certainty that Jessica had inherited. And concluded that parents were the last people on earth to organize.

My parents, born in Russia, didn't like the war but wouldn't tell a soul; their philosophy: no one can fight city hall and win, so why bother? Also it was dangerous, someone could be arrested, lose a job, end up in the poorhouse, better to live and let live, but what they meant was, leave us alone. I disagreed violently, and worked to prove them wrong. To my delight we did manage to move the Leviathan an inch or two in a just direction. My father, declaring enough is enough, signed a petition against the bombing.

Still, I didn't take Jessica to meet my family because I feared her questions would unnerve them. "Why work at Grummans? Don't they make warplanes? How can you be a policeman during these times? Doesn't it shame you?" I agreed with her assessments, but these relatives didn't know how else to make a living, and their consciousness hadn't been raised.

As we stood together on the front lines against war and racism, injustice and imperialism, a new ism presented itself, one that grew like a balloon but never seemed to burst. For nights on end we talked about sexism, male chauvinism, how identifying with the struggles of others helped us to understand why people fight to the death for independence, liberation, their place on this earth. Now suddenly, amazingly, here we were confronting our own oppression. And we didn't have to look far. In the male-dominated movement, women cooked dinner while men discussed theory. However, it would all change, and rapidly.

Jessica and I lived with men. But she decided to move out, declaring she could not confront and fight her oppression or that of other women while living with a man. I disagreed, but we remained close friends. My partner was active only peripherally. However, her boyfriend was a "movement heavy," someone too embedded in his views to be able to consider hers. Leaving him freed her in many ways. She went on to create a radical feminist organization. I joined a consciousness-raising group. Still, we met often to plan women's actions and to discuss our lives. We kissed hello, good-bye, remained devoted to each other.

When a hail of police bullets in Chicago murdered Black Panther leader Fred Hampton, the anger of many in the movement was palpable. We wanted to do something, and decided to pull together a women's march to protest the sudden jailing of several Black Panther women whose efforts against racism had become legion. The arrests also disrupted many of the Party's activities, including the breakfast program for children. In particular we would focus on one woman in Connecticut, incarcerated for her politics, outspokenness, and ability to draw crowds. Needless to say, much passion went into organizing the march; our slogan was "Free Our Sisters, Free Ourselves, Power to the People." We anticipated fifty thousand demonstrating women descending on New Haven. Jessica and I traveled across the country, rallying them to rally others to participate. We wrote and mimeographed thousands of leaflets, distributed them at Laundromats, subway stations, movie houses, campuses, supermarkets, religious institutions, street corners; we went everywhere to talk about the upcoming event.

Some days Jessica and I worked out of an office on upper Broadway in Manhattan, a clearinghouse for whatever still needed to be done. Women often dropped by to pick up flyers and travel information. The energy was endless, the dedication priceless, the outcome had to be a major success.

Two weeks before the scheduled march, as I was sitting behind a desk sorting mail, Jessica arrived with two women I didn't know. No introductions were made. Jessica pulled up a chair; the two women remained standing. Something scary was about to happen but I wasn't sure what. Jessica didn't look angry, upset, just certain, the way people do before a pronouncement. I chattered on about our progress, about who was doing what, even shoved a pile of new flyers across the desk for their perusal. All these decades later, I can still recall most of the conversation.

"Beverly, we've heard some news that involves you."

"What's that?" My mind no doubt searching for possible scenarios.

"We heard you agreed to allow the Black Panther men march with us."

"That's true," I said. "I think it's a wonderful idea."

"This is a women's march," she said matter-of-factly, as if another decision had already been made in some secret chamber of the universe.

"And it remains a women's march," I countered.

"Not if they come."

"If men want to shout, Free our sisters, why stop them?" I felt this deeply. Plus, telling Panther brothers they couldn't march to support the women was unthinkable.

Jessica said the issue was not closed. I would be contacted to attend a meeting for another go-round. Her imperious tone, a knife thrust.

Although the office visit continued to bother me, I never imagined we wouldn't arrive at some sort of agreement. I called together the women who shared my view. None of us wanted to see any block of women pull out of the march. So it was decided I should attend the meeting.

We learn a great deal from friends but are strangely averse to saying so. Jessica's opinions had often challenged my own and nudged my perspective in various ways. However, this felt differ-ent. But was it? We were best friends, yes, but best "political" friends. What did that mean? We shared an ideology, and were immersed in a struggle that defined everything in our lives, including the meaning of success. We each wanted women to know and fight their oppression, to identify their needs and meet them, to take on and break free from male institutions and male expectations. And, finally, for women to wrest power in every arena of society. Jessica and I signed off on these goals a million times. Yet the particulars of how to pursue them were threatening our relationship. Friendship forged in the birth of a movement creates its own rules. One was loyalty to the cause above all else. Sharing such a belief system can be as heavy as love itself. Ask any war veteran.

Reluctantly, I considered several possibilities for the upcoming meeting. Develop cogent arguments and stick to them no matter what; take on the role of resident reporter and refuse to participate; simply beg them to change their minds, appealing to sisterhood, their concern for the women in prison, their desire not to be divisive, and so on. Still, I sensed a miserable outcome, remembering Jessica's influence at another meeting a year before. About fifty women had come together to plan a sit-in at a radio news station in order to read a Declaration of Truth about the war over the airwaves. Three-quarters of the group wanted to inform the station of our intentions, hoping to stave off police or any violence. Jessica explained in considerable detail how it would be detrimental to prepare them for our sit-in. How the element of surprise would give us the edge. Expecting them to collude with us or meet our demand was infantile thinking, she said, and gave convincing historic examples. By the end of her riff, everyone agreed with her.

So it was with trepidation that I made my way to Jessica's meeting. It was held in someone's brownstone basement, converted into a lovely apartment with wood-paneled walls, indirect lighting, gorgeous leather couch and chairs, terra-cotta-tiled floor. About fifteen women sat around chatting. I had invited eight women (my side of the argument), but only four were there. Jessica arrived. She waved to the room, then took a seat away from me.

A few minutes later in walked three very well-known Black Panther women, whose activism, charisma, and great resiliency were respected by all. Ahead of her fury, I saw the question in Jessica's eyes: Who invited them? I had told one of the women about the situation, never expecting she'd attend. But there she was with two others. Chatter ended.

Jessica was the first to speak. She said we were a new movement and needed to declare our sovereignty before we could be inclusive. That meant a women's march should be only women.

Once more I responded that anyone wanting to work for women's liberation was welcome, how could it be otherwise? And round we went, various people saying the same things in different ways. The Panther women, though, remained quiet, making us hear our words ever louder until nothing we said resonated.

Jessica, however, was spurred on to even more eloquent pronouncements: Men have too often come between women, she said. Men have not yet learned to let women lead. Men will have to see the power of women before they will change. She warned if we continue to do what others want, if we always comply as women have done for aeons, we will never achieve our liberation. Therefore a women's march attended by men could only be undermined. How strange to agree with her analysis but not her conclusion.

When we had gone around too many times to find new arguments, one of the Panther women stood to speak.

"Listen, sisters, we appreciate this march for one of ours, we want to see it succeed, we believe it'll be a powerful demonstration of women together fighting for political justice. Freeing our sisters and freeing ourselves is a monumental part of a long struggle, but it is part of a struggle. And for us the struggle for justice is a struggle against racism, it's what it is. Therefore we insist that men, particularly black men, who wish to fight for the freedom of political prisoners be welcomed. Those women who refuse to march with black men can only seem racist. We demand the right of our brothers to march with us to free our sisters. It's the way it must be."

Then the Panther women excused themselves and left. There we sat, not in our usual circle but on two sides of the room. Nothing had been resolved. No one had convinced anyone differently. When I looked at Jessica, she turned away, which broke my heart. Although my sense of loss was immediate, I refused to reconsider my position.

The march turned out to be a huge success. Tens of thousands of women came from across the nation. New Haven was shut down in anticipation of our presence. And our presence was powerful. Women of all ages, colors, creeds, from all walks of life, with children and without, were there. So were the Black Panther men and women, but not Jessica or the women who agreed with her.

It was a memorable day for those who came, those who watched, and for the women in prison. It was also a day that marked a split in our never-to-be-whole-again movement. A split the media were happy to define as between the women who would relate to men and those who wouldn't, which was both too glib and too simplistic. More accurately, those who advocated "women only" saw it as a temporary but necessary time to get together without negative interference from men, who historically benefited from keeping women down. Other women continued to believe we could organize the men we lived and worked with to change. Eventually, I left the male-dominated political movement to join with women for our liberation.

Yet Jessica and I never spoke to each other again, although we remained active for years after. At mass gatherings and protests, it was easy to avoid meeting. However, coming together in someone's apartment was painful and awkward for both of us, I'm sure. But her stance was to ignore me, and I followed suit. Eventually she moved to another state and the difficult encounters ended.

What irony! Embedded in the struggle for women's liberation was the idea of sisterhood. That was to be our strength: women cooperating, not competing with each other, no more domination and hierarchy, gone the schism between the personal and the political. We would demand better birth control as well as an end to the war and racism. Unfortunately, because we were the children of a patriarchal society, sisterhood was not a given but an ideal for which to strive. Neither Jessica nor I could get past our righteousness.

It seems ludicrous now to have forfeited our deep friendship then over the issue of who could march. Why didn't we struggle it through? What in heaven's name did we have to lose? I've thought a great deal about this and concluded that back then any disagreement threatened the entire structure of our beliefs. We were young, and our politics hadn't been honed to a place of strength and confidence.

In one's twenties being right is important, being wrong, humiliating, devastating. But it felt more complicated. What changes with time is not our moral sense of right or wrong or our principles per se but the rigidity with which we hold them. And therein lies the problem for political friends: the possibility of allowing a sliver of disagreement to upend or taint an entire friendship.

So, yes, looking back I wish we had handled it differently, tried to save what was there between us, not let it flow away so easily. We may never have agreed about the march, but there was so much we did agree on.

Not long ago, I was on a panel about the subversive aspects of women's writing and saw Jessica in the audience. We hadn't shared the same space in more than ten years, and my eyes kept sliding to her face. I found her presence disquieting. So much time gone by, so many chunks of our lives hidden from each other. Should I seek her out at the end of the conference? What would I say? Clearly she knew I was there. Maybe pass by and smile, wave, or make some other kind of neutral but friendly gesture to give her an opportunity to express a word or two. I feared and wondered what her response would be. And a strange thought fizzed in my brain. After all, she'd been right, men had been the reason our friendship ended; unwittingly, it was true, but there we are. Would I share this with her if she offered to rummage through those days?

As the panel came to a close, Jessica slid quickly up the aisle and disappeared, her departure a statement. Disappointment and relief vied inside me. Now I'd never know if future possibilities existed. Then again, the burden of trying to recapture the past had been lifted, leaving my memories intact.

WANT

_____

Nuar Alsadir

WHEN I MET Ava, I was in my early twenties, living a life typical of many young women who come to New York City to find themselves. My quest for identity—a rummage for things that held traces of the person I wanted to become—played out in my every decision: whether to eat an egg special at Sidewalk Café or pierogies at Veselka, to see an old Hal Hartley film at the Film Anthology Archives or the art-house movie of the month at the Angelika. My apartment (like all apartments, a storehouse for remnants of my psyche) was decorated with flea-market finds: an antique birdcage, a banjo without a neck, a globe lamp that didn't light up—items picked up, like so many things in my life at the time, less for functionality than for appearance and mood. Insomniac hours were spent trying to figure out how to convert the storage space above the bathroom door into a giant fish tank, viewable from both kitchen and shower. One-off pieces of clothing—a pair of purple suede pants with red iron-on stars, which I wore until the last iron-on star had fallen off—hung off the edge of my wardrobe below vintage hats I'd bought in Paris. I was drawn to these things not only for their attractiveness but for the story they would tell about me. I seized upon items I wouldn't see on each passing woman or in anyone else's apartment. Whatever else I wanted from life, I wanted to be singular.

When you're young and female, however, singularity often comes in twos. Ava, sharing in my desire to be unique, joined my quest, and for a time we were driving toward the same point, in parallel. Critical to our closeness were some essential differences that kept our paths from colliding: I was an aspiring writer, she was an actor; I was eternally serious, she was a comic; she grew up in a rural town in the East, I was from a midwestern city; I was quiet, dark, an Arab ("exotic," as people say); she was blond, blue-eyed, and spoke bluntly. What we most had in common was that we liked to go out. Dressing up and exploring the city gave us the chance to figure out who we were.

AVA AND I met each other soon after we'd each moved to New York. We were at a party thrown by a mutual friend, a woman who had been an actor in high school and college but eventually tired of auditions and became a banker. The crowd was mostly dominated by guests from her new world, and I wasn't particularly close to the few people I already knew. Feeling bored, I scanned the room for someone to talk to. I spotted a short, thin blonde in a pink sixties A-line dress with bright white flowers and bell sleeves. Huge blue eyes that made her look childlike, almost angelic, quickly turned mischievous as she mimicked a guy holding forth to a group of women across the room. I gravitated toward her—that night and for months after—because I could tell that, with Ava, life would never be dull. She could transform a dud of an evening into a theater for her own amusement, disarming even the most reserved people by giving them an absurd challenge. Marching up to a stranger, she would say, "Try to smile without letting your eyes smile." As the corners of the person's mouth slowly turned upward, eyes fixed with maniacal focus on the opposite wall, he or she would inevitably break into laughter. Ava would then show how it was done—mouth smiling, eyes not—looking like one of the twin girls in *The Shining*.

She won people's attention by making them laugh—a talent I admired, although when it came to men, it frequently locked her in the role of perpetual best friend. To compensate, she often used her training as an actress to play (or, rather, overplay) the role of a seductress, emphasizing her sexuality to Jackie Collins extremes: gyrating when she danced, flirting with any boy who showed the slightest interest, and sleeping around with no thought of the consequences.

Ava didn't believe in regret. My first glimpse of how little she worried over what others thought of her came when we took a salsa class together. The studio was run by a stunning Cuban man, Eduardo, widely known as one of the best salsa dancers in the city. We both fell into mad crushes and would often imagine various unlikely schemes to win his attention. Bored at parties, we would sit in a corner dreaming of what would happen if, just then, Eduardo walked in, took us each by the hand, and spun us around the floor, dazzling our friends as well as the tired-looking boys who sat on the couches sipping their beers.

Once during class, as we did a basic three-step in front of the mirror, Eduardo looked over at Ava, clapped his hands to stop the music, and blurted with mock alarm, "No! Not so *obvious*—you not *segsy*!" He then turned back to the class and gave an impassioned, impromptu lecture on the erotic nature of subtlety. Ava kept her back erect and looked straight ahead, as though taking acting notes from a director. Rather than feel any embarrassment, she turned his rant into a joking part of our lexicon. The following evening, Ava cycled through a series of poses in front of my bedroom mirror, addressing herself in a Cuban accent, "Not so *obvious*—you not *segsy*!"

FOR AVA, IF you wanted to be a certain kind of person, all you had to do was act the part. Change came from the outside and burrowed its way in. "I can turn my feelings on or off like water," she would brag, dancing through the doorway of my apartment after a breakup, headphones overflowing with distortion and rave. Surrounded by people who affirmed her way of being, she'd hit on a strategy I respected, then coveted. I, too, wanted to transform myself into someone not weighed down by history.

I learned through Ava a new kind of thrill—the thrill of viewing oneself as a character that could be tweaked, edited, re-created. Before going out for the evening, we would meet at one of our apartments to swap clothing, style each other's hair, exchange makeup, share glitter. Borrowing each other's outfits—especially something unusual, like Ava's black pleather Avengers' dress, or my steel-tipped stilettos—allowed us to step outside of ourselves. Once in costume, we'd consider whom we might run into, discussing every conceivable social permutation and deciding which character would best handle these imagined encounters. Our night out would then be compared against these expectations, as though we were acting out a story we had already told ourselves, feeling our way through a script we'd already read.

This creativity carried over to more significant events too; everything became alterable in the retelling. Whenever something upset one of us, the other was there to recast things in a more positive light ("He didn't break up with you, he *set you free*"). We'd rearrange details so that the bad was muted and the good accentuated to such an extreme that we lived in an alternate universe, in which we could do no wrong. It was a friendship formed on hope and possibility. We were never just *being* but always *becoming*. "One must always live," we told ourselves, "as if on the brink of love." We were living, always, on the brink of love, desire, and countless other transformations one dreams of when young and living alone for the first time in a new city. As with most lifestyles lived at the brink, however, on the other side of exhilaration was the inevitable fall.

THE FIRST NOTICEABLE downturn in my friendship with Ava took place around my twenty-third birthday, almost a year after we'd become friends. My mother had sent me a hundred-dollar bill to buy myself a present. I wanted to spend it on something exotic, to feel a burst of novelty, like the sensation I'd had biting into salmon roe for the first time at a sushi bar on Avenue A. I phoned Ava, who, always up for an adventure, agreed to come out shopping with me. We met on the corner of Broadway and Fourth Street, beginning our quest in the center Village and radiating outward, through SoHo and Chinatown, then into NoLita and the East Village.

After an hour or so of desultory window-shopping, we stumbled into a shoe store on Second Avenue, a narrow space filled almost exclusively with black shoes, many covered with metal rings and studs. The salesperson—a glum woman in her twenties with blue hair, multiple piercings and tattoos, and a dog collar around her neck—refused to make eye contact with us until I asked to try on a pair of square-toed mules. The shoes were clearly *different*, if not quite attractive. I slipped them on, strutted around the store, and announced, "I'll take them!"

"You're making the right decision," Ava encouraged, looking me up and down. "They're really cool."

Turning to the saleswoman, I said, "I'd like to wear them out."

"Good idea," she muttered, hooking the inside heels of my old Mary Janes with two fingers as though they were dirty diapers being transferred to a boiling vat with tongs. After placing my old shoes in a box, she calculated the bill, and I paid with my birthday cash. As we walked out, I turned to Ava to describe my excitement over the purchase, but before I could speak she said, "You know what, I think I'm going to get a pair, too."

I looked at her in disbelief. "Why don't you just borrow mine?"

"I want my own pair," she said, annoyance creeping into her tone. Heading back into the store, she added under her breath, "What's the big deal?"

"No big deal," I said, feeling guilty for being possessive. But my exhilaration had turned to discomfort. I looked down at the shoes. The more I studied them and imagined Ava wearing an identical pair, the less I liked them. In fact, I didn't want them anymore. But they had already touched the street. There was no returning them.

DESIRE, EVEN FOR a pair of shoes, often conceals a complicated agenda—much in the way the word *want* has two definitions: to desire, and to lack. Combine these meanings, and you get the essence of longing, to desire what you lack. In order to understand a person's desire, you must first identify the lack it conceals.

I had no access to such depths within Ava, but what I was beginning to see made me think that her outward, imitative gestures were taking the place of an inner life. Ava, I decided, was a bit like Tom Ripley, the title character in Patricia Highsmith's *The Talented Mr. Ripley*, who used imitation to define himself. "If you wanted to be cheerful, or melancholic, or wistful, or thoughtful, or courteous," Ripley said, "you simply had to *act* those things with every gesture." In the novel, Ripley imitates to the point of murder, killing a man to usurp his identity. Although I certainly didn't fear that Ava would kill me, there was still a sense of violence in her imitation, some small death of self I experienced each time she used an inflection, a laugh, or an expression that I thought belonged to me. She was slowly, I thought in my most paranoid moments, cannibalizing me.

As I watched Ava shift through countless small transformations—some drawn from my identity, some from my closet, and others from the various people she encountered in her life (the way she tilted her head to look contemplative when she wasn't listening, which she'd adopted from a woman in her acting class, or the piratelike head scarf she'd seen on the model-waitress at our local café)—I began to wonder if I knew her at all. Her mercurial moods, which at the start of our friendship I'd found so intriguing, began to disturb me. The more conflicted my feelings became, the more the closeness I had thrived on turned oppressive. As I searched for ways to distance myself from her, I found myself keeping a close mental account of her every action.

Under this new, less compassionate scrutiny, Ava appeared to be taking greedy advantage of me. If we ordered pizza, I now noticed, she always reached first for the largest piece. When we ate out, even if she ordered a drink and I didn't, we would split the bill down the middle; if, on the other hand, I had a cocktail and she didn't, she would tabulate the difference and insist that I pay more. I invited her to parties, but she rarely reciprocated. If we planned to get ready to go out at my apartment, around dinnertime, she would show up with food for herself, or walk in carrying just one beer. Yet she would squeeze my bottle of expensive hair gel as if she were sucking out the last dollop through a straw.

Soon she moved beyond my wardrobe and possessions to my opinions. Once, we were having a conversation about anorexia, a subject that for Ava cut scarily close to her own anxieties about weight. Referring to *The Best Little Girl in the World* (a young adult novel told from the perspective of an anorexic teen), I said that when I'd read the book in high school, I'd found the story oddly inspirational—the psychological control the main character exerted over her body showed a steely resolve that I found compelling. Even as I expressed this sentiment, I knew that I was being more than a little sadistic—one of Ava's primary issues had always been a lack of impulse control, particularly when it came to eating. To maintain her figure, she paid for binges with starvation, and though to me she looked thin, she often complained she was fat.

If I felt a slight tinge of guilt then, months later, when I heard her parrot the same idea about anorexics and self-control in front of a mutual friend, I felt only annoyance. "That's sick," I said. "How can you go around *espousing* anorexia? Do you have any idea what it does to people? Next, you'll say you admire torturers for their precision." As the two listened to my tirade, Ava kept quiet. She couldn't point out that I was contradicting something I'd said earlier, because it would mean acknowledging that she'd stolen the idea. It was manipulative and downright mean on my part, but I couldn't help myself. When I saw my words strut out of her mouth, I had to stick out my tongue to trip them.

I'd hoped this little contretemps would slow her encroachment, but I was too late. Ava had already moved beyond imitation and was circling in on my desires. If I had a crush on someone, she would encourage me, then flirt with the guy when she thought I was out of sight. When I had a boyfriend, she would find an excuse to e-mail him, saying she was arranging plans for all of us yet somehow making me feel like the odd one out. Still, most of her behaviors could be interpreted in multiple ways, so I was never sure that I wasn't simply being paranoid. Even so, I stopped introducing her to the new people in my life and slowly became downright secretive. If she wanted to know where I'd bought a new article of clothing, I'd lie and tell her that I couldn't remember the name of the store or that it had been a gift. Anything she wanted to borrow was "at the cleaners" or "had a tear." Our friendship began to feel unsteady.

AS I LOOK back and try to explain why I continued my friendship with Ava, I tell myself that we shared a strange love, which—whatever its other effects—was flattering to me. At the most basic level, she paid meticulous attention to my thoughts and actions. Once, I had a boyfriend who was apartment-sitting for me while I was out of town. Realizing that I'd left my journal in the apartment, I panicked and immediately called him to beg, "If you see my journal lying around, *please* promise not to read it." He was tuning his guitar as I asked this, only half listening to me as he turned a peg to get a sharper note. I understood instantaneously—even as my words mingled with his twangs—that he would never bother to read my journal. He wasn't curious about me in a way that would compel him to poke through my private thoughts. Knowing Ava not only listened to me but would remember something I'd said as though she were quoting Nietzsche kept me close to her. When we talked, I felt brilliant, fascinating; she brought out the version of myself I liked most, a person self-consciousness normally held down.

"There are thousands of him, but only one *you*," she told me once. I'd called her late at night, months after the last incident with my boyfriend, when I was again feeling disappointed. I said whoever I was, I didn't want to be that person any longer. I wanted to be more like her, the kind of person who refuses to *take it*, someone a person could lose for good if he screwed up. If she were in my position, she would have behaved as though she didn't care, assuming that eventually her emotions would fall into place.

Yet the flip side of the belief that you are free to try on identities like clothing is that you don't have to be held responsible for your actions—as long you keep moving and changing, there's no accountability. This is rarely the case in a romantic relationship because, inevitably, a conversation will take place, and your true feelings will come out, as mine did with my boyfriend in the wee hours of that night. Such a working through of issues was impossible for me and Ava, even though I was much closer to her than I was to my boyfriend. No matter how intimate, friendships are rarely like romantic relationships. Nothing is owed, and there is a tacit understanding that you do not have to "work on things"—you would never "break up" as you might do with someone you were dating. After all, how often do friends go to therapists together the way couples see counselors?

As I backed away from any opportunity for a discussion with Ava, a gaping hole formed at the heart of our friendship. Just as when someone ignores you, it is natural to repeat yourself in louder and louder tones until the person responds, my passivity made her bolder, and more pathological in her dealings with me.

THAT SUMMER, I was going home to visit my family for three weeks, and Ava had agreed to look after my cat, Flotsam. Although this was a huge favor to me, I knew it would also give Ava an opportunity to have a break from her roommate and to use my phone to make long-distance calls. The second week I was away, Ava was invited to a party by my boyfriend, whom at that point I'd been dating for about eight months. He was co-hosting a big bash with friends—the kind of party that had been in the planning stages for a long time, the kind that, as a new girlfriend, you feel a certain anxiety about missing. I'd become increasingly uncomfortable with the way Ava interacted with this boyfriend, especially since she knew how insecure I was about the relationship. It seemed she was always finding excuses to touch him, whether to fix his hair, pick lint off his sweater, or dab imaginary ketchup from the side of his mouth with her finger.

"I invited Ava," he told me over the phone as he listed who would be at the party.

"That's good," I said, not telling him that she hadn't mentioned it to me or that the idea of her being there made me ill. I decided to hide my anxiety—afraid that making a big deal of her coming would only intrigue him—and changed the subject.

When Ava called later that night, I didn't bring up the party, nor did I react when she did, saying in passing, "I'll keep an eye on him for you." Instead, I decided I would call another friend who'd be there and ask her to spy for me.

When the night of the party arrived, I couldn't eat, read, or concentrate on anything. I envisioned scenarios both at and after the party, scenarios that eventually threw me into a fit of paranoia. I became convinced that something had been going on between Ava and my boyfriend for some time and decided to search his e-mails for evidence. All I had to do was log on with his username and try to figure out his password (it was made up of six characters, which meant there were only about seventeen billion permutations). I distracted myself by sitting in front of the computer typing in password possibilities, starting with his cat's name, his mother's name, his favorite bands and, eventually, just hitting the keys haphazardly. After a few hours, I gave up and went to sleep feeling not quite as desperate as I had before.

The next morning, I called my spy. "How was the party?" I asked casually.

"Fun," she told me, listing who had been there and then relaying a long story about an incident involving two friends of hers I barely knew. Finally, I got up the nerve to ask if she'd seen Ava. "Yeah," she said. "She was there with that friend of hers, the one who always drinks too much and ends up—"

"Was she talking to him?" I interrupted, getting to the point.

"Who? Her friend?"

"No, Ava."

"Talking to who?" she asked.

"My boyfriend," I said.

"Not really," she said, trying to remember. "She seemed pretty out of place—though, come to think of it, I do remember seeing her with him on the dance floor." She paused for a few seconds, then asked, "Why was she wearing your clothing?"

Although I had fully expected to hear that she had been flirting with my boyfriend, I hadn't imagined that Ava had the cojones to do so in one of my outfits. To go after him, that is, as me.

"She was wearing your long black skirt and green silk Chinese top," she continued. "I think the shoes may have been yours, too. They were black with red flowers."

My suspicions had been realized, I thought. This new form of imitation—which seemed more a way of supplanting me than anything else—made me realize that I had to be on my guard. I imagined Ava flitting about in my black skirt, which was too tight for her and now no doubt misshapen, and knew I would never wear that skirt again.

"IMITATION IS THE highest form of flattery," my mother used to say when I complained about copycats in school. Easily one of the stupidest platitudes in our language, the proverb disturbed me, particularly coming from my mother, whose view on stealing stood in stark contrast to what she was telling me. "It is stealing," she would say, "to take a pen from an office where you work, to take more packets of ketchup than you need from McDonald's, to be given too much change and keep it." Because of this, I had developed such anxiety around stealing that it became difficult for me to take anything, even trivial things, from anyone.

The primal scene of my anxiety transpired when I was five. I was with my mother in Mr. G's, a local grocery store a few blocks from where I grew up on the South Side of Chicago. As we walked down the baking aisle, I spotted a bag of walnuts, plastic ripped open just under the paper label. Although I didn't particularly like walnuts, I reached in, took one, popped it in my mouth, and continued down the aisle with a vague sense of triumph. Later, as my mother loaded the groceries into the back of our Chevy wagon, I told her about the walnut, thinking she'd be proud because she was always encouraging me to eat raisins and nuts instead of candy.

She put the last grocery bag in the way back, turned, placed one hand on her hip, and lowered her eyebrows. "That's stealing," she said and, gripping my arm, marched me back into the store to the manager's booth. She knocked on the pane and—I now know—somehow communicated to the manager that she wanted to teach me a lesson. "Go ahead," my mother said, nudging me forward. "Tell her what you did."

"I saw an open bag of walnuts," I said, utterly terrified, "and took one." I had often seen adults try nuts and olives from the big barrels at the health food store and didn't quite understand how what I'd done was any different.

"Well," the manager began in a deep voice, "you know you're not supposed to take things that aren't yours. Now, give it back."

"I don't have it anymore!" I gasped, horrified. "I ate it."

"What do you mean," she asked, looking down at me over her glasses, "you *ate it*? It wasn't yours to eat."

"I'm sorry," I said. "I can't give it back. It's gone."

Stealing has always disturbed me because it's not only a taking but a kind of *incorporation*, a transformation that prevents the stolen item from returning to its original state. One morning when I was seven, we woke to discover that my parents' Buick Regal was gone. A week later, my father received a call telling him the police had tracked the car down. After he got off the phone, he said, flatly, "They found it," and walked out of the room. Later I heard him tell my mother, when he thought my brother and I were sleeping, that the car had been hot-wired and driven to the other side of town to be used as a venue in which to "turn tricks." I pictured peeking through its windows and seeing a diorama-scale circus act, and thought my father was going to surprise us with our new car-turned-circus-tent in the morning. When it wasn't back in our driveway a week later, I asked when we were going to get the Regal back. Thinking my father hadn't heard when he didn't answer, I asked again. He looked up and, angry at me, I thought, for asking twice, said, "You'll never set eyes on that car again."

ALTHOUGH YOU'D THINK I would have learned my lesson, the next time I had plans to go out of town for more than a few days, I turned to Ava. I don't know whether I was testing her, trying to give her a second chance, or just needed a cat sitter and was in a convenient state of denial. Either way, in hindsight, I realize how bizarre it was that I asked Ava to look after Flotsam again.

My boyfriend would soon be moving out of the city to start a new job, and I decided to throw a going-away party for him. Because I was returning from my vacation only one day before the party, I would have to hustle to get the place ready. I wanted to make enough food so that people wouldn't have to leave the party to get something to eat, but I didn't have much in the fridge and didn't really know how to cook. I made the only thing I knew well—pasta sauce—and called it "Italian salsa." It sat untouched in a big bowl next to bread and a variety of cheeses.

I'd invited thirty-five or forty people, and when they all showed up and crammed themselves into my three-hundred-square-foot studio apartment, they appeared to be huddling for warmth. Flotsam spent most of the party perched on the stereo high atop the fridge. As the guests arrived, I gave what I would call a "tour" of the place, extending my hand to the right, toward the stove, I'd say, "The Kitchen," then, pointing to the couch, "The Living Room." Taking approximately five steps forward, I'd extend my hand toward the desk and say, "The Study," and to the mattress on the floor, "The Bedroom." There was no point in the apartment where one could stand and not see all other points. Periodically, I'd hear my boyfriend say to someone,

"And this is Italian salsa." Plastic cups with wine dregs and cigarette butts sat next to my computer, empty beer cans covered a stack of unfinished work, green bottles balanced precariously on the edges of my bookshelves, on top of my medicine cabinet, on the ledge of the tub beside my shampoo. For weeks after the party, I would wake in the middle of the night to the sounds of Flotsam swatting and chasing a lost cork she had found under the furniture.

Ava showed up with her special artichoke dip and helped me host, spending much of the party near the intercom buzzing people in and greeting them at the door. Periodically, she'd pull me toward her by the arm and whisper, "I'm sending someone out for more beer." Or "We're shuffling through Hole again—I'm going to change the CDs." That night, she was radiant, introducing herself to everyone, accepting little scraps of paper with numbers scrawled on them every time I glanced in her direction. She walked out of my apartment, well past 3:00 A.M., with a bag of clanging bottles in either hand.

The night after the party, as I was getting ready for a bon voyage dinner with my boyfriend, I went to my closet to get a red leather jacket my brother had picked up for me at a flea market in Spain. It wasn't there. I emptied the closet, figuring the jacket had to be somewhere inside since there was no other place in my tiny studio where it could be. Perhaps in my rush to straighten up, I thought, I'd absentmindedly stuffed it in an unusual spot to get it out of the way. I searched the room methodically but couldn't find it anywhere.

Could someone have stolen the jacket during the party? I wondered. I didn't want to ask my boyfriend until I was absolutely sure it was missing. Most of the people at the party had been friends of his I didn't know well, and the question might seem accusatory. Plus, I'd been leaning on reticence since the earlier disappointments in our relationship—working things out in my head rather than in the open—happy with what seemed to be the effects of pretending to be just blasé enough to make *him* the one who was scrambling to make things work.

Besides, I told myself, people had been filing through the apartment all night—it was unimaginable that someone could have rifled through my closet and taken the jacket without anyone seeing. Afraid of being late, I grabbed a sweater and, as I walked to the restaurant, ran all the possibilities of what could have happened to the jacket through my mind.

When I got home, I called Ava, to thank her for all her help and to see what she thought. She knew my apartment well, had been overseeing the party, and would be able to sort through my suspicions with me. I told her about the jacket, how I'd looked everywhere, but as I began my analysis she cut me off.

"I'm sure no one at the party stole it—you probably just forgot where you put it," she said, biting into what sounded like an apple. Slurping the juice into her mouth in order to speak, she added dismissively, *"I'hill tur up."* Then, sounding distracted, she changed the subject and made an excuse to get off the phone.

I hung up the receiver. A hollow feeling came over me as I thought the unthinkable: Ava stole my jacket. I wouldn't have suspected her had she not already crossed a boundary by borrowing my clothing without asking, but at that point I knew anything was possible. Most irritatingly, the jacket had meant something special to me because it had been a gift from my brother. To anyone else, it would be just an old, worn-out item— its leather cracked and stained, its lining ripped at one armpit so that you'd hit a dead end when you slipped your hand into the sleeve. I couldn't understand how the jacket could be the object of anyone's desire.

There was a man I'd once known who confessed to me that he stole something from every woman he slept with. Soon after the party, Ava entered my dream life and was often displaced by this man in the midst of scenes. She would turn the corner and he would walk toward me, confident, lit from behind, wearing my jacket.

I FELT DEPLETED. I couldn't think about Ava or the jacket anymore, and as our friendship seemed to be on hold, I became more and more comfortable putting her out of my mind. Three months later I received a letter from Ava. She explained the mystery of the missing jacket as though it had been an honest mistake: she'd borrowed it, forgotten to return it before I came back into town, and didn't know why she hadn't told me about it when I'd called. She then figured she'd use the set of keys she still had to sneak back into my apartment and place the jacket somewhere, gaslighting me into thinking I'd overlooked it—but she never got around to it.

She'd understand, the letter continued, if I never wanted to speak to her again, but she wanted to return the jacket. "Call me and let me know how you want me to get it back to you," she wrote.

I called and told her I'd received her letter. Yet I couldn't bear to enter into her reasoning. I imagined she would explain away the action or try to turn it into a joke. Instead of either scenario, I asked a simple question, "Are you still in therapy?"

"Yes," she answered, slightly bewildered.

"Then why don't you give me the jacket back the next time you see me and we'll continue being friends without discussing it. Just promise me you'll talk to your therapist about what you did." I didn't want to hear her explanations, to embarrass her, or to be embarrassed myself. I didn't want to make her say aloud what, at some level, I already knew. We had become like bitter lovers who could only taste the bitterness and didn't know how to talk about our love.

I reverted to the approach to life I'd learned from Ava, shifting to a new persona rather than taking responsibility for the one that may have done wrong. Ironically, Ava and I both loved a Madonna song that was popular at the time, "Human Nature," in which she sings the line "I'm not your bitch don't hang your shit on me." The funny thing is that I'd always missed the point of the song, that she was singing to someone who wouldn't let her speak her mind—"You wouldn't let me say the words I longed to say." I'd always chosen to see only the perspective of the person refusing to be dumped on.

My friendship with Ava remained cordial but was maintained in the way something you stick in the freezer and forget about is maintained—even if it's still "good," much of the flavor has escaped. The intensity the relationship had possessed in the early years was gone, and we passed through year after year with minimal contact, meeting only for coffee or a drink every six months or so.

Shortly after our friendship cooled, Ava got married, and it was only many years later, after I was also married and had given birth to my daughter, that I had any insight into what had precipitated our breaking point. One day, while I was watching my daughter kick on her play mat, the buzzer rang. It was the UPS man with a package. I carried the small box into the apartment and was stunned to find Ava's return address scrawled in the upper left corner. Inside was a gift for my daughter—a stylish little girl's dress, which Ava had obviously put a great deal of care into selecting. We hadn't spoken in years, but we had friends in common who must have told her I'd had a baby.

She'd enclosed a note wishing me well and apologizing for being out of touch. In a long paragraph explaining why she hadn't contacted me and her perspective on why our friendship had faltered, she slipped in a sentence that stuck in my mind because of its peculiarity: "I figured you no longer had any use for me." There was no mention of the jacket.

Still puzzling over all of this a few days later, I stumbled on another insight. As I was trying to determine whether or not my daughter was teething, I turned to T. Berry Brazelton's *Touch-*

points: Your Child's Emotional and Behavioral Development. Flipping through the chapters, I came to a section on stealing, which, as I read it, made me think of Ava:

> A more subtle reason for stealing is the desire to identify with others. As the intense desire to identify with his parents, his siblings, or his schoolmates increases, he may take important things from them. In his own concrete way of thinking, he will believe that having a possession of the other person's amounts to being like the other person.

I wondered whether imitating me and, more significantly, stealing from me, could have been Ava's reaction to my having pulled away from our friendship. Maybe, I thought, as we moved apart and I began to detach myself from her, stealing was her way of clinging to our former friendship, returning to the relationship that once made us feel excited to be ourselves.

Yet even as I recognized that Ava's stealing my jacket had been a complicated act, not only of covetousness but also of identification and love, this insight did not make me return to her. Our friendship had become like my family's Regal, a car in which someone had been turning tricks. What it had once meant, where it might have taken us, was gone. There was no way to recover it.

TENURE

Patricia Marx

I F YOU AND I ever become friends, we will remain friends forever. This is not because you are such a terrific person, though I'm sure you are. (I've heard great things about you!) No. The credit—I hope you won't mind—must be assigned to me. I am the most easygoing, accommodating, nonjudgmental, and unassuming friend in the world, and if we ever meet, you better agree or else.

Ask Audrey.

Audrey and I had been great pals for years when she stopped talking to me with no warning and, as far as I could tell, for no reason. We went from a few phone conversations a day to zero. If I ran into Audrey at a party, she conspicuously snubbed me. I could be wrong about this, but I think I once saw Audrey cross the street to avoid me. Most people in a similar situation would say something like "Hey, Audrey, I couldn't help but notice that when I walked into the Lincoln Plaza Cinema last night, you ran out of the theater as if it were on fire."

And what did I say to Audrey about her strange behavior? Absolutely nothing. Audrey had steered clear of me for a year, and my response was to act as if nothing out of the ordinary had happened. Then one day, I found myself on the same airplane as Audrey. It crossed my mind that she might jump out the window. Instead, she arranged to sit next to me. We chatted merrily during the flight. Though I was curious, I never once asked her for an explanation of that year of silence. I figured: whatever the reason, it couldn't be good. Besides, she had gotten over it. Our friendship had resumed. So why rock the plane?

I do not believe in the power of Meaningful Talks, except when they relate to problems arising out of hair or makeup. Otherwise, confrontations, in my opinion, serve only to make the plaintiff feel better for making the other person feel bad—and to make both parties embarrassed (imagine being inside a self-help book). Does anybody really change as a result of self-conscious dialogue? I don't think so, at least not for the better.

LET ME GIVE you an example of how much I hate honest discourse. A few years ago, I received a phone call from Nancy, a childhood frenemy of mine. (A frenemy is half friend, half enemy—a modern-day mythical being.) "I was wondering if you could give me some advice about a problem I am having with my best friend, Charlotte," Nancy said in an earnest tone that immediately caused me to worry. I hadn't talked to Nancy since high school, which had been about thirty years earlier. Nancy explained that Charlotte had recently told her she "needed more space" and asked that they not see each other for a few months. "I remembered," said Nancy, "that you had also withdrawn from me in high school, and I thought if you could tell me why you did that, it might help me in my relationship with Charlotte."

Oh, boy. The truth was I had never liked Nancy very much and I liked her less after she began to copy my mannerisms and speech patterns and to wear the same clothes that I did. I felt her attention had been, to put it generously, cloying. "I guess I was just jealous of you," I said, improvising. "For being a cheerleader."

"You were jealous of me?!" said Nancy, obviously relieved. "I was jealous of you for being on Student Council."

I may not believe in self-conscious talks between friends, but I do believe in "Friend Tenure." If I like you enough and for a long enough time—as was the case with Audrey but not with Nancy—then you will be rewarded with permanent friend status. As my everlasting friend, you can get away with whatever is less than murder, and even murder in certain circumstances—I'm thinking of a few people in particular—is acceptable. The jealousies, resentments, and squabbles that tear apart so many others will never undo us because, out of respect, I hold those I am really fond of to a lower standard than I do other people.

That's not all! As part of your tenure package, here's what you get:

You don't have to return my phone calls. If I must know, for instance, the name of the dry cleaner you swear is terrific and you fail to get back to me, I'll call again—and, if need be, again. I don't keep a mental ledger of phone calls. I am Patty of Little Pride.

Nor do you have to invite me to all your parties. I fully understand that you have many friends and a small place. To tell you the truth, I like gossiping about the party more than I like being at the party. So do me a favor: have your party without me and give me a juicy report the next day.

If we are supposed to go to the movies tomorrow night and you want to cancel tomorrow afternoon—let's say, you got a better invitation—go right ahead. I adore a night off. If you want to make me especially happy, e-mail with the news that, although you and I have no plans for tonight, if we had, you are busy and we must reschedule.

If you buy the same dress I just bought, that's okay. But if you decide to wear it to Susan's party after I told you that's what I'd be wearing, I'd prefer you to be a few pounds heavier than I am that night.

If you tell me that I can have your extra ticket to the Madonna concert and then you decide to give the ticket to your mother instead of to me, I will forgive you even though I like Madonna better than I like you.

I don't have any children, so you can't possibly offend me by saying something nasty about them. Ditto my husband. I'm not married, but if I were, he'd probably be getting on my nerves by this time anyway.

If you'd like to tell me in painstaking detail about the dream you had last night, I will pretend to be engrossed.

There will be no rows. I only like arguing with people I agree with. Also, no gifts. Please do not be offended, but upon meeting you, if it looks as if a friendship may develop, I may ask you to sign a "no gift" agreement.

And of course, as Audrey will attest, there is no way to drop me (though, as Nancy discovered, I may drop you). If you decide never to talk to me again, I will consider you a strong, silent friend, or even elusive. If you move away without letting me know your new whereabouts, I will consider you a friend on sabbatical.

Finally, as part of the tenure package, you get *me*, the friend who is easier to take care of than a Teflon pan. By the way, there is one slight problem. Since I never get rid of friends, I have at present no vacancies.

You'll Be All Right

Elissa Schappell

ON LOOKS ALONE, I would never have picked
Monica to be my friend, not in a million years. It wasn't
just that we didn't live in the same neighborhood, or go to the
same school. My public high school prided itself on being the
private school of public schools. When kids got kicked out of private school, or sent home from boarding school, my school was
where they ended up. Some of the public school girls were
invited to the Junior League's cotillions and hunt club balls. But
despite the invitations and our airs, despite dating the occasional
du Pont relative, make no mistake, we were just passing. That
knowledge, that I was just passing, gave me great solace at
times—I wasn't one of these spoiled and petty bourgeois pigs in
the Lilly Pulitzer dresses and the pearl earrings the size of
olives—and other times it caused me great torment. I wanted
the power that came with acceptance by these people, and it
blinded me in ways I am still ashamed of.

The summer of my junior year of college, I was living at

home with my parents and working at a TV station in Wilmington, Delaware. My boyfriend, Tim, was in Philadelphia working at a law firm; we saw each other on weekends. Tim, always the patriotic one, wanted us to lose our virginities together on Memorial Day (I had lied to him and told him I too was a virgin), and so in the side yard of my parents' house—with the words *cherry bomb* going off in my head—I got pregnant.

In the beginning when I felt queasy, I told myself it was my nervous stomach. I was developing an ulcer at college, and I attributed the nausea to nerves. After all, it was only the second week of work at the TV station and the first week hadn't gone so well because, while I had no problem in my other part-time job—which involved taking hits off the nitrous tank and delivering singing balloon telegrams to children's birthday parties and new orthodontic practices—I had no idea what it meant to work in a newsroom. I was a fiction writer, my experience in journalism limited to a class in journalistic ethics (an oxymoron), in which we worshiped Edward R. Murrow.

I thought about calling in sick, but my mother was home, and under no circumstances did I want my mother to suspect what I feared was true, what I didn't even allow myself to ponder. I didn't want anyone to know. Not my sister, and certainly not my college friends—all of whom adored Tim—and not my childhood friends, with whom I had gone through a sort of stages of sexuality, not unlike Kübler-Ross's stages of dying—first came denial of sexuality, then anger, then bargaining, and depression, and finally acceptance.

In our little hothouse of a universe, talking about sex was like talking about money. Only no money and new money talk about money. Reputations, and sex lives, were treasured and polished like the family silver. What did you have, really, but your reputation?

Anyway, as soon as I'd gotten the results of my test, I'd scheduled an abortion for the next month. The doctor insisted it was the earliest time she could give me, but I couldn't help thinking that she was trying to punish me, for what I felt most deeply was a sin. What was there to talk about?

I couldn't not tell Tim, I had to tell him.

I'd wanted to tell him in person that weekend when he came to visit but instead had blurted it out during our evening phone call.

"How can this be happening to us?" he said over and over again, seemingly stunned. "This isn't supposed to happen."

"I know." I felt tricked, and small and dirty.

There was no sound on the line for a few seconds. I could hear him breathing hard, trying not to cry.

"Are you sure?" he said.

"Yes, I'm sure."

"Ah shit," he said. "You know what, I love you."

"I love you too."

"Okay, so let's do it."

"What?" I said, my stomach clenching, not wanting him to say another word.

"Elissa," he said, "will you marry me?"

I started to cry. It was all so wrong, and sad.

"I mean it," he pleaded. "Let's have the baby. We can have the baby. It's our baby. We'll move in together, get an apartment, we can do it."

"Are you joking?" I said.

"No."

"Okay, sure, we can have a baby—and what will we tell your parents?" I said, knowing this would sober him up. "Hmm? That we're babysitting it? Or maybe we could hide it and tell them the place is trashed and reeks because we got a puppy?"

"I mean it."

"I know."

I knew, and Tim knew, that having a baby and getting married in college was something we would never do. We swore each other to secrecy.

It was a hard secret to keep, but we'd keep it.

When I met Monica, she was tearing copy from the AP machine. She was wearing glasses and looked about ten years older than me, though she wasn't. I guessed she'd gone to Del Tech or Christiana High School, both located in a part of town known mostly for its mall and racetrack. I bet she'd been on the silk squad, one of those girls in hot pants and boots who twirled the flags while the band played, or maybe, once, she'd been one of those smoking lounge kids who hung out outside the building, her hair shading her eyes. Either way, I bet she knew how to fight, both kids and grown-ups.

Monica was dressed to impress, and the combination of her looks and her ambition—she was going to be on the nightly news—made me aware of how silly I looked, and it also made me feel her vulnerability. She was serious about this, and thus she could be disappointed. I protected myself at all costs from ever appearing serious about anything, simply for this reason. Her outfit—dictated it seemed by *What Color Is Your Parachute?*—was a dove gray midthigh skirt, a blazer and white silky necktie blouse, and despite the heat and humidity she was wearing suntan-colored panty hose (over a gold anklet) and sensible bone-colored pumps. Her face was fully made up: foundation, powder, cover-up, blush, eyeliner, eye shadow, mascara, lip liner, lipstick, and gloss, like she was going to be on the news, not making coffee in the newsroom. Already she had blond anchorwoman hair, set curls that did not move. I wondered what she thought of my own mop of hair, cut short in the back and left long in the front, like a punk rock Veronica Lake, which I had in assorted fits of depression, or drunkenness, streaked blond and white. No doubt she wondered how in the world my face, with its desperately pale skin, heavily mascaraed lashes, and frosted lips, would register on camera.

It fell to Monica to show me the ropes—the Xerox machine, the dictionaries, the coffeemaker, the AP news service, where we tore news and turned it into copy, chronicling a day's worth of Delaware news: a small fire behind the Burger King, the vandalizing of a statue of William Penn in a local park. While she sat and typed up stories, I hunted and pecked along the typewriter keys, wishing to hell I hadn't cut typing class to make out in the car of some forgettable boy. After an hour I'd used up an entire roll of eraser tape.

She barely seemed to notice me.

Days later, after we'd eaten lunch together side by side, I found out that, unlike me, Monica didn't live with her parents. In fact, she said nothing about her parents at all. She had gone to the University of Delaware, and was taking a semester off. She was living in a new subdivision, one of those that had (to my family's horror) sprouted up like a fungus in the farmlands near to our house over the past few years. She said she lived with her fiancé, Ron, but I didn't think the ring she wore on her left hand was an engagement ring. The house was her fiancé's place, she said; she'd moved in a year ago.

"I like the area," she said. "The grass and all, the trees, you know."

"It's nice." I shrugged. My parents still lived in the house I grew up in.

"Yeah." She laughed. "It'll do."

I wasn't sure if she was being sarcastic or honest.

She asked if I had a boyfriend, and I told her about Tim. "Sounds nice," she said—which was what everybody said about Tim.

"Yeah, well . . . ," I said. It seemed everybody, from Tim's friends to my own, thought he was too much of a nice guy for me. Even my own parents thought he was the perfect gentleman.

"I know," Monica said. "You never really know what goes on with people, do you?"

———

I BEGAN RIDING to work with Monica after two weeks of my mother driving me the half an hour into Wilmington to drop me off and my father bringing me home after work, this despite my polite objections—I didn't want to put her out—and my fear that it would be awkward to be alone with her in a car—what would we talk about?

The first morning I agreed to let Monica drive me to work, I had to knock twice. At first when she opened the door I thought she was sorry I'd come.

"Hi," she said, talking through a crack in the door. "I'll just be a minute."

She shut the door, but I could hear her talking to someone in the house. As I stood on the porch leaning against the windows, I listened while pretending interest in the houses around me. Tiny azalea and holly bushes had been planted far apart, which made them seem very small and suggested a kind of hope, a dream that one day they'd grow so they filled up the spaces. In every other way the houses were identical gray and brown, nearly undistinguishable one from another. Monica didn't have an American flag on her door, or a chickadee painted on her mailbox. If I ever lost her address, I'd never find her again.

"And don't run the air conditioner . . . ," I heard a man inside say. "I mean it. . . ."

Even though it was just 8:00, it was already hot and humid. I looked through the window—there was the shadow of a man, with a flat-top haircut, the kind you see on gym teachers and ROTC guys. I couldn't really tell, but he seemed a lot older than Monica.

Monica slammed the front door behind her. "Come on," she said, walking briskly to her car and getting into the little blue Toyota.

"Is that your fiancé?" I asked, dumbly following her.

"Yep," she said as she backed up fast out of the driveway.

Monica didn't run the AC. We stopped at the 7-Eleven and bought Big Gulp–size Tabs, and despite the fact I'd had bacon and toast for breakfast, I got donut gems. Monica never ate any of that crap. She was watching her weight, one day it would matter, as the camera, cruel as it was, added at least ten pounds to a body. At lunchtime, she always ate a salad she'd brought from home, or a yogurt and an apple. Meanwhile, I ate the peanut butter and Marshmallow Fluff on wheat sandwich my mother had packed me "just in case," as a sort of emergency sandwich should there not be time for me to grab lunch, or should I be, as in this case, just too chicken to venture out alone. I ate fast, embarrassed by the Fluff. How old was I?

If she wondered how I'd ever gotten the internship, Monica never said, or perhaps she just knew, just assumed that for girls like me there would always be someone to write a letter, a call that could be made by a family friend. Weren't girls like me used to getting what we wanted?

The copy we wrote was for the anchor, an older man who was handsome in a tired, dinner-theater Don Quixote sort of way. He patrolled around our tiny newsroom like a king, surveying his kingdom. He would on occasion pause at our little communal desk to talk to us, and when he did, he never missed an opportunity to flirt with Monica, touching her shoulder and making jokes. Although I'd attracted my share of older men and had boyfriends in college, I was invisible to him.

When he wanted something from us, like an update on a story, it was Monica he called into his office, and she'd rise obediently; other times, when he called out for a cup of coffee, she'd get up and roll her eyes like this was something she was used to, men calling to her, maybe putting their hands on her, and she could handle it. I didn't know if I could, and I never got a chance to try it. Monica was always there, a step ahead of me.

Sometimes while Monica was talking to the anchor, or working, looking up some reference, I'd slip away and talk to one of the women reporters who did double duty as the weather girl; sometimes I got to call the National Weather Service and take down the meteorology report; sometimes, while the weather girl was taking the shine off her nose, she'd let me affix the suns and storm clouds to the map.

I don't remember when it became clear that Monica wasn't actually on staff at the TV station. She'd never told me she was, I had just inferred it, but the longer I was there the clearer it became to me: despite the fact that Monica worked harder than I did, and was more professional than I was, the newsroom staff seemed nicer to me, more respectful. I didn't understand it. Perhaps the women felt threatened by her, by the attention the anchor gave her, not that she seemed to care.

I couldn't imagine how she was making ends meet. It wasn't just the bagged lunches, or the fact that, if you paid attention you could see she was rotating the same three outfits week in and week out. I knew that, while her fiancé supported her working at the station, and thought it was all well and good that she had this dream, she was soon going to have to get a real job.

The morning after Fourth of July weekend was the first day I threw up, and the first day Monica didn't meet me at the door ready to go. She opened the door and let me in. She'd woken up late, she said. She let me into the house; the radio on the windowsill was on the morning Zoo station, and she was still taking the hot rollers out of her hair. I thought it made her nervous to have me inside. There was a black-and-white picture of a man on the refrigerator. Why was Monica with him? Sure he had a job, and a house, but what else?

"Is that him?" I asked.

"Yep," she said. "That's from the church directory," she said. I didn't ask why she wasn't in the picture. Maybe it was an old picture.

"He's cute," I said, but it wasn't true exactly. He looked serious, intense, in a way that seemed both exciting and scary. He was wearing a short-sleeved dress shirt and a tie, which I bet was part of his job's uniform.

"I'll be right back, I ran my stocking," she said. As soon as she headed up the stairs, I started to look around the house. It had a strangely vacant, unlived-in feeling. Like whoever was living there was living very carefully, or maybe it was that the place seemed almost like a set, equipped as it was with the stock kitchen table, two chairs and a couch, a rocking chair, a grandfather clock, and a TV. I saw no traces of Monica anywhere.

In contrast, the living room, which was off the hallway, was full of furniture, all of it covered with clear plastic.

"All that's from his mother's house," she said, surprising me as I stood there staring. "I'm not supposed to go in there."

"Why not?" I was embarrassed to be caught spying.

"I am not allowed to sit on the furniture, not even supposed to even think about sitting on the furniture," she said. She was serious.

"What?" I'd never heard anything like that in my life.

"She hates me," Monica said, running her hands up her legs to check for runs. "Like I care."

I couldn't imagine anyone hating Monica. I wondered if maybe her fiancé was still married to somebody else—he seemed old enough—maybe his mother was on that woman's side.

After seeing Monica's house that day, I found myself telling her things I told only my closest friends. That my grandmother had had another stroke and so now couldn't speak at all or feed herself, that the food sometimes fell from her lips and spilled on her blouse, but still she insisted on being taken out to lunch. It took her hours to eat. I loved my grandmother and hated that I sometimes felt humiliated when I went out with her because of the way people stared. I told her my sister had to wear a back brace for years, and that although my father's cancer was in remission, I was sure he'd die soon.

We also talked about innocuous stuff, our weekends and what we'd done—I'd gone to Philadelphia, she'd gone to a baseball game, though she confessed, "We don't see that many people."

I wasn't sure if that meant Monica didn't have a lot of friends and wanted to be my friend or was telling me to keep my distance. Underneath our chatter was the sense that, at any minute, the line "maybe we could get together sometime" could pop up, each of us just waiting for the other to say it, or not say it.

As soon as we got into the car that day, I felt ill. I wanted to go home, but I couldn't, my mother was there, and I most certainly couldn't explain why it was I was home and crawling up into bed. What would I say—"I think I have a touch of the fetus"?

After about a mile, Monica turned to me. "What's wrong with you? Are you sick?"

"No," I said, though the motion of the car was making me nauseated. I stuck my head out the window and tried to breathe through my nose. I was afraid I was going to throw up, and I didn't want to do that in her car. I could only imagine what Ron would say about that.

"I'm fine." I felt tears start to come into my eyes.

"Where did you go last night?"

"Nowhere." I wiped my eyes on my sleeve. "You're right, maybe it's the flu."

"Right," she said; then after a minute, she said, "Roll up your window. I'm putting on the AC."

I knew I shouldn't let her do it, but I did.

When we got to work, she said, "Go sit down, I'll bring you some water."

She watched me drink it. I waited for her to say something, to tease me for being hungover or scold me for what I suspected she was already figuring out.

"How are you feeling?" she said quietly, like she knew already it was a secret.

"So much better," I lied.

By the time five o'clock came around, I did feel better. I'd had a lemon ice for lunch, and that seemed to help. Maybe everything was going to be all right, maybe, I thought, it would pass. So when the rest of the staff said they were going to go to a softball game some of them were going to be playing in, Monica and I decided to go too. We were flattered to be invited, and there was the giddy sense of escaping the routine of our usual friendship.

We stopped on the way to the game and picked up beer. We drove up to the diamond, parked, then walked over to the sideline and sat down in the grass. Suddenly, I felt a terrible pain in my stomach. I started to sweat and my mouth filled with saliva. When I stood up my legs felt weak and elastic as old rubber bands, but I knew I had to get away from everyone. I was walking as fast as I could, and as far as I could, almost making it over to the trees lining the street before I fell to my knees and threw up.

Moments later, Monica was beside me.

"I'm fine," I said.

"Come on," she said. "I'm taking you home."

When we got into the car, I told her. I told her what had happened, how bad I felt, how Tim was going to skip out of work next Friday and we were going to go to the hospital together, and how if his parents, conservative Republicans, ever found out, they would kill him and hate my guts forever, slut that I was.

My own parents couldn't know either.

"They'd kill me," I said. "No, they'd cry. They'd feel bad for me, disappointed. . . ."

I started to cry harder because this was the truth.

"It's good he's coming down." Monica said this like it meant something.

"He asked me to marry him," I said and laughed out loud. "Ha!"

"For real?" Monica said, and I could tell that she thought I was lucky.

"He's like that," I said. "He didn't mean it, not really."

"Are you going to be okay?"

"He's got money, I've got some," I said, suddenly so angry with myself. "I am so stupid. You know what he said? He said wearing a condom is like riding a bicycle with a noose around your neck."

"Men are idiots," she said.

"... And I was like, okay ..."

"... You're not the first."

"Well, I feel like I am going to hell." I was aware of how ridiculous it sounded but how true it felt. "I'm going to be punished."

"It was an accident," she said. "It's not like you're a bad person."

Monica didn't say anything for a moment, she just handed me tissues she found in her purse and squeezed my shoulder. Then she said, "*You'll* be all right. You know that." She looked me in the face, stared at me, like she could see the future, and then started the car.

If she said more than that on the ride home, I don't recall it. I just remember that: *You'll be all right.*

Of course, I didn't believe her then, but it was the truest thing she could have said. I would—be all right. Because of her, because of my parents, because of my boyfriend, because, because, because ...

And *she*, Monica, would be all right, but for different reasons. Not because of my friendship, sadly—no, none of the things that would save her would have anything to do with me.

Right then, though, nothing was, or would seem, all right for a very long time. However, that night, after telling Monica, I slept through the night for the first time in weeks.

THE ROUTE TO the hospital was the same way Monica and I went to work. As Tim drove, I stared out the window cursing myself, digging my nails into my palms with agitation and remorse—why had I told her? Because I wanted to tell her. But I didn't have to tell her. I could have told her that I was carsick, that it was my ulcer, anything . . . Why her? I barely knew her. Was that the point? I certainly knew nothing about her that would ensure her silence. How did I know she wouldn't tell, hadn't already told people? Why hadn't I kept it to myself? Why had I been so weak?

It was this sort of weakness that had gotten me into my situation in the first place. Tim would never tell anyone, why had I? I didn't tell him I had told her. I had promised to keep it secret, and I kept promises then. I knew he'd be upset, he wouldn't understand how I could tell someone who was, to him, a virtual stranger. I couldn't make him understand, because I didn't understand how it was that I trusted her.

Afterward, on the way back home, I leaned my head out the window, so I couldn't hear anything Tim was saying, or not saying. I liked the dull roar of the wind, the feeling of my tears streaking back into my ears. I felt sick when he suddenly pulled off the road and into the parking lot of a florist that advertised in the window with a giant horseshoe made out of yellow carnations.

"Please don't," I said, wishing Tim hadn't stopped the car but had just kept driving, kept moving farther and farther away from the scene of the crime. "Come back."

But he didn't. When he returned, he had a bouquet of long-stemmed red roses.

"What are these for?" I asked. "Did I just win the Kentucky Derby?"

IN MY BED at home that night, Tim sleeping downstairs in the library as we weren't allowed to sleep in the same room in my parents' house, I thought about Monica. I didn't want Tim right now. I wanted Monica. I wondered what she was doing, if I could call her, if there was anything to say if I did call her. What would I say? It hurt. Ask her, Do you know if I can take a bath? Ask her, Do you hate me? Ask her, Will I ever be the same again?

That night I moved from one life into another, leaving behind my girlfriends, my ideas of what was right and wrong. It was like passing into another time zone; the world was still the same, only I was out of sync. I belonged in this new place but wasn't yet able to speak the language, and I didn't know that I wanted to learn.

ON MONDAY WHEN I rang the bell at Monica's house, I heard her voice call out, "Come on in!"

I let myself in and was surprised to see Ron standing in the kitchen, drinking his coffee over the sink, his hand on his tie to keep it from getting splashed.

"Good morning," he said. "You must be Elissa." He took my hand and shook it the way salesmen or men who worry about making a good impression do. I wondered if he knew how strong he was. He smiled, and I knew she'd said nice things about me. I couldn't imagine what, but this being let into the house like this, meeting him, it meant something.

"Okay," he said. "Gotta go." He grabbed a lunch bag off the counter; it looked just like Monica's and I imagined her making both of their lunches the night before. Did he get a tuna fish on white bread sandwich? Did he get salad and a yogurt?

Monica strolled into the kitchen, a hot roller still in the front of her hair.

"See ya, babe," he said and kissed her on the cheek. She didn't kiss him back. Instead, she kept her eyes on me. "Hi," she said, looking me over like she was examining me for damage. He pulled slowly out of the drive, like I thought maybe he was watching us.

"So," she said, after his car had disappeared. "How *are* you?"

"I am fine," I said. "I am just fine."

What I thought was, Tim had pulled out of the driveway, then stopped and backed up to kiss me good-bye again—this should have endeared him to me—but it just annoyed me. Just go, I thought, please just go. What kind of a person was I?

"Really?" she said.

"Yes, really," I said, sounding a little too curt. I didn't want to talk about it.

"Okay," she said, and I wondered for a moment if I'd hurt her feelings. I hadn't said anything, I reasoned, but that was it, I hadn't said anything. We rode in silence for a few minutes until she put on the radio. When we stopped at 7-Eleven, she got out.

"Want anything?" she asked.

"No thank you," I said. I was glad that it was almost time for me to return to school. Next summer I would work in Philadelphia at a big TV station—Tim's family had connections—or I'd work at a radio station, intern for a disc jockey maybe. Where would Monica be? I could help her too, couldn't I? I owed her that. Unlike me, she had drive, and certainly could handle the work. What would that be like, though? I could see her showing up in Philadelphia for an interview in her polyester blouse and gray-blue suit, her bone-colored pumps, and I winced.

At work, I could feel her looking at me; when I returned her stare, she just smiled; I felt known in a way I had rarely ever experienced in my life, and while it was like a gift in that moment, I regretted it too. It scared me.

At work, when I was done writing my copy, I didn't ask Monica if she wanted to go get a lemon ice like I usually did. Instead, the moment her back was turned, I sought out the weather girl and gossiped with her at her desk. I told her I was only going to be working there a couple more days and asked, maybe, couldn't I once do the weather?

She laughed at me. Monica, looking over, just smiled and shook her head like I was some dumb kid. I couldn't help it, I was giddy with freedom.

Later I asked Monica, perhaps too loudly, "How much longer are you going to be working here?"

"We haven't decided yet," she said, shooting a look at the anchorman's office. She looked nervous. "We'll see . . . ," she said, and smiled in a way that made me know she didn't like the question.

ON THE WAY home, I drilled her with questions. When are you and Ron getting married? How does he feel about you not making money? What will happen if you don't get a job at the station? What will happen? Where will you go?

I don't remember what she said.

That next week was my last week. I wanted to take two weeks off before school started and go to the beach with Tim.

"We'll go out for drinks after work," Monica said.

I said, "Okay."

Then on my last day I told Monica that I couldn't have drinks with her.

"Oh," she said. "Okay."

"My father is going to pick me up, and . . ."

"Whatever," she said.

I thought she looked sad, a little sad, but just for one minute, and maybe I wanted to see that in her eyes. She hugged me.

"So," she said, "don't be a stranger."

"Just be strange," I said back.

She laughed and shook her head. "You're so funny."

"Oh, go on," I said. "I mean it, go on . . ."

"Let me know when you're home for Christmas," she said. "You get a big break then, right?"

"I will. I'll call," I said. I wanted to hug her again, but I didn't.

"Take care of yourself," she said.

"You too."

I wanted to say something more; there was more to say, but I couldn't say it. I wanted to say, Thank you for taking care of me. Thank you for keeping my secret. Thank you for not making me feel like I was no good. But I didn't.

So I went back to school. I broke up with Tim. I went a little crazy. Tim became a Republican. I became a writer. I hated myself for the abortion, though every day, not talking about it, never speaking it, not to anyone, ever, made it seem less and less like reality. It was my secret and mine alone. If I didn't tell it, if no one knew, then it was as though it never happened. After a while I stopped thinking about it. Still, over the years, when I visited home, when I couldn't sleep at night, I would sometimes think about Monica. I would wonder where she was, what she was doing. Did she ever think about me? In fits of paranoia, I willed her to not think about it, to forget me. I wanted my secret to just break down one day like a rock into sand and sift away, and then to Monica I'd be just another spoiled girl, who got what she wanted the way kids like me always did.

YEARS LATER, WHILE I was driving cross-country with my husband, Rob, we stopped in a tiny town in New Mexico, outside of Albuquerque. There was nothing there but a church, some pawn shops, and a little cantina where we ate two-dollar burritos and drank a few Tecates. By the time we got back to the hotel, it was late. While Rob was in the shower, I turned on the TV, which was chained to the nightstand. Judging by the reception, if you didn't pay for cable, you had the choice of two local stations, so I flipped between them, one snowier than the other. Then I heard a voice that froze me; it was Monica. I leaned closer to the screen, but instead of making her face clearer, it made her hazier, but it was Monica's voice, or I thought it was. I slid back on the bed. There she was, the outline seemed true, as did the voice, the slight southern accent, she was there, there on my TV. Right there. Or that's what I want to think.

THE KINDNESS OF STRANGERS

Jennifer Gilmore

Late one night, in between dry heaves, I was watching the remake of *A Streetcar Named Desire* when Abigail called. Jessica Lange—Blanche, of course—was saying, "I don't want realism. I want magic! Yes, yes, magic!" I remember because my throat had welled up with tears: I wanted magic too!

When I heard Abby's voice on the phone, I turned down the volume, but I could still watch Blanche getting drunk and moving her arms as she tried to say what was in her heart.

"Hi," I said. Abigail had called a lot since I'd been sick. And her parents sent a huge bouquet of happy flowers: delphiniums, asters, yellow snaps, and liatris. My mother put the cheery arrangement next to the balloon bouquet that sprouted from the paw of a teddy bear, from my mother's cousins, who clearly thought I was eleven.

"Not a whole hell of a lot," I answered. It must have been difficult to talk to me, but still Abby tried to.

Three weeks earlier, a disease had struck me violently and swiftly, landing me in a hospital in upstate New York, where I had just started graduate school. I was soon told it was ulcerative colitis, which caused ulceration and inflammation of the inner lining of the colon and made me shit blood and vomit bile twenty-three hours a day.

My mother came to retrieve me from that hospital upstate and take me to D.C., where she and my father lived. In the helicopter that transported me, I lay on the gurney, a coffin, and she held my hand. I remember it was twilight, and a fleshy pink leaked in through the tiny windows. There's the Statue of Liberty! my mother said. And then: Here comes the Washington Monument, sweetie! I strained my neck to see, but the nurse who held my IV gently kept my head down. Slowly I was turning into a child again.

Abby listened to the daily update, which was pretty much the same each day she called: Save the colon! Save the colon! This was my mother's mantra, and the surgeon listened to her, always smirking. We can pretend, he seemed to be saying as he crossed his arms over his big belly, but it's going to have to come out one of these days. Sooner or later. Your daughter, the surgeon told my parents as if I was too young to understand, is very very sick.

"I'm sorry," Abby said, after I told her the doctor said it was going to have to come out sometime.

"Yeah," I said. I couldn't really talk about it, and I watched Blanche gasp beneath the glare of the light.

I had already lost fifteen pounds, though my face had grown large: a round, pocked moon, a side effect of the high dosage of steroids I took when all the other medications seemed to fail. My face looked prenatal, with no evident bone structure. I had been taken off solid foods. To hydrate you and let the bowel rest, my doctor had told me. When he said this, I pictured that wretched, massive, twisting snake that was wreaking such havoc in my body snoring soundly beneath a soft baby blanket, for a moment, calmed. My only nourishment was that milky TPN teeming through my veins that sat in a bag like a see-through teat on my IV stand.

I wore a paper-thin hospital gown that revealed how my breasts were practically history.

Perhaps this is why the technician who came in to change my IV told me, "Don't worry, hon, you'll be out by the prom."

The prom! I'm fucking twenty-five years old! And by my calculations, the prom was eight months away. "I don't want to go to the prom," I told the nurse.

"Well I have some good news," Abby said over the phone.

Where was she anyway? For a fleeting moment, I wondered where all my friends were. They didn't live in D.C., to be fair. And sometimes—no, often—someone would call and in between spasms of abdominal pain, or a wave of nausea, I would listen to her talk about her life. After all, what did I have to say? Yup, view's the same. Yup, still sick.

My friend Laura was studying to be a teacher. Julia had just gotten a position at the *Times*—the *Times*! she'd said, as if I hadn't heard her the first time—and Abigail was on her way to becoming a painter. Right after college, she had moved to New York and gone to art school. Abby was living pretty much as I had imagined I would live, whereas I had just started graduate school and was now trying to keep hydrated and let my bowel rest.

Talking to my friends made me even less connected to a world outside, as if the tenuous thread by which I was tethered to the living was readying to snap. My old life of wanting—success, recognition, many bylines—was useless to me now. It felt shallow and wrong and did not incorporate the idea that something like this—as in *this*—could happen to me or anyone else. Ambition had transformed into something far more primal: I would have liked my life.

"I'm going to have a show!" Abby said.

Just then I remembered being in Australia with Abby when we both went to spend the semester abroad, which was how we'd met. We had gone to the middle of that massive country, to Darwin, and had gone camping in Aboriginal territory, at Kakadu. There were huge gorges that cut like scars into dry land, and we paddled our way around them and under waterfalls, set up camp beneath an entirely different sky than the mottled suburban stars James and I had kissed beneath in high school. I remembered climbing to the top of an enormous hill, feeling that singing in my legs, and looking out at the land, so different from anything I had ever seen. The horizon was on fire. Standing there with Abby beneath the baking sun, I felt like we were on a distant planet surrounded by a terrible ring of fire we would have to jump over if we ever wanted to leave.

On television, Blanche threw herself on the bed. My heart went out to her, she who had slept with strangers simply for protection. What would that be like? I began to wonder but stopped myself. Sleeping with strangers. Better to think about food, so much more difficult to live without but far easier to need.

"A show," I said to Abigail. "How fantastic."

I guess I thought I would be first. Abby had always planned to go to law school. But it will be environmental law, she had told me, as if that changed anything. I was at the beginning of everything then and, now that I think about it, which I tried not to in the hospital and I try not to even now, my dreaming was so large it seemed not so much like dreaming but like expectation. I had expectations, unknowing, of course, how hard it is to get so little in life.

"It's in six months," Abby said. "You're going to be better by then."

"Well it's before the prom anyway," I said.

I remembered then how, when we got back from Australia, Abigail just changed her major and started painting at the campus art studio until very late at night. Sometimes I would come over and sit with her while she worked. Part of me felt robbed, that she had stolen some process that was only mine. Just who does she think she is? I'd thought upon leaving the building and heading out into the night, the campus illuminated under the blue, humming safety lights. I must have believed I held ownership over all creation.

"The prom?" Abby asked.

I laughed, and a shot of pain bit into my side. I could just picture her show: a group of disaffected people standing around wearing berets and looking at the fish paintings Abby had started doing our senior year.

Talking to Abigail made me think about everything that was falling away: all my new graduate school friends were writing but me. They had to be. What else would they be doing in that tiny, freezing town? It was only early October when I went in, and already a layer of frost had covered the waxy ivy bordering my first-floor apartment each morning. The hills and deep ravines and gorges, so breathtaking the summer I had looked at the school, were already becoming part of a fierce and alien landscape. I remembered driving to a new friend's house far out of town, past faded, sloping farmhouses and rolling hills, the country illuminated beneath a rising and alarming harvest moon, and I remember wondering: Where am I, and what on earth am I doing here?

In between shitting blood, I made lists: send this story here, send this one there. Why not write a poem! As soon as I get out—tomorrow!—I will write a brand-new beautiful story. My story will not be about this—what is there to say?—but it will do what I was trained to do. I will take the grief and transform it. Who else but me has this to say?

When I got like this, pain was, in a small way, relief. I remember thinking: If I die here, right now, at least I won't have to write anymore.

"I'll be there," I said to Abby. It was ridiculous. I didn't know if I'd even be alive.

I hung up with Abby and thought of being in that tiny hospital upstate. It was not my mother coming in from the cold, clutching her tiny suitcase, that I remembered. It wasn't the doctor bending over me to put in a central line, a catheter inserted into one primary vein, as the veins in my arms were already filled and stopped from so many IVs, or his hot breath blowing over my chest as he cut into me with his little scalpel. I remembered my writing professor, who had come a few mornings to sit by my bed. I hardly knew her, but she sat next to me, knitting. No one I knew—not even my grandmother—was a knitter, and the steady icicle click of those needles gave me great comfort. Like breathing.

I went back to the television movie, still on mute. Mitch had left and Blanche was again drinking alone, but I knew exactly what was about to happen.

All this talk of the prom must have been why I thought of high school: the leaves turning in September, polyurethane hallways, walking in groups of three and four. My roommate, Juanita, must have heard me sniveling as I remembered kissing James Mallon in the back of a truck as we sailed down Bradley Boulevard, toward Great Falls. Would I ever feel that way again? "Blue Suede Shoes" was playing from the front as we kissed until the truck stopped suddenly at a red light and threw us apart. Now sexual adventure seemed as irretrievable as childhood.

As some kind of benevolent gesture I still don't completely understand, the doctors had put me on the cancer ward. Though it's true I couldn't catch cancer, I caught on to the fact that no disease is pretty. After two weeks, I'd had three roommates who came for chemo one after the other. They came in dressed in their street clothes, got into their thin white gowns, took off their wigs, suffered like hell for three days, put their clothes and their wigs back on, and left.

We all talked about eating.

With all of the roommates who came and went, we asked each other the same thing: what would we eat if we could eat?

"Spare ribs, potato salad, biscuits," the last one had said.

I'd told her, "Sautéed soft-shell crabs in hazelnut sauce over radicchio. Foie gras."

"Who?" she said.

"Foie gras. Jesus," I had muttered beneath my breath.

I was such an ass.

THE NIGHT ABBY told me about her upcoming show, I woke up crying from my dream of standing at the edge of a burning world. All the nurses thought I was so young, and in that thick hospital dark, I too felt I was receding into the deep, sad crevices of childhood, or even before that, my bones not yet formed, my features still questionable. Who would I become? I wondered when I got up the courage to look at my bloated face. Sometimes I thought to feel for gills. But really, and this feeling has not entirely left me, I was becoming an old woman. I was aging without any of the experience age normally affords. I had not married or had children. I had not written that damn book. I had not yet asked my grandmother to tell me everything. My body had betrayed me—would it ever be strong enough to get on a plane and just go somewhere, and I don't mean with a nurse in a medevac? Would my body ever make it to the top of a giant hill to witness a country on fire?

Each morning as dawn broke across that city I'd grown up in and always hated, the university hospital medical students came in groups of two and three to assess my progress. "Are you naawwzeeated, Miss . . . ?" There was always a ruffle of papers as they tried to find my name among their many files. "Have you had a bowel movement?" they all asked brightly. One leaned over to touch my stomach.

Are you kidding me? At this point I was one big bowel movement. Have you read the damn charts? Have you seen the IV of lorazepam leading straight to my nauseated heart? But these were only thoughts. What I said was "Please don't touch me."

NOT LONG AFTER Abby told me about her show, my stomach became as hard as a wooden door. It was still rising like yeasty bread, inflating to the point of megatoxicity, on the very brink of exploding, when that surgeon came in and with a regular Bic pen marked my lower abdomen where the ileostomy bag would attach. The crude X he drew on me, and the randomness of the placement, was startling. Somehow I had thought science to be more assured, far more high tech.

"You'll be okay," Juanita said when she heard me sniffling. "It'll be over soon."

But I was such a fool; I wasn't thinking about the operation, what was about to happen to me. I was remembering my life before. I thought of the time Abigail and I took a bus up the coast of Australia to Cairns, and how we had gone scuba diving in the Great Barrier Reef. We weren't certified, but we went with an instructor, and when the surgeon came in to take me to the OR, I remembered how we had practiced using scuba masks in shallow water around this little island. I'd had this strange urge to take off my mask while underwater. That's normal, the instructor told me. But you have to resist it. Then, as soon as we went under again, I tore off the mask and my oxygen, and I remember the feeling now, of thinking I could breathe and trying to, and then realizing I couldn't, as I was underwater. The instructor had pulled me up in his strong arms. No worries, he said, cheerfully. Happens all the time. When I caught my breath, I could see the quick, fishlike flash of Abby as she tooled around underwater with no evident breathing problems at all.

Later, when we hopped off the boat and really went under, I had learned to keep my mask on and was rewarded with an amazing universe below: giant clams with velvet insides we could stick our arms into. Clown fish, enormous corals and anemones, their colored tentacles swaying to the rhythm of some moon-linked tide I couldn't see. Little reef sharks that the instructor fed with mullet.

I haven't gotten over the wonder of that day, but I never wrote a word about that feeling of being underwater, in a completely new and beautiful world. Abby, though, began painting fish and also dot paintings, just like we saw the Aboriginals do, the moment we got back to the States. I admired Abby's ability to take what she saw around her and make art of it as I was stuck in some inner dialogue, which prevented me from registering what happened around me. But her paintings caught me by surprise. We had seen the same thing, and she had recorded it. Or replicated it. Was there a difference? When the doctor and his harem of students came in to put me under, I thought how maybe I would never write about anything again.

THAT NIGHT THEY took out my large intestine, pulling an inch of the small one out of my abdomen, a cinnamon stick through the skin of an orange, just like I'd made in school. They created a stoma to slip inside a ten-inch plastic bag, which, in turn, would collect stool.

When I woke up, I had an ileostomy bag, which I would wear for nearly a year. Next to the bag was the incision, a line from the apex of my rib cage all the way down, where I'd been shaved clean. Metal staples clamped the wound closed, and there was this pain in and through the middle of me so pure, I am sure I will always remember it.

The students came in: "Have you had a bowel movement lately?"

"Fuck you," I told them. "Do your homework."

I was on cardiac watch, hooked up by my nose and throat and the tips of my fingers to a machine. My legs were strapped into these plastic wraps, secured by Velcro, and they made my legs move. I was a little Rockette, if only I didn't have the wires and tubes that made me look more like a Rockette marionette. No one would give me a mirror but I am told my face was the size of a basketball, though, due to the uneven distribution of fluids, was swollen disproportionately to itself and therefore appeared to be lumpy, which didn't sound much like a basketball to me.

Kick, kick went my legs, as my mother held my hands and wept.

Late that night Abigail called. "How *are* you?"

I think she had called before, and I know now she had talked to my parents, but I couldn't really talk then or now.

"Hmmphghao," I said.

"I'm thinking of you," she told me.

And I know that she was, and if I'd been able to feel a thing I know I would have appreciated her doing so. But Abby was making art and I was learning how to change an ileostomy bag. Just hours before, the nurse had come in: First this, she'd said, then this. I felt a slight tug as she lifted the bag to show me how it was attached. Then shut it here, she said, clamping the bottom closed. I looked up at the ceiling. You'll catch on later, the nurse said, placing a pamphlet, "About Your Ileostomy," on the table by the bed. You'll have to.

"I really am," Abby said.

At some point I hung up with Abby and at some point my mother and father went home. Still the machine that watched my heart hissed and beeped. Still some grand puppeteer made my legs kick in the air. I was in and out of sleep and dreams and memory and anesthesia and morphine. At some point I was awakened out of that terrible darkness, to the feel of a hand on my shoulder.

"Shh," the voice said. "Shhh."

The voice turned me onto my stomach but somehow didn't hurt me. From behind, it untied my robe, gently touched my shoulders, my back, the backs of my thighs, with a warm towel. *Swish. Swish.* I could see white tennis shoes peeking out from beneath pink scrubs.

"There," the voice said. "Usually the people are much older," it said.

I turned on my back again and could make out a small figure attached to the shoes, long blond hair swinging through the semidarkness. The towel dipped into the water, and I could hear the trickle as it was being wrung out, dipped again.

"Older?" I asked.

"Their skin. It's thinner. It moves."

The washcloth moved expertly around the needles and wires, over my arms, over the bruises in my stopped-up veins.

"That feels good." I realized then that all I had wanted this whole time was to feel better.

The cloth moved toward my abdomen. Warmth.

"I try to do this for the patients. At least once. I know what it can be like in here—was it last night? Yes, it was in this exact room. A man had been here for over two months and no one had bathed him. He cried the whole time I washed him. Bypass." The nurse lifted up that terrible bag and ran the towel beneath it. "Ileostomy," she said. The washcloth moved over my hips. *Swish, swish.*

"Yeah."

I heard the nurse squirting lotion into her hands. She wasn't wearing gloves, and her warm hands hovered above my stomach for a split second. I could feel the pain of the incision, from simply having turned over.

She spread the lotion around the staples, never touching them, and I could hear the crinkle of the plastic bag. She rubbed lotion into my legs, my ankles, each toe.

The water sloshed in the basin as the blond-haired nurse picked it up to leave.

"I'll check on you later," she said. "Try and sleep before they drag you up for breakfast."

Light came in through the windows: it was dawn, and the students would be back soon. My mother would be there soon, planning my menu for the next day—hmm, Jell-O! she'd say. How about the beef consommé, sweetie?—when I would be able to have solid food—at least that's what they were calling it—for the first time in over a month.

"Thank you," I told the nurse. I heard her slowly open the door and walk out into the hallway.

I HAVE THOUGHT so often about the moment that nurse came in, all the time really, because I think it's what I've always wanted from a friendship and never been able to have. How hard is it to let someone help you? I'll tell you: when you are stripped of your self and rendered an anonymous girl in an anonymous hospital bed, it's hard. Sickness closed me off to anyone but my surgeon, whom I had no choice but to let cut in. But my surgeon is not my friend. When you are aching perhaps it is mere presence, the click of metal knitting needles, a washcloth moving slowly over grieving skin, that's what's needed. I did not need to talk to my friends about how I was being left behind. Sometimes, I think, it takes a stranger.

I FORGAVE SO many of my friends their absence. Why ditch my old friend from kindergarten because she didn't send flowers? I accepted this, as I accepted the dream or the memory of my experience.

A week after the surgery, I finally left the hospital I had been in for over a month. I learned how to change my bag—suffice it to say it involved an inordinate amount of science to figure out

the exact proportion of putties and pastes and plastics and pow-
ders to ensure the bag stayed closed—and went back to graduate
school. But I didn't write about being sick. It's like being drunk,
I reasoned, an old story. Instead I wrote about James Mallon,
who in my story falls out of the truck when it stops suddenly at
that light. I jump out to try to help him back in. It's so obvious
to me now: At the height of weakness, who doesn't want to be
able to save someone?

Four months later, I got an invitation to Abigail's art show in
Manhattan. Though I was still weak, I'd tried to get back to
some semblance of a normal life. Having the bag precluded that
a bit: I spent a lot of time fantasizing—and this was not a pleasant fantasy—that I would be sitting in someone's home drinking tea and talking about the structure or point of view of some
story when the clasp would unclamp and shit would pour out
everywhere. It reminded me of my mother, whom I'm told carried a jar of pickles everywhere she went when she was pregnant
with me so if her water broke she could drop the jar and no one
would know the difference. What jar would I carry around? God
only knows.

I DROVE DOWN to Manhattan with a philosophy major who
was also heading to the city for the weekend. We left the day of
the event, and I was supposed to meet Abigail at her apartment
in the East Village, drop off my stuff, and go have a drink before
her opening. I had wanted to thank her for all the calls and the
flowers and the way she had done what she could to let me know
she had been there.

I remember rifling through my closet to find something to
wear: my options were limited as, despite the nurses' claims that
I could wear whatever I chose, some pants rubbed against the
stoma, which was terribly irritating. And with skirts I had to
stuff the bag into tights or stockings. When it began to fill, I

would worry that it would show through my clothes, a huge, bulbous balloon that, I also feared, could pop at any moment.

I decided on black pants and a cute little sweater that dipped into a V at the neck, showing off my breasts, which were slowly growing back, a sign I was finally reaching puberty again. I remember leaning into the mirror and putting on eyeliner and mascara, running blush along my cheeks, the bones I'd inherited from my mother returning to my face once I was weaned off the steroids. I had never worn much makeup, but now I felt the need to cover over something I couldn't name but I could see on my skin—sickness, perhaps—that seemed to skim my skin like an oil slick sliding over water. Putting on dark red lipstick, I watched myself painting on a smile.

As luck—mine at least—would have it, we got a flat tire on the way, which made me late for Abigail's opening. When I finally got to the city, about an hour into it, I went straight to the gallery. Running up the two flights of stairs to the space, I could feel the bag pulling me down as I stretched my legs with each step: it was always there.

The small room was filled with people, but I could see the walls, painted black. As I got accustomed to the bright gallery lights, a wave of nausea, the likes of which I had not experienced since before I'd had my surgery, came over me. Does it sound extraordinary to say that each wall was covered in large intestines? There were paintings and also wall murals, and some three-dimensional colons coming out of the black walls, which must have been made from layers and layers of acrylic. Each colon had a different shape, and each one had bits of blood painted on the end of it.

No worries! the scuba instructor told me as Abby and I came up from the water for air. Just breathe, he said. Whatever you do, don't take off the mask.

People milled about—none of them was wearing a beret—

and I recovered my breathing. I looked at the walls, and for a moment the twisting, impossible shapes were beautiful. They seemed to be shot through with a luminous light, which gave the illusion that the forms moved across the canvases and the walls, like rays of sun beneath the sea. If I hadn't seen them for what they were, I would have admired Abby's progress, as if, for the first time, she'd been able to trace some remarkable inward process. Only that process she recorded was mine.

Abigail came toward me, a plastic cup of wine in her hand. She looked the same as when we were traveling together: casual and young and tall and strong and comfortable in her black jeans and a loose black sweater. I felt withered and old in comparison, unable to stand up straight from the constant tug of the not-yet-healed incision.

"Hi," she said. "I was hoping you'd come in earlier, so I could have talked to you about this."

I nodded. "The phone is sometimes useful," I said.

"I thought it would be better to talk in person," she said.

"Like this," I said. "In person, like this you mean."

"What do you think?" Abby asked.

"Of the art?" I asked her.

"Of everything," she said.

"I don't really see this as your material," I said. How had she made art of this first? When would I ever in my life sit down and write an ileostomy story? Never. "What happened to the fishes?"

Abigail took a sip of her wine, and I ran my fingers through my hair unconsciously, forgetting that it had been coming out in big clumps from the anesthesia and touching it in any way was never a good idea. I was looking at my hands, marked with stray hairs like life lines, when someone came up to congratulate her. She kissed him on both cheeks and then turned back to me.

"Look," she said. "Your sickness really affected me."

"Me too," I said.

Someone else approached. "This is Wright," Abby said to me.

"Oh my god!" Wright said when Abby introduced me. "You're the inspiration for all this!" His arms swept the expanse of the room. "Abby has talked so much about you. How *are* you?"

"I'm fine," I said, crossing my arms over my chest. "How are you?"

I STAYED THERE through the opening and even went to the dinner after, and then I decided to leave town that night. It wasn't even Abigail really, I just panicked: What if I have an accident? What if the bathroom is miles from the bedroom? Or worse, what if it's so close that Abigail will hear me emptying the bag all night?

I remember hugging her good-bye on the wet cobblestone street. "It was a great show," I told her. It was important to me that she know I was fine with it. Because if I was fine with it, then I had put it—the hospital, the needles, the nurses who never came when I called them, the roommates who I knew were all dying—behind me. If I was okay, then hadn't I moved on?

But of course I was not fine with it. I'd not yet had the chance to figure out for myself how I would handle being in the world, and Abigail had managed to make that decision for me: I was the girl without the colon. How *interesting*! She had formed my identity. The people sitting around the table stuffing themselves with homemade pasta in that crowded Italian restaurant had smiled at me brightly. Yes, I live upstate, I said, and everyone nodded furiously, encouraging me to speak as if it was my voice that had been lost. Why yes, it certainly *is* cold there, but sure is pretty!

The stoma was spewing liquid—which is what it is when you do not have a colon—into the bag. This always registered as a benign little tickle, a twitch in the eye.

I looked up and around the table: Who there could not see right through me?

———

IT IS A terrible lesson, but it's one of the many things I have taken with me from that time that, though it is over, has defined me in so many ways. I remember seeing a brand-new world with Abigail. We went up to the top of the world and watched it burning, and we dove down beneath it to watch it teeming with life: I have never had that feeling before or since, but I have also never been stolen from by someone I love. What I take from that is this: strangers—nurses, a professor who knits, even that policeman who took pity on me upon being met by my tearstained, mascara-smeared face when he pulled me over for speeding along the Palisades on my way home that night—can often offer comfort that those we know can't. You will never have to see the stranger you were laid bare before again. And in a single moment a stranger cannot let you down.

She *stole* it, I thought, driving out of the city, the George Washington Bridge behind me, strung with a million lights, and into the long, expansive sky, the endless stretch of black land. Isn't my grief mine? I didn't know that it would be months before I talked to Abby and that when she called I wouldn't mention that evening, not ever. I would never be vulnerable to her again. Driving along the highway, I didn't know that talking to Abby from now on would always be like talking to a stranger. As I headed north, I longed for that feeling of being beneath the sea, cushioned by water and moving surely and fluidly through a brightly colored universe.

That beautiful nurse had taken each one of my hands in hers and massaged each finger, my wrist, my arm. Had she been real? "I'll check on you later," she'd said before she left. She had offered me everything I needed in a single moment, but I never did see her again.

JENNY OFFILL is the author of the novel *Last Things*, which was chosen as a Notable or Best Book of the Year by *The New York Times*, *The Village Voice*, the *Los Angeles Times*, and *The Guardian* (U.K.). It was also a finalist for the *Los Angeles Times* First Book Award in 2000. Her fiction and nonfiction have appeared in *Story*, *Epoch*, *Travel & Leisure*, and *The Washington Post*.

ELISSA SCHAPPELL is the author of *Use Me*, a novel in stories, which was a runner-up for the PEN-Hemingway award; a cofounder of the literary magazine *Tin House*; and a contributing editor at *Vanity Fair*. Her essays, interviews, and stories have appeared in places such as *The Paris Review* and *The New York Times Book Review*, as well as *The Mrs. Dalloway Reader*, *The KGB Bar Reader*, and *The Bitch in the House*. She lives in Brooklyn, New York.

ABOUT THE CONTRIBUTORS

HEATHER ABEL is a writer living in Brooklyn, New York. She previously was a reporter and editor with *High Country News* and the *San Francisco Bay Guardian*.

DIANA ABU-JABER is the author of the novels *Arabian Jazz* and *Crescent*. Her memoir, *The Language of Baklava*, is coming out in spring 2005. She lives in Miami, Florida.

DOROTHY ALLISON is the author of *Bastard Out of Carolina*, *Cavedweller*, *Two or Three Things I Know for Sure*, and *Skin: Talking About Sex, Class, and Literature*. She makes her home in Northern California with her partner, Alix Layman, and her eleven-year-old son, Wolf Michael.

NUAR ALSADIR'S poetry and prose have appeared in numerous periodicals, including *Grand Street*, *The Kenyon Review*, *Ploughshares*, *The New York Times Magazine*, *Slate*, *Tin House*, and *Bookforum*. She teaches writing at New York University.

KATE BERNHEIMER is the author of a novel, *The Complete Tales of Ketzia Gold*, and editor of the collection *Mirror, Mirror on the Wall: Women Writers Explore Their Favorite Fairy Tales*. She recently taught in the MFA Program for Poets and Writers at the University of Massachusetts.

EMILY CHENOWETH is a writer living in Brooklyn, New York, whose work has appeared in *Tin House* and other publications. She received her M.F.A. from Columbia University, and she currently works as an editor at *Publishers Weekly*.

JENNIFER GILMORE'S work has appeared in magazines and journals including *Alaska Quarterly Review, Allure, Biography, Bookforum, CutBank, Epoch, Nerve*, and *Salon*. She has recently completed her first novel.

BEVERLY GOLOGORSKY'S novel *The Things We Do to Make It Home* was a *New York Times* Notable Book, a *Los Angeles Times* Best Fiction, and a finalist for the Barnes & Noble Discover Great Writers Award. Her book reviews and op-ed pieces have appeared in various newspapers and magazines. She is currently at work on her next novel, *Who Do You Think You Are?*

VIVIAN GORNICK is an essayist and a memoirist. She has written eight books, among them the noted *Fierce Attachments* and *The End of the Novel of Love*.

ANN HOOD is the author of seven novels, including *Somewhere off the Coast of Maine* and *Ruby*; a memoir, *Do Not Go Gentle: My Search for Miracles in a Cynical Age*; and a short story collection, *An Ornithologist's Guide to Life*.

NICOLE KEETER is a freelance writer living in Brooklyn, New York. Her work has appeared in *Allure, Glamour, Interview*, and *O, The Oprah Magazine*. She was previously a film critic for *TimeOut New York*.

PATRICIA MARX writes comedy for movies, television, and print. Her books include *Meet My Staff*, illustrated by Roz Chast, and *The Skinny*, cowritten with Susan Sistrom.

LYDIA MILLET'S third novel, *My Happy Life*, won the 2003 PEN-USA Award for Fiction. The year 2005 sees the release of her fourth and fifth novels, *Everyone's Pretty* and *Oh Pure and Radiant Heart*, by Soft Skull Press.

MARY MORRIS is the author of twelve books: five novels, three collections of short stories, three travel memoirs, and along with her husband, Larry O'Connor, an anthology of travel literature. The recipient of the Rome Prize in Literature, Morris teaches writing at Sarah Lawrence College. Her next novel, *Revenge*, will be published by St. Martin's in 2005.

FRANCINE PROSE is the author of ten works of fiction, including *Blue Angel*, *Household Saints*, *Hunters and Gatherers*, *Primitive People*, and *Guided Tours of Hell*. Her work has appeared in *The New Yorker*, *The Atlantic*, *GQ*, and *The Paris Review*. She is a contributing editor at *Harper's* and writes regularly on art for *The Wall Street Journal*.

KATIE ROIPHE is the author of *Still She Haunts Me* and *The Morning After*. Her work has appeared in *The New York Times*, *Vogue*, *Esquire*, *McSweeney's*, *Tin House*, and *Harper's*, among many other places. She holds a Ph.D. in literature from Princeton University and lives in Brooklyn, New York, with her husband and baby.

HELEN SCHULMAN is the author of the novels *Out of Time*, *The Revisionist*, and *P.S.*, which has recently been made into a feature film starring Laura Linney and Topher Grace. She has also published a story collection entitled *Not a Free Show* and coedited, with Jill Bialosky, the essay anthology *Wanting a Child*. Her fiction and nonfiction have appeared in places such as *Vanity Fair*, *Time*, *The New York Times*, *Vogue*, *GQ*, *Travel & Leisure*, *Food & Wine*, *The Paris Review*, and *Tin House*. She is currently the Acting Fiction Coordinator of the Writing Program at the New School.

ELIZABETH STROUT is the author of the novel *Amy and Isabelle*. Her short stories have appeared in a number of magazines, including *The New Yorker*. She makes her home in Brooklyn, New York.

EMILY WHITE is the author of *Fast Girls: Teenage Tribes and the Myth of the Slut*. Her nonfiction has appeared in *The New York Times Magazine, Nest, Bookforum,* and *The New York Times Book Review,* and other venues. Her novel, *The Third River,* will be published by Clear Cut Press in 2005. She is currently at work on a book about the disgraced celebrity money manager Dana Giacchetto and the 1990s.